Minding the Store

Minding the Store

Great Writing About Business,
from Tolstoy to Now

Edited by
Robert Coles and Albert LaFarge

THE NEW PRESS

NEW YORK
LONDON

For Elizabeth

Pages 302–3 constitute an extension of this copyright page.

Requests for permission to reproduce selections from this book should be mailed to:
Permissions Department, The New Press, 38 Greene Street, New York, NY 10013.

Published in the United States by The New Press, New York, 2008
Distributed by W. W. Norton & Company, Inc., New York

LIBRARY OF CONGRESS CATALOGING-IN-PUBLICATION DATA

Minding the store : great writing about business, from Tolstoy to now /
edited by Robert Coles and Albert LaFarge.
p. cm.
ISBN 978-1-59558-355-0
1. Business—Fiction.   2 Short stories, American.   3. Short stories.
I. Coles, Robert.   II. LaFarge, Albert.
PS648.B89M56   2008
808.83'93553—dc22
2008014413

The New Press was established in 1990 as a not-for-profit alternative to the large,
commercial publishing houses currently dominating the book publishing industry.
The New Press operates in the public interest rather than for private gain, and is
committed to publishing, in innovative ways, works of educational, cultural, and
community value that are often deemed insufficiently profitable.

www.thenewpress.com

Composition by NK Graphics
This book was set in Janson Text

Printed in the United States of America

2   4   6   8   10   9   7   5   3   1

CONTENTS

PREFACE

Robert Coles

During the early 1950s I was greatly privileged to get to know the writer and physician Dr. William Carlos Williams, and to accompany him on his daily "house rounds," he called them—visits to his ailing patients in the New Jersey homes where they lived. In between seeing people, talking with them, figuring out what had gone wrong in this or that part of their bodies, he would stop and think about the work he did, its possibilities, its responsibilities, its satisfactions, its hazards. Once, upon leaving the bedside of a child sick with a serious ear infection, and on the way to see another child who was stricken with polio, I heard a worried but insistently determined, car-driving physician speak some words meant to address himself, let alone his young, medical student listener:

"Look, going on my rounds, seeing patients, listening to them, figuring out what is wrong, and why, and what needs to be done, and why, is—well, going to work, trying to do the best possible job: running a business with as much intelligence and energy as we can muster, and yes, with your conscience running in high gear, so you do the right thing, and don't end up slipping, and falling flat on your face, your conscience in tatters. Yes, I say 'running a business'"—he may well have seen a look of surprise on my face, or had decided, as was his wont, to challenge conventional thinking with a poet's strong, metaphorical energy—"because what a businessman has to do is work with customers, seek their assent, connect with them just as a doctor or lawyer or teacher has to do with a patient, a client, a student. There's drama in all of our lives, and plenty of it in the world of business: people wanting, needing, looking, seeking customers—people figuring out what to make (manufacturers), what to sell, and how to do both so that money is spent, money is made. I remember President Coolidge saying that 'the business of America is business,' and he was getting at a lot there—apart from his politics or social beliefs: hey, look at how that word business can absorb so many implications that in their sum tells us about ourselves: we get busy, we give people the business (tell them off), we say that someone really knows his business, or minds his own business, or gets right down to business, or is businesslike (methodical, earnest): a lot going on with that word, which tells us a big lesson: business is a world of folks going about their various ways—so a poet, novelist, and playwright is naturally going to bear down on the business world, see its makings, its workings as a place to explore, convey, bring to life: business activity as human activity finding its various and particular forms of expression."

Those words surely and strongly echoed in my mind when I was asked by a dean at the Harvard Graduate School of Business Administration whether I would be willing to teach "a course like one of those humanities seminars you've been teaching at the [Harvard] medical school, or to the college's undergraduates or at the School of Education, using literature to help other students think about life, about what they'll be doing later on, and why, and to what effect." The result was several years of a seminar at the Harvard Business School, and some of what those students and I read together now appears in the following pages, along with other readings that Albert LaFarge and I feel also merit consideration, as instruments of social consideration and personal introspection, moral reflection: the standby consequences of art become a kind of continuing companionship—and in that last regard, I ought to say that to this day some of those Harvard graduate students in its Business School still keep in touch with one another, with their teacher: remembering moments in books read, discussed, taken to mind and heart—literature worked into lives even as it tells of them.

INTRODUCTION

Albert LaFarge

This book exists to give readers—and not just students at business schools—an opportunity to appreciate the variety of behavior and experience that attends the quest for survival in the business world. Here you will find a raft of distinguished writers reflecting, however obliquely, on the ironies, agonies, ethical challenges, misunderstandings, and moments of grace in the world of commerce. The writers gathered here were not chosen for their expertise in finance or accounting or anything like that. Many would likely echo one contributor, who concedes, "I don't know much about business, alas." But they all have vital things to teach us about character and conduct, in and out of the business world; they've found ways to hold our attention long enough to show us a little about how the world works, and how the mind works—and how we all try our best as we work, whether it's behind a desk in a corporate office, or on the road as a traveling salesman, or in some other avenue of commerce, striving to put bread on the table and keep a roof over our head, at the very least. This book contains portrayals of brilliant salesmanship—of one character we are told, "You couldn't deny him"—as well as befuddlement and dismay and floundering and worry about flagging careers, overbearing bosses, mounting unpaid bills, competitors. Resilience and humor and resourcefulness abound, as well as despair and defeated ambition.

The book is divided, somewhat arbitrarily, into five parts that reflect major aspects of a life in business.

Part 1 (The Hard Sell) shows selling in action. The characters are crafty dealmakers who throw all their inventiveness and determination into the job at hand. They encounter obstacles that make their negotiations interesting and revealing of larger truths of the human predicament.

We can all learn a thing or two from these players, even those we wouldn't emulate.

Part 2 (The Office) is about the gestalt of the workplace: a couple of light takes on office atmospherics (Joseph Heller, Franz Kafka), then two somewhat more sober looks at corporate life through the lens of two people (Jill Nelson and Gwendolyn M. Parker) who find themselves questioning their career paths, not to mention the whole culture they have to contend with at the office. All of these selections, even the lighthearted ones, probe the psychopathology of daily life in the office. (If this book could hold moving images it might include a clip from the 1999 movie *Office Space* or an episode of Ricky Gervais's BBC sitcom *The Office*.) The section concludes with a piece from Walker Percy's *The Moviegoer*, which yearns beyond the office space, inclining toward a wider search, courtesy of a philosophically minded New Orleans stockbroker.

Part 3 (The Rich Man's House) is set in the domestic spaces of the white-collar class. John Cheever's "The Housebreaker of Shady Hill" gives a wry, robust, ultimately charitable picture of a businessman whose home, and that of a neighbor, are the terrain of a moral crisis. Ann Beattie's "Janus" concerns a successful but anxious real estate agent. Then we visit with the protagonist of Sinclair Lewis's classic *Babbitt*, whose name has become synonymous with what H.L. Mencken derogated as the "booboisie." The rich man in the title of Jean Thompson's quietly unsettling story appears only briefly, but his house tells us volumes about him, even in his absence.

Part 4 (Coming Up Short) chronicles failure. Failure abounds in business, of course, and rears its head in virtually every story in this book, if you look close enough; but in this section the observations about failure are especially pointed, sometimes veering toward overt parable, as in the stories of Flannery O'Connor and O. Henry, two pioneering masters of the short story. And in a novel set in the present day, Michael Thomas, a young writer from New York City, shares the agonied insights of a character who will not lose heart, despite grinding challenges in his past and present. James Agee shows us grind without much hope to speak of, through an accounting of the lives and prospects of farmworkers in Alabama in the 1930s. Studs Terkel gives an oral history of a father who comes up short, his words echoed by those of an empathetic daughter.

Part 5 (You Can't Take It With You) affirms that death, no matter your station or profession, will not be outstripped. In Arthur Miller's classic play *Death of a Salesman*, Willy Loman is seen at the end of his tether. Joseph Conrad's "An Outpost of Progress" carries themes reminiscent of his famous novella *Heart of Darkness* (in which Kurtz utters perhaps the most famous dying words in the literature of business: "the horror, the horror"). John Updike, in "My Uncle's Death," touches on the ways in which young people carry forth the lessons of their elders, in this case a rarely seen uncle who leaves a lasting mark. And the book closes with Leo Tolstoy's "Master and Man," a morally urgent parable of commercial ambition and the possibility of redemption.

Minding the Store is the tip of a mighty iceberg—a mere sampling of writers whose work invites (and will reward) further exploration. Their stories promise to be a source of deep and lasting pleasure and will stand up to repeated readings, yielding new layers of insight with each return.

PART 1

The Hard Sell

Raymond Carver

ARE THESE ACTUAL MILES?

Raymond Carver *(1938–1988) was born in Clatskanie, Oregon, to a family in uncertain circumstances; his mother worked as a retail clerk and waitress, and his father was a Dust Bowl refugee who found employment in the lumber mills. He lived most of his life in the Pacific Northwest. His writing—poetry, essays, and short stories—is a source of wonderment and insight. His first collection,* Will You Please Be Quiet, Please? *(1976), where the story below first appeared (under the title "What Is It?"), was nominated for a National Book Award. Two other collections,* Cathedral *(1983) and* Where I'm Calling From: New and Selected Stories *(1988), were nominated for a Pulitzer Prize and the National Book Critics Circle Award. He never wrote a novel—couldn't find the time, he said, amid the pressures of other jobs, parenting, doing the laundry, what have you—but his short fiction is among the most emotionally penetrating we have, in America or anywhere, and has been translated into more than twenty languages. In this story, a couple is forced to part with a prized possession, under trying circumstances: a hard sell if there ever was one.*

Fact is the car needs to be sold in a hurry, and Leo sends Toni out to do it. Toni is smart and has personality. She used to sell children's encyclopedias door to door. She signed him up, even though he didn't have kids. Afterward, Leo asked her for a date, and the date led to this. This deal has to be cash, and it has to be done tonight. Tomorrow somebody they owe might slap a lien on the car. Monday they'll be in court, home free—but word on them went out yesterday, when their lawyer mailed the letters of intention. The hearing on Monday is nothing to worry about, the lawyer has said. They'll be asked some questions, and they'll sign some papers, and that's it. But sell the convertible, he said—today, *tonight*. They can hold onto the little car, Leo's car, no problem. But they go into court with that big convertible, the court will take it, and that's that.

Toni dresses up. It's four o'clock in the afternoon. Leo worries the lots will close. But Toni takes her time dressing. She puts on a new white blouse, wide lacy cuffs, the new two-piece suit, new heels. She transfers the stuff from her straw purse into the new patent-leather handbag. She studies the lizard makeup pouch and puts that in too. Toni has been two hours on her hair and face. Leo stands in the bedroom doorway and taps his lips with his knuckles, watching.

"You're making me nervous," she says. "I wish you wouldn't just stand," she says. "So tell me how I look."

"You look fine," he says. "You look great. I'd buy a car from you anytime."

"But you don't have money," she says, peering into the mirror. She pats her hair, frowns. "And your credit's lousy. You're nothing," she says. "Teasing," she says and looks at him in the mirror. "Don't be serious," she says. "It has to be done, so I'll do it. You take it out, you'd be lucky to get three, four hundred and we both know it. Honey, you'd be lucky if you didn't have to pay *them*." She gives her hair a final pat, gums her lips, blots the lipstick with a tissue. She turns away from the mirror and picks up her purse. "I'll have to have dinner or something, I told you that already, that's the way they work, I know them. But don't worry, I'll get out of it," she says. "I can handle it."

"Jesus," Leo says, "did you have to say that?"

She looks at him steadily. "Wish me luck," she says.

"Luck," he says. "You have the pink slip?" he says.

She nods. He follows her through the house, a tall woman with a small high bust, broad hips and thighs. He scratches a pimple on his neck. "You're sure?" he says. "Make sure. You have to have the pink slip."

"I have the pink slip," she says.

"Make sure."

She starts to say something, instead looks at herself in the front window and then shakes her head.

"At least call," he says. "Let me know what's going on."

"I'll call," she says. "Kiss, kiss. Here," she says and points to the corner of her mouth. "Careful," she says.

He holds the door for her. "Where are you going to try first?" he says. She moves past him and onto the porch.

Ernest Williams looks from across the street. In his Bermuda shorts, stomach hanging, he looks at Leo and Toni as he directs a spray onto his begonias. Once, last winter, during the holidays, when Toni and the kids were visiting his mother's, Leo brought a woman home. Nine o'clock the next morning, a cold foggy Saturday, Leo walked the woman to the car, surprised Ernest Williams on the sidewalk with a newspaper in his hand. Fog drifted, Ernest Williams stared, then slapped the paper against his leg, hard.

Leo recalls that slap, hunches his shoulders, says, "You have someplace in mind first?"

"I'll just go down the line," she says. "The first lot, then I'll just go down the line."

"Open at nine hundred," he says. "Then come down. Nine hundred is low bluebook, even on a cash deal."

"I know where to start," she says.

Ernest Williams turns the hose in their direction. He stares at them through the spray of water. Leo has an urge to cry out a confession.

"Just making sure," he says.

"Okay, okay," she says. "I'm off."

It's her car, they call it her car, and that makes it all the worse. They bought it new that summer three years ago. She wanted something to do after the kids started school, so she went back selling. He was working six days a week in the fiber-glass plant. For a while they didn't know how to spend the money. Then they put a thousand on the convertible and doubled and tripled the payments until in a year they had it paid. Earlier, while she was dressing, he took the jack and spare from the trunk and emptied the glove compartment of pencils, matchbooks, Blue Chip stamps. Then he washed it and vacuumed inside. The red hood and fenders shine.

"Good luck," he says and touches her elbow.

She nods. He sees she is already gone, already negotiating.

"Things are going to be different!" he calls to her as she reaches the driveway. "We start over Monday. I mean it."

Ernest Williams looks at them and turns his head and spits. She gets into the car and lights a cigarette.

"This time next week!" Leo calls again. "Ancient history!"

He waves as she backs into the street. She changes gear and starts ahead. She accelerates and the tires give a little scream.

In the kitchen Leo pours Scotch and carries the drink to the backyard. The kids are at his mother's. There was a letter three days ago, his name penciled on the outside of the dirty envelope, the only letter all summer not demanding payment in full. We are having fun, the letter said. We like Grandma. We have a new dog called Mr. Six. He is nice. We love him. Good-bye.

He goes for another drink. He adds ice and sees that his hand trembles. He holds the hand over the sink. He looks at the hand for a while, sets down the glass, and holds out the other hand. Then he picks up the glass and goes back outside to sit on the steps. He recalls when he was a kid his dad pointing at a fine house, a tall white house surrounded by apple trees and a high white rail fence. "That's Finch," his dad said admiringly. "He's been in bankruptcy at least twice. Look at that house." But bankruptcy is a company collapsing utterly, executives cutting their wrists and throwing themselves from windows, thousands of men on the street.

Leo and Toni still had furniture. Leo and Toni had furniture and Toni and the kids had clothes. Those things were exempt. What else? Bicycles for the kids, but these he had sent to his mother's for safekeeping. The portable air-conditioner and the appliances, new washer and dryer, trucks came for those things weeks ago. What else did they have? This and that, nothing mainly, stuff that wore out or fell to pieces long ago. But there were some big parties back there, some fine travel. To Reno and Tahoe, at eighty with the top down and the radio playing. Food, that was one of the big items. They gorged on food. He figures thousands on luxury items alone. Toni would go to the grocery and put in everything she saw. "I had to do without when I was a kid," she says.

"These kids are not going to do without," as if he'd been insisting they should. She joins all the book clubs. "We never had books around when I was a kid," she says as she tears open the heavy packages. They enroll in the record clubs for something to play on the new stereo. They sign up for it all. Even a pedigreed terrier named Ginger. He paid two hundred and found her run over in the street a week later. They buy what they want. If they can't pay, they charge. They sign up.

His undershirt is wet; he can feel the sweat rolling from his underarms. He sits on the step with his empty glass in his hand and watches the shadows fill up the yard. He stretches, wipes his face. He listens to the traffic on the highway and considers whether he should go to the basement, stand on the utility sink, and hang himself with his belt. He understands he is willing to be dead.

Inside he makes a large drink and he turns the TV on and he fixes something to eat. He sits at the table with chili and crackers and watches something about a blind detective. He clears the table. He washes the pan and the bowl, dries these things and puts them away, then allows himself a look at the clock.

It's after nine. She's been gone nearly five hours.

He pours Scotch, adds water, carries the drink to the living room. He sits on the couch but finds his shoulders so stiff they won't let him lean back. He stares at the screen and sips, and soon he goes for another drink. He sits again. A news program begins—it's ten o'clock—and he says, "God, what in God's name has gone wrong?" and goes to the kitchen to return with more Scotch. He sits, he closes his eyes, and opens them when he hears the telephone ringing.

"I wanted to call," she says.

"Where are you?" he says. He hears piano music, and his heart moves.

"I don't know," she says. "Someplace. We're having a drink, then we're going someplace else for dinner. I'm with the sales manager. He's crude, but he's all right. He bought the car. I have to go now. I was on my way to the ladies and saw the phone."

"Did somebody buy the car?" Leo says. He looks out the kitchen window to the place in the drive where she always parks.

"I told you," she says. "I have to go now."

"Wait, wait a minute, for Christ's sake," he says. "Did somebody buy the car or not?"

"He had his checkbook out when I left," she says. "I have to go now. I have to go to the bathroom."

"Wait!" he yells. The line goes dead. He listens to the dial tone. "Jesus Christ," he says as he stands with the receiver in his hand.

He circles the kitchen and goes back to the living room. He sits. He gets up. In the bathroom he brushes his teeth very carefully. Then he uses dental floss. He washes his face and goes back to the kitchen. He looks at the clock and takes a clean glass from a set that has a hand of playing cards painted on each glass. He fills the glass with ice. He stares for a while at the glass he left in the sink.

He sits against one end of the couch and puts his legs up at the other end. He looks at the screen, realizes he can't make out what the people are saying. He turns the empty glass in his hand and considers biting off the rim. He shivers for a time and thinks of going to bed, though he knows he will dream of a large woman with gray hair. In the dream he is always leaning over tying his shoelaces. When he straightens up, she looks at him, and he bends to tie again. He looks at his hand. It makes a fist as he watches. The telephone is ringing.

"Where are you, honey?" he says slowly, gently.

"We're at this restaurant," she says, her voice strong, bright.

"Honey, which restaurant?" he says. He puts the heel of his hand against his eye and pushes.

"Downtown someplace," she says. "I think it's New Jimmy's. Excuse me," she says to someone off the line, "is this place New Jimmy's? This is New Jimmy's, Leo," she says to him. "Everything is all right, we're almost finished, then he's going to bring me home."

"Honey?" he says. He holds the receiver against his ear and rocks back and forth, eyes closed. "Honey?"

"I have to go," she says. "I wanted to call. Anyway, guess how much?"

"Honey," he says.

"Six and a quarter," she says. "I have it in my purse. He said there's no market for convertibles. I guess we're born lucky," she says and laughs. "I told him everything. I think I had to."

"Honey," Leo says.

"What?" she says.

"Please, honey," Leo says.

"He said he sympathizes," she says. "But he would have said any-thing." She laughs again. "He said personally he'd rather be classified a robber or a rapist than a bankrupt. He's nice enough, though," she says.

"Come home," Leo says. "Take a cab and come home."

"I can't," she says. "I told you, we're halfway through dinner."

"I'll come for you," he says.

"No," she says. "I said we're just finishing. I told you, it's part of the deal. They're out for all they can get. But don't worry, we're about to leave. I'll be home in a little while." She hangs up.

In a few minutes he calls New Jimmy's. A man answers. "New Jimmy's has closed for the evening," the man says.

"I'd like to talk to my wife," Leo says.

"Does she work here?" the man asks. "Who is she?"

"She's a customer," Leo says. "She's with someone. A business person."

"Would I know her?" the man says. "What is her name?"

"I don't think you know her," Leo says.

"That's all right," Leo says. "That's all right. I see her now."

"Thank you for calling New Jimmy's," the man says.

Leo hurries to the window. A car he doesn't recognize slows in front of the house, then picks up speed. He waits. Two, three hours later, the telephone rings again. There is no one at the other end when he picks up the receiver. There is only a dial tone.

"I'm right here!" Leo screams into the receiver.

Near dawn he hears footsteps on the porch. He gets up from the couch. The set hums, the screen glows. He opens the door. She bumps the wall coming in. She grins. Her face is puffy, as if she's been sleeping under se-dation. She works her lips, ducks heavily and sways as he cocks his fist.

"Go ahead," she says thickly. She stands there swaying. Then she makes a noise and lunges, catches his shirt, tears it down the front. "Bankrupt!" she screams. She twists loose, grabs and tears his under-shirt at the neck. "You son of a bitch," she says, clawing.

He squeezes her wrists, then lets go, steps back, looking for something heavy. She stumbles as she heads for the bedroom. "Bankrupt," she mutters. He hears her fall on the bed and groan.

He waits awhile, then splashes water on his face and goes to the bedroom. He turns the lights on, looks at her, and begins to take her clothes off. He pulls and pushes her from side to side undressing her. She says something in her sleep and moves her hand. He takes off her underpants, looks at them closely under the light, and throws them into a corner. He turns back the covers and rolls her in, naked. Then he opens her purse. He is reading the check when he hears the car come into the drive.

He looks through the front curtain and sees the convertible in the drive, its motor running smoothly, the headlamps burning, and he closes and opens his eyes. He sees a tall man come around in front of the car and up to the front porch. The man lays something on the porch and starts back to the car. He wears a white linen suit.

Leo turns on the porch light and opens the door cautiously. Her makeup pouch lies on the top step. The man looks at Leo across the front of the car, and then gets back inside and releases the handbrake.

"Wait!" Leo calls and starts down the steps. The man brakes the car as Leo walks in front of the lights. The car creaks against the brake. Leo tries to pull the two pieces of his shirt together, tries to bunch it all into his trousers.

"What is it you want?" the man says. "Look," the man says, "I have to go. No offense. I buy and sell cars, right? The lady left her makeup. She's a fine lady, very refined. What is it?"

Leo leans against the door and looks at the man. The man takes his hands off the wheel and puts them back. He drops the gear into reverse and the car moves backward a little.

"I want to tell you," Leo says and wets his lips.

The light in Ernest Williams' bedroom goes on. The shade rolls up.

Leo shakes his head, tucks in his shirt again. He steps back from the car. "Monday," he says.

"Monday," the man says and watches for sudden movement.

Leo nods slowly.

"Well, goodnight," the man says and coughs. "Take it easy, hear? Monday, that's right. Okay, then." He takes his foot off the brake, puts it on again after he has rolled back two or three feet. "Hey, one question. Between friends, are these actual miles?" The man waits, then clears his throat. "Okay, look, it doesn't matter either way," the man says. "I have to go. Take it easy." He backs into the street, pulls away quickly, and turns the corner without stopping.

Leo tucks at his shirt and goes back in the house. He locks the front door and checks it. Then he goes to the bedroom and locks that door and turns back the covers. He looks at her before he flicks the light. He takes off his clothes, folds them carefully on the floor, and gets in beside her. He lies on his back for a time and pulls the hair on his stomach, considering. He looks at the bedroom door, outlined now in the faint outside light. Presently he reaches out his hand and touches her hip. She does not move. He turns on his side and puts his hand on her hip. He runs his fingers over her hip and feels the stretch marks there. They are like roads, and he traces them in her flesh. He runs his fingers back and forth, first one, then another. They run everywhere in her flesh, dozens, perhaps hundreds of them. He remembers waking the morning after they bought the car, seeing it, there in the drive, in the sun, gleaming.

John O'Hara

THE HARDWARE MAN

John O'Hara *(1905–1970) started as a cub reporter at a newspaper in his hometown of Pottsville, Pennsylvania. He wrote short stories for the* New Yorker *early in its history (it launched in 1925) and over the years contributed more than two hundred stories, helping shape the classic "*New Yorker *story," the gold standard of short fiction during the magazine's midcentury heyday. He was indeed prolific—eleven short-story collections, three volumes of novellas: more than four hundred pieces of short fiction in all (he also wrote novels). "The Hardware Man," which first appeared in the* Saturday Evening Post, *showcases O'Hara's uncanny ear for dialogue and his attunement to the nuances of American life, not least in the arena of commercial ambition.*

Lou Mauser had not always had money, and yet it would be hard to imagine him without it. He had owned the store—with, of course, some help from the bank—since he was in his middle twenties, and that was twenty years ago as of 1928. Twenty years is a pretty long time for a man to go without a notable financial failure, but Lou Mauser had done it, and when it has been that long, a man's worst enemies cannot say that it was all luck. They said it about Lou, but they said it in such a way as to make it sound disparaging to him while not making themselves appear foolish. It would have been very foolish to deny that Lou had worked hard or that he had been a clever business man. "You can't say it was all luck," said Tom Esterly, who was a competitor of Lou's. "You might just as well say he sold his soul to the devil. Not that he wouldn't have, mind you. But he didn't have to. Lou always seemed to be there with the cash at the right moment, and that's one of the great secrets of success. Be there with the cash when the right proposition comes along."

Lou had the cash, or got hold of it—which is the same thing—when Ada Bowler wanted to sell her late husband's hardware store. Lou was in his middle twenties then, and he had already been working in the store at least ten years, starting as a stock boy at five dollars a week. By the time he was eighteen he was a walking inventory of Bowler's stock; he knew where everything was, everything, and he knew how much everything was worth; wholesale, retail, special prices to certain contractors, the different mark-ups for different customers. A farmer came in to buy a harness snap, charge him a dime; but if another farmer, one who bought his barn paint at Bowler's wanted a harness snap, you let him have it for a nickel. You didn't have to tell Sam Bowler what you were doing. Sam Bowler relied on your good sense to do things like that. If a boy was buying a catcher's mitt, you threw in a nickel Rocket, and sure as hell when that boy was ready to buy an Iver Johnson bicycle he would come to Bowler's instead of sending away to a mail-order house. And Lou Mauser at eighteen had discovered something that had never occurred to Sam Bowler: the rich people who lived on Lantenengo Street were even more appreciative when you gave them a little something for nothing—an oil can for a kid's bike, an ice pick for the kitchen—than people who had to think twice about spending a quarter. Well, maybe they weren't *more* appreciative, but they had the money to show their appreciation. Give a Lantenengo Street boy a nickel Rocket, and his father or his uncle would buy him a dollar-and-a-quarter ball. Give a rich woman an ice pick and you'd sell her fifty foot of garden hose and a sprinkler and a lawn mower. It was all a question of knowing which ones to give things to, and Lou knew so well that when he needed the cash to buy out Sam Bowler's widow, he actually had two banks to choose from instead of just having to accept one bank's terms.

Practically overnight he became the employer of men twice his age, and he knew which ones to keep and which to fire. As soon as the papers were signed that made him the owner, he went to the store and summoned Dora Minzer, the bookkeeper, and Arthur Davis, the warehouse man. He closed his office door so that no one outside could hear what he had to say, although the other employees could see through the glass partitions.

"Give me your keys, Arthur," said Lou.

"My keys? Sure," said Arthur.

"Dora, you give me your keys, too," said Lou.

"They're in my desk drawer," said Dora Minzer.

"Get them."

Dora left the office.

"I don't understand this, Lou," said Arthur.

"If you don't, you will, as soon as Dora's back."

Dora returned and laid her keys on Lou's desk. "There," she said.

"Arthur says he doesn't understand why I want your keys. You do, don't you, Dora?"

"Well—maybe I do, maybe I don't." She shrugged.

"You two are the only ones that I'm asking for their keys," said Lou.

Arthur took a quick look at Dora Minzer, who did not look at him. "Yeah, what's the meaning of it, Lou?"

"The meaning of it is, you both put on your coat and hat and get out."

"Fired?" said Arthur.

"Fired is right," said Lou.

"No notice? I been here twenty-two years. Dora was here pretty near that long."

"Uh-huh. And I been here ten. Five of those ten the two of you been robbing Sam Bowler that I know of. That I know of. I'm pretty sure you didn't only start robbing him five years ago."

"I'll sue you for slander," said Arthur.

"Go ahead," said Lou.

"Oh, shut up, Arthur," said Dora. "He knows. I told you he was too smart."

"He'd have a hard time proving anything," said Arthur.

"Yeah, but when I did you know where you'd be. You and Dora, and two purchasing agents, and two building contractors. All in it together. Maybe there's more than them, but those I could prove. The contractors, I'm licked. The purchasing agents, I want their companies' business, so all I'm doing there is get them fired. What are you gonna tell them in Sunday School next Sunday, Arthur?"

"*She* thought of it," said Arthur Davis, looking at Dora Minzer.

"That I don't doubt. It took brains to fool Sam Bowler all those years. What'd you do with your share, Dora?"

"My nephew. I educated him and started him up in business. He owns a drug store in Elmira, New York."

"Then he ought to take care of you. Where did yours go, Arthur?"

"Huh. With five kids on my salary, putting them through High, clothes and doctor bills, the wife and her doctor bills. Music lessons. A piano. Jesus Christ, I wonder Sam didn't catch on. How did *you* catch on?"

"You just answered that yourself. I used to see all those kids of yours, going to Sunday School, all dolled up."

"Well, they're all married or got jobs," said Arthur Davis. "I guess I'll find something. Who are you gonna tell about this? If I say I quit."

"What the hell do you expect me to do? You're a couple of thieves, both of you. Sam Bowler treated everybody right. There's eight other people working here that raised families and didn't steal. I don't feel any pity for you. As soon as you get caught you try to blame it all on Dora. And don't forget this, Arthur." He leaned forward. "*You were gonna steal from me.* The two of you. This morning a shipment came in. Two hundred rolls of tarpaper. An hour later, fifty rolls went out on the wagon, but show me where we got any record of that sale of fifty rolls. That was this morning, Arthur. You didn't even wait one day, you or Dora."

"That was him, did that," said Dora. "I told him to wait. Stupid."

"They're all looking at us, out on the floor," said Arthur.

"Yes, and probably guessing," said Lou. "I got no more to say to either one of you. Just get out."

They rose, and Dora went to the outer office and put on her coat and hat and walked to the street door without speaking to anyone. Arthur went to the back stairs that led to the warehouse. There he unpacked a crate of brand-new Smith & Wesson revolvers and broke open a case of ammunition. He then put a bullet through his skull, and Lou Mauser entered a new phase of his business career.

He had a rather slow first year. People thought of him as a coldblooded young man who had driven a Sunday School superintendent to suicide. But as the scandal was absorbed into local history, the unfavorable

judgment was gradually amended until it more closely conformed with
the early opinion of the business men, which was sympathetic to Lou.
Dora Minzer, after all, had gone away, presumably to Elmira, New York;
and though there were rumors about the purchasing agents of two
independent mining companies, Lou did not publicly implicate them.
The adjusted public opinion of Lou Mauser had it that he had behaved
very well indeed, and that he had proven himself to be a better business
man than Sam Bowler. Only a few people chose to keep alive the story
of the Arthur Davis suicide, and those few probably would have found
some other reason to be critical of Lou if Arthur had lived.

Lou, of course, did not blame himself, and during the first year of his
ownership of the store, while he was under attack, he allowed his resentment to harden him until he became in fact the ruthless creature
they said he was. He engaged in price-cutting against the other hardware stores, and one of the newer stores was driven out of business because of its inability to compete with Lou Mauser and Tom Esterly.

"All right, Mr. Esterly," said Lou. "There's one less of us. Do you
want to call it quits?"

"You started it, young fellow," said Tom Esterly. "And I can last as
long as you can and maybe a *little* bit longer. If you want to start making a profit again, that's up to you. But I don't intend to enter into any
agreement with you, now or any other time."

"You cut your prices when I did," said Lou.

"You bet I did."

"Then you're just as much to blame as I am, for what happened to
McDonald. You helped put him out of business, and you'll get your
share of what's left."

"Yes, and maybe I'll get your share, too," said Tom Esterly. "The Es-
terlys were in business before the Civil War."

"I know that. I would have bought your store if I could have. Maybe
I will yet."

"Don't bank on it, young fellow. Don't bank on it. Let's see how
good your credit is when you need it. Let's see how long the jobbers
and the manufacturers will carry you. I *know* how far they'll carry Esterly Brothers. We gave some of those manufacturers their first orders,

thirty, forty years ago. My father was dealing with some of them when Sam Bowler was in diapers. Mauser, you have a lot to learn."

"Esterly and Mauser. That's the sign I'd like to put up some day."

"It'll be over my dead body. I'd go out of business first. Put up the shutters."

"Oh, I didn't want you as a partner. I'd just continue the name."

"Will you please get out of my store?"

Tom Esterly was a gentleman, a graduate of Gibbsville High and Gettysburg College, prominent in Masonic circles, and on the boards of the older charities. The word upstart was not in his working vocabulary and he had no epithet for Lou Mauser, but he disliked the fellow so thoroughly that he issued one of his rare executive orders to his clerks: hereafter, when Esterly Brothers were out of an article, whether it was a five-cent article or a fifty-dollar one, the clerks were not to suggest that the customer try Bowler's. For Tom Esterly this was a serious change of policy, and represented an attitude that refused to admit the existence of Mauser's competition. On the street he inclined his head when Mauser spoke to him, but he did not actually speak to Mauser.

Lou Mauser's next offense was to advertise. Sam Bowler had never advertised, and Esterly Brothers' advertising consisted solely of complimentary cards in the high school annual and the program of the yearly concert of the Lutheran church choir. These cards read, "Esterly Bros., Est. 1859, 211 N. Main St.," and that was all. No mention of the hardware business. Tom Esterly was shocked and repelled to see a full-page ad in each of the town newspapers, announcing a giant spring sale at Bowler's Hardware Store, Lou Mauser, Owner & Proprietor. It was the first hardware store ad in Gibbsville history and, worse, it was the first time Mauser had put his name on Sam Bowler's store. Tom Esterly went and had a look, and, yes, Mauser not only had put his name in the ad; he had his name painted on the store windows in lettering almost as large as Bowler's. The sale was, of course, a revival of Mauser's price-cutting tactic, even though it was advertised to last only three days. And Mauser offered legitimate bargains; some items, Tom knew, were going at cost. While the sale was on there were almost no customers in Esterly Brothers. "They're all down at Mauser's," said Jake Potts, Tom's head clerk.

"You mean Bowler's," said Tom.

"Well, yes, but I bet you he takes Sam's name off inside of another year," said Jake.

"Where is he getting the money, Jake?"

"Volume. What they call volume. He got two fellows with horse and buggy calling on the farmers."

"Salesmen?"

"Two of them. They talk Pennsylvania Dutch and they go around to the farms. Give the woman a little present the first time, and they drive their buggies right up in the field and talk to the farmers. Give the farmers a pack of chewing tobacco and maybe a tie-strap for the team. My brother-in-law down the Valley told me. They don't try to sell nothing the first visit, but the farmer remembers that chewing tobacco. Next time the farmer comes to market, if he needs anything he goes to Bowler's."

"Well, farmers are slow pay. We never catered much to farmers."

"All the same, Tom, it takes a lot of paint to cover a barn, and they're buying their paint off of Mauser. My brother-in-law told me Mauser's allowing credit all over the place. Any farmer with a cow and a mule can get credit."

"There'll be a day of reckoning, with that kind of foolishness. And it's wrong, *wrong*, to get those farmers in debt. You know how they are, some of them. They come in here to buy one thing, and before they know it they run up a bill for things they don't need."

"Yes, I know it. So does Mauser. But he's getting the volume, Tom. Small profit, big volume."

"Wait till he has to send a bill collector around to the farmers. His chewing tobacco won't do him any good then," said Tom Esterly.

"No, I guess not," said Jake Potts.

"The cash. I still don't see where he gets his cash. You say volume, but volume on credit sales won't supply him with cash."

"Well, I guess if you show the bank a lot of accounts receivable. And he has a lot of them, Tom. A lot. You get everybody owing you money, most of them are going to pay you some day. Most people around here pay their bills."

"You criticizing our policy, Jake?"

"Well, times change, Tom, and you gotta fight fire with fire."

"Would you want to work for a man like Mauser?"

"No, and I told him so," said Jake Potts.

"He wanted to hire you away from me?"

"A couple of months ago, but I said no. I been here too long, and I might as well stay till I retire. But look down there, Tom. Down there between the counters. One lady customer. All the others are at Mauser's sale."

"He tried to steal you away from me. That's going too far," said Tom Esterly. "Would you mind telling me what he offered you?"

"Thirty a week and a percentage on new business."

"Thinking you'd get our customers to follow you there. Well, I guess I have to raise you to thirty. But the way it looks now, I can't offer you a percentage on new business. It's all going in the opposite direction."

"I didn't ask for no raise, Tom."

"You get it anyway, starting this week. If you quit, I'd just about have to go out of business. I don't have anybody to take your place. And I keep putting off the decision, who'll be head clerk when you retire. Paul Schlitzer's next in line, but he's getting forgetful. I guess it'll be Norman Johnson. Younger."

"Don't count on Norm, Tom."

"Mauser been making him offers?"

"I don't know for sure, but that's my guess. When a fellow starts acting independent, he has some good reason behind it. Norm's been getting in late in the morning and when ha' past five comes he don't wait for me to tell him to pull down the shades."

"Have you said anything to him?"

"Not so far. But we better start looking for somebody else. It don't have to be a hardware man. Any bright young fellow with experience working behind a counter. I can show him the ropes, before I retire."

"All right, I'll leave that up to you," said Tom Esterly. On his next encounter with Lou Mauser he stopped him.

"Like to talk to you a minute," said Tom Esterly.

"Fine and dandy," said Mauser. "Let's move over to the curb, out of people's way."

"I don't have much to say," said Tom Esterly. "I just want to tell you you're going too far, trying to hire my people away from me."

"It's a free country, Mr. Esterly. If a man wants to better himself. And I guess Jake Potts bettered himself. Did you meet my offer?"

"Jake Potts wouldn't have worked for you, offer or no offer."

"But he's better off now than he was before. He ought to be thankful to me. Mister, I'll make an offer to anybody I want to hire, in your store or anybody else's. I don't have to ask your permission. Any more than I asked your permission to run a big sale. I had new customers in my store that I never saw before, even when Sam Bowler was the owner. I made *you* an offer, so why shouldn't I make an offer to fellows that work for you?"

"Good day, sir," said Tom Esterly.

"Good day to you," said Lou Mauser.

Tom Esterly was prepared for the loss of Norman Johnson, but when Johnson revealed a hidden talent for window decorating, he felt cheated. The window that attracted so much attention that it was written up in both newspapers was an autumnal camping scene that occupied all the space in Mauser's window. Two dummies, dressed in gunning costume, were seated at a campfire outside a tent. An incandescent lamp simulated the glow of the fire, and real pine and spruce branches and fake grass were used to provide a woodland effect. Every kind of weapon, from shotgun to automatic pistol, was on display, leaning against logs or lying on the fake grass. There were hunting knives and compasses, Marble match cases and canteens, cots and blankets, shell boxes of canvas and leather, fireless cookers, fishing tackle, carbide and kerosene lamps, an Old Towne canoe, gun cases and revolver holsters, duck calls and decoys and flasks and first-aid kits. Wherever there was space between the merchandise items, Norman Johnson had put stuffed chipmunk and quail, and peering out from the pine and spruce were the mounted heads of a cinnamon bear, a moose, an elk, a deer, and high above it all was a stuffed wildcat, permanently snarling.

All day long men would stop and stare, and after school small boys would shout and point and argue and wish. There had never been anything like it in Bowler's or Esterly Brothers' windows, and when the display was removed at Thanksgiving time there were expressions of regret. The small boys had to find some place else to go. But Norman Johnson's hunting-camp window became an annual event, a highly profitable one for Lou Mauser.

"Maybe we should never of let Norm go," said Jake Potts.

"He's right where he belongs," said Tom Esterly. "Right exactly where he belongs. That's the way those medicine shows do business. Honest value, good merchandise, that's what we were founded on and no tricks."

"We only sold two shotguns and not any rifles this season, Tom. The next thing we know we'll lose the rifle franchise."

"Well, we never did sell many rifles. This is mostly shotgun country."

"I don't know," said Jake. "We used to do a nice business in .22's. We must of sold pretty close to three hundred of the .22 pump gun, and there's a nice steady profit in the cartridges."

"I'll grant you we used to sell the .22 rifle, other years. But they're talking about a law prohibiting them in the borough limits. Ever since the Leeds boy put the Kerry boy's eye out."

"Tom, you won't face facts," said Jake. "We're losing business to this fellow, and it ain't only in the sporting goods line or any one line. It's every which way. Kitchen utensils. Household tools. Paints and varnishes. There's never the people in the store there used to be. When you's first in charge, after your Pa passed on, just about the only thing we didn't sell was something to eat. If you can eat it, we don't sell it, was our motto."

"That was never our motto. That was just a funny saying," said Tom Esterly.

"Well, yes. But we used to have funny sayings like that. My clerks used to all have their regular customers. Man'd come in and buy everything from the same clerk. Had to be waited on by the same clerk no matter what they come in to buy. Why, I can remember old Mrs. Stokes one day she come in to borrow my umbrella, and I was off that day and she wouldn't take anybody else's umbrella. That's the kind of customers we used to have. But where are those people today? They're down at Lou Mauser's. Why? Because for instance when school opened in September every boy and girl in the public and the Catholic school got a foot-rule from Lou Mauser. They maybe cost him half a cent apiece, and say there's a thousand children in school. Five dollars."

"Jake, you're always telling me of those kind of things. You make me wonder if you wouldn't rather be working for Mauser."

"I'll tell you anything if it's for your own good. You don't have your Pa or your Uncle Ed to tell you no more. It's for my own good too, I'll admit. I retire next year, and I won't get my fifty a month if you have to close down."

"Close down? You mean run out of business by Mauser?"

"Unless you do something to meet the competition. Once before you said Mauser would have trouble with the jobbers and the manufacturers. Instead of which the shoe is on the other foot now. Don't fool yourself, Tom. Those manufacturers go by the orders we send in, and some articles we're overstocked from last year."

"I'll tell you this. I'd sooner go out of business than do things his way. Don't worry. You'll get your pension. I have other sources of income besides the store."

"If you have to close the store I'll go without my pension. I won't take charity. I'll get other work."

"With Mauser."

"No, I won't work for Mauser. That's one thing I never will do. He as good as put the gun to Arthur Davis's head, and Arthur was a friend of mine, crook or no crook. I don't know what Mauser said to Arthur that day, but whatever it was, Arthur didn't see no other way out. That kind of a man I wouldn't work for. He has blood on his hands, to my way of thinking. When I meet Arthur Davis in the after life I don't want him looking at me and saying I wasn't a true friend."

"Arthur would never say that about you, Jake."

"He might. You didn't know Arthur Davis as good as I did. There was a man that was all worries. I used to walk home from work with him sometimes. First it was worr'ing because Minnie wasn't sure she was gonna marry him. Then all them children, and Minnie sick half the time, but the children had to look just so. Music lessons. A little money to get them started when they got married. They say it was Dora Minzer showed him how they could knock down off of Sam Bowler, and I believe that. But I didn't believe what they said about something going on between him and Dora. No. Them two, they both had a weakness for money and that was all there was between them. How much they stole off of Sam Bowler we'll never know, but Arthur's share was put to good use, and Sam never missed it. Neither did Ada Bowler. Arthur wouldn't of stole that money if Sam and Ada had children."

"Now you're going too far. You don't know that, and I don't believe it. Arthur did what Dora told him to. And what about the disgrace? Wouldn't Arthur's children rather be brought up poor than have their father die a thief?"

"I don't know," said Jake. "Some of it was honest money. Nobody knows how much was stolen money. The children didn't know any of it was stolen money till the end. By that time they all had a good bringing-up. All a credit to their parents and their church and the town. A nicer family you couldn't hope to see. And they were brought up honest. Decent respectable youngsters, all of them. You can't blame them if they didn't ask their father where the money was coming from. Sam Bowler didn't get suspicious, did he? The only one got suspicious was Lou Mauser. And they say he kept his mouth shut for six or seven years, so he was kind of in on it. If I ever saw one of our fellows look like he was knocking down off of you, I'd report it. But Lou Mauser never let a peep out of him till he was the owner. I sometimes wonder maybe he was hoping they'd steal so much they'd bankrupt Sam, and then he could buy the store cheaper."

"Well, now that's interesting," said Tom Esterly. "I wouldn't put it past him for a minute."

"I don't say it's true, but it'd be like him," said Jake. "No, I'd never go to work for that fellow. Even at my age I'd rather dig ditches."

"You'll never have to dig ditches as long as I'm alive, and don't say you won't take charity. You'll take your pension from Esterly Brothers regardless of whether we're still in business or not. So don't let me hear any more of that kind of talk. In fact, go on back to work. There's a customer down there."

"Wants the loan of my umbrella, most likely," said Jake. "Raining, out."

Esterly Brothers lasted longer than Jake Potts expected, and longer than Jake Potts himself. There were some bad years, easy to explain, but there were years in which the store showed a profit, and it was difficult to explain that. Lou Mauser expanded; he bought the store property adjoining his. He opened branch stores in two other towns in the county. He dropped the Bowler name completely. Esterly Brothers stayed put and as is, the middle of the store as dark as usual, so that the electric lights had to burn all day. The heavy hardware store fragrance—something between the pungency of a blacksmith's shop and the sweetness of the apothecary's—was missing from Lou Mauser's well-ventilated buildings, and he staffed his business with young go-getters. But some of the old Esterly Brothers customers returned after temporarily defecting to Mauser's, and at Esterly's they found two or three of the aging clerks whom they had last seen at Mauser's, veterans of the Bowler days. Although he kept it to himself, Tom Esterly had obviously decided to meet the go-getter's competition with an atmosphere that was twenty years behind the times. Cash customers had to wait while their money was sent to the back of the store on an overhead trolley, change made, and the change returned in the wooden cup that was screwed to the trolley wire. Tom never did put in an electric cash register, and the only special sale he held was when he offered a fifty percent reduction on his entire stock on the occasion of his going out of business. Three successive bad years, the only time it had happened since the founding of the store, were unarguable, and he put an ad in both papers to announce his decision. His announcement was simple:

50% Off

Entire Stock

Going Out of Business

Sale Commences Aug. 1, 1922

ESTERLY BROTHERS

Est. 1859

Open 8 A.M.—9 P.M. During Sale

All Sales Cash Only—All Sales Final

On the morning after the advertisements appeared, Tom Esterly went to his office and found, not to his surprise, Lou Mauser awaiting his appearance.

"Well, what can I do for *you*?" said Tom.

"I saw your ad. I didn't know it was that bad," said Lou. "I'm honestly sorry."

"I don't see why," said Tom. "It's what you've been aiming at. Why did you come here? If you want to buy anything, my clerks will wait on you."

"I'll buy your entire stock, twenty cents on the dollar."

"I think I'll do better this way, selling to the public."

"There'll be a lot left over."

"I'll give that away," said Tom Esterly.

"Twenty cents on the dollar, Mr. Esterly, and you won't have to give none of it away."

"You'd want me to throw in the good will and fixtures," said Esterly.

"Well, yes."

"I might be tempted to sell to you. The stock and the fixtures. But the good will would have to be separate."

"How much for the good will?" said Lou Mauser.

"A million dollars cash. Oh, I know it isn't worth it, Mauser, but I wouldn't sell it to you for any less. In other words, it isn't for sale to you. A week from Saturday night at nine o'clock, this store goes out of business forever. But no part of it belongs to you."

"The last couple years you been running this store like a hobby. You lost money hand over fist."

"I had it to lose, and those three years gave me more pleasure than all the rest put together. When this store closes a lot of people are going to miss it. Not because it was a store. *You* have a *store*. But we had something better. We never had to give away foot-rules to schoolchildren, or undercut our competitors. We never did any of those things, and before we *would* do them we decided to close up shop. But first we gave some of the people something to remember. Our kind of store, not yours, Mauser."

"Are you one of those that held it against me because of Arthur Davis?"

"No."

"Then what did you hold against me?"

"Sam Bowler gave you your first job, promoted you regularly, gave you raises, encouraged you. How did you repay him? By looking the other way all the time that you knew Arthur Davis and Dora Minzer were robbing him. Some say you did it because you hoped Sam would go bankrupt and you could buy the business cheap. Maybe yes, maybe no. That part isn't what I hold against you. It was you looking the other way, never telling Sam what they were doing to him. *That* was when you killed Arthur Davis, Mauser. Sam Bowler was the kind of man that if you'd told him about Arthur and Dora, he would have kept it quiet and given them both another chance. You never gave them another chance. You didn't even give them the chance to make restitution. I don't know about Dora Minzer, but Arthur Davis had a conscience, and a man that has a conscience is entitled to put it to work. Arthur Davis would have spent the rest of his life trying to pay Sam back, and he'd be alive today, still paying Ada Bowler, no doubt. Having a hard time, no doubt. But alive and with his conscience satisfied. You didn't kill Arthur by firing him that day. You killed him a long time before that by looking the other way. And I'm sure you don't understand a word I'm saying."

"No wonder you're going out of business. You should of been a preacher."

"I thought about it," said Tom Esterly. "But I didn't have the call."

Colson Whitehead

from *JOHN HENRY DAYS*

Colson Whitehead *(1969–) writes knowingly of the vulnerability of American consumers to their own affectations. One wily character born to exploit such vulnerability is Lucien, a comic confection of American worldliness and mojo. But Lucien is no fake or counterfeiter; he is exactly as he appears to be. Colson Whitehead was born and raised in New York City. In addition to* John Henry Days, *from which this excerpt is reprinted, his novels include* The Intuitionist *(1999) and* Apex Hides the Hurt *(2006). He lives in Brooklyn.*

There is a peaceful listlessness in the way the towncar glides through these valleys that makes Lucien think this is the way things were meant to be all along. That in the shrinking dregs of the Ice Age glaciers retreated and scraped through mountains in order to facilitate these modern highways; the final and supreme use of accumulated eons of pulverized stone is gravel for highway shoulders; the succession of rivers they pass merely affirms their progress like milestones, and the water cycle is just a little something on the side. He has come to believe that the intent of geological dynamism is modern convenience. Everything, in fact, all these ancient mechanisms. Somehow four fingers becomes the most practical arrangement, the opposable thumb and that whole mess, and on this day the driver steers the luxury automobile across tempered asphalt with accomplished digits. Is there a liquid that makes the air conditioner work, the way there is Freon in refrigerators? This substance biding its time through humdrum epochs for its ultimate deployment against Southern humidity, the prevention of perspiration stains on Lucien's suit. The inexorable tending towardness of all things.

Heady thoughts of a p.r. flack on a Saturday morning.

Lawrence Flittings, his right-hand man, dependable lieutenant, sits to his left and answers Lucien's questions with care. Lucien gazes at the passing hills and inquires about the preparations without listening to Lawrence's rehearsed answers. He knows Lawrence has taken care of every grubby detail but understands that the man needs to prove his efficiency, and hence this game. Lawrence is as close as Lucien has ever come to having an efficient gay assistant without having a bona fide efficient gay assistant. Lucien asks, How is the hotel, how was the dinner last night, which junketeers have made the trip?

What Lucien really wants to know is if Lawrence can name those trees. Crawling along the mountainside, all the way up to the cracked peaks, the trees march unperturbed by the incline, stand up straight despite the insinuations of gravity. They must have strong roots, all intertwined underground. They work together to keep from rolling down the slope, to provide for Lucien's delectation a calming introduction to the natural beauty of West Virginia. The hotel is small but comfortable, Lawrence says, the dinner last night was enjoyed by all, the usual suspects from the media pool are in attendance, and now Lucien lobs a poser: Do you know the names of those trees, Lawrence?

There is nothing in his laptop or in his post-it-festooned clipboard to aid him. Lawrence says swiftly, "I don't know," and Lucien nods, looking out the window all the while. If the driver can help them out with a little native lore, he does not say. Lucien has to keep Lawrence on his toes. He looks into the future: Next time they have an out-of-town event, Lawrence will research all the local flora and fauna, just in case. But Lucien will not ask the next time. Lawrence will wait for the question but it will not come, then he'll try to slip his new knowledge into the conversation somehow. Listen to that red-breasted robin, Lucien, it's their mating season and that is their mating call.

These trees do not dissemble. They are true to their natures, like Lucien. Lawrence his first day on the job probably imagined he was coming to work for a Mike Ovitz, or a fashioner of summer blockbusters. A postmodern Barnum in a slimming Italian suit. All who meet Lucien expect such, such is his reputation, misearned. Certainly he surprised Lawrence immediately, in those first few days (he must have) with his humility and soft, careful speech. Oh, he thunders now and again, but

only at those who understand thunder and will listen to nothing else.
Certainly he surprised Lawrence with his sincerity over time. (Ticking
off here his favorite attributes.) Lucien is not, as many believe him to be,
fake. Such a label implies premeditation, that the inner man does not
match the outer man and fakery is involved. But he is no counterfeiter.
From time to time, after the lights have been turned out and the surly
emanations of the streetlights fill his bedroom or in odd moments at
well-attended events when he is in between greetings and small talk and
alone in a crowd before he has decided on his next strategic interaction,
Lucien will find himself lost in his landscape. How he stumbled there is
not important, which sign he misinterpreted that led him into this intro-
spective cul-de-sac, what is important is that he is face to face with his
character and must account for what he has become, and in those moments he will not flinch. He can describe the man he sees with merciless
acuity, recognize the hunched and shriveled creature before him and
there, it happens, he extends his arms without reluctance or disgust to
embrace his true self. And there is no disagreement between Lucien at
that moment of sudden confrontation and Lucien at this very moment,
on the job, timecard perforated, en route to his latest assignment. No
false front, he does not dissemble, he is exactly as he appears to be.

The miles retreat. Lawrence says it's not that much farther, and Lucien thinks, all these trees are for me. To delight his eye. He wonders if
the natural drift of his thoughts makes him a narcissist, but then reas-
sures himself that he is only substituting the concept of Lucien for the
larger family of man. For simplicity's sake. He's thinking about all humanity, not just himself. That business about the jungle shaping four
fingers and a thumb and thus their smooth ride this morning: all three
of them, Lucien, Lawrence and the driver, enjoy the monkey's good fortune. And everyone on the road ahead and behind him, on all the roads
leading to and shunting off this highway. Lucien's I is a democratic
beast, many-headed, fork-tongued. Neolithic toolmakers shaped arrow-
heads, these skills developed over time and now the chrome doorhandle
of this vehicle is shaped just so. The magnitude of chrome doorhandles
disproves his narcissism once and for all. There are millions and millions of chrome doorhandles in use around the globe, turned by peasant and king alike, facilitated by perfected manufacturing process,

millions, allowing swift and easy egress from vehicles, nooked betwixt palm and metacarpals. He is not alone in receipt of the neolithic tool-makers' gifts. Heck, people are opening doors everywhere.

The miles retreat and Lawrence says again, it is not much farther. Soon they will be in Talcott. Lucien has a patchwork idea of the town stitched by pop culture. He has borrowed elements of that idea on more than one occasion, to underscore the home-style virtues of a new home-style lemonade or to reconfigure a dull-witted celebrity's plati-tudes into a front-porch wisdom that journalists will pick up on and in turn deliver to the people. To present things just so. Folks pick up on these flourishes very quickly. When he first started in this business and was coming to understand his facility for making people believe things and was much taken with the language of his therapist, Lucien thought he was tapping into the collective unconscious. But now he thinks it's simply the atmosphere. That air is an admixture of nitrogen, oxygen, trace gases, and one of these trace gases is American cliché and we breathe it in with our first breath. Peering past miles they have yet to travel, Lucien pictures Talcott and sees the tall spire of the town church, a crowd of parishioners glad-handing with the pastor on Sun-day morning, a blond child in a bright striped shirt waving a sparkler on July Fourth and a glass pitcher of lemonade pimpled by condensation. We know that the lemonade is homemade because there are seeds swirling in the bottom of the pitcher and that detail is what makes it true. Talcott is an American small town and contains virtues.

Lucien thinks, maybe the trick about doing a town is making the thing into the idea. He has never done a town before.

Thinks back. He treated Mayor Cliff as he would any other client. He did not talk down to the man just because he was from another neck of the woods and knew nothing about being seated at the best table. No one client is dumber than another; they are all merely clients. Mayor Cliff had just departed the matinee of a popular Broadway show and had sunset plans for the observation deck of the Empire State Building. He had rolled the Playbill into a grubby tube and from time to time during the discussion it unfurled and he rolled it anew. The mayor ex-plained that the wife had never been to the Big Apple and this trip was a perfect opportunity to mix business with pleasure. The wife was out shopping, he said as he unzipped his purple track jacket to reveal a joke T-shirt. The joke was lost on Lucien. Something about woodchucks. Lucien did not allow this miscommunication, this symbol of their cultural difference, to alter his prepared remarks although perhaps he was a little sad that Mrs. Cliff had not come along as well, so that afterward the couple could discuss his words, and an hour or two hours from then, Lucien would feel his ears burn.

Lucien said to the mayor, "This is my office and that is my guest chair. We have a process we have to do now and I want you to be comfortable. This is what I do in the getting to know the client stage, you have questions and want to be reassured. Your time is valuable so I'll be honest with you: I sell light bulbs. Yes. It generally takes time for the appropriateness of this analogy to settle in so I will ask you, do you know how fragile light bulbs are? It's always the filament that breaks before the glass. You've knocked over lamps, I've knocked over lamps, knocking over lamps is the side racket of every American. They're very fragile. It's the filament. Fil-a-ment. Sounds like a word you'd use to describe a god. 'A thousand lovely filaments falling down her divine shoulders.' Fragile and yet they light up the whole world. These tiny crimps of metal. Hit the switch and a million electrons jump off the filament into darkness and light up the room. These are tiny electrons that are full of energy.

"My point takes a bit to get around to. I go, and what are we? We are energy too. This is Einstein talking here, not me. Just then. Now I'm back. Look at my hand. Yours will do just as well of course, but look at my hand. The knuckles here say that's where the bones meet, so I have bones. The tendons stretch here and so I have muscles beneath my skin. If I pinch my fingertip like this it goes white because I cut off the blood flow. I have capillaries and veins and inside them blood. You understand my point. There are smaller and smaller systems, down to blood cells and the specialized tiny bits inside them and we can go smaller still into atoms. Blood cells and tiny atoms that you and I need to live and that's energy. Split the atom and that's energy. Energy to destroy a city or light it up or power a sun. These are natural processes. The windows of my office are tinted to cut out the UV—too much of that will give you cancer, but the point is that the sun is a giant light bulb. I'm reinforcing my opening gambit. It is a series of atomic explosions, a billion splitting atoms. The light of the sun takes a day or two to reach us, there is universal constant involved, but there it is. The sun is a big ball of splitting atoms that allows life on earth and in my hand I have atoms, I have a sun. We all have suns in our hands, inner light, every object, and all they need are a little something to initiate the reaction. That's why I say I'm in the light bulb business. I'm just trying to let a little something out.

"I handle celebrities. I handle shiny new cars from Europe. These cars have a power in their names, these European imports, because to American ears they sound exotic and so they want them straight out the gate and this makes my job a little easier. They are already leaking light before I ever get my hands on them. Look into my eyes. Then some things come to me dull and I have to get to work. Otherwise they remain dim. The duller something is the duller you feel and that's where the elbow grease comes in. I have handled paperweights and toasters and politicians. Organized events for them that are like setting up mirrors to reflect their inner radiance to best effect. No, I can't name any of my political clients, I have signed nondisclosure agreements and such things are the holy word, but rest assured you have seen the light glinting off the teeth of my political clients and have pulled the lever for them, chum. A company that produces lawn sprinklers once approached me, and now I feel the satisfaction of a job well done when I drive through upstate suburbs to visit friends or clients and see rainbows caught in the spray of sprinklers I have helped out. This is missionary work. I've helped TV pilots get along. Some are still in syndication as we speak. I have never done a hubcap, but I hope with all my heart that one day I will. I've had my eye on a few and now it's a matter of contacting the manufacturers. Pro bono. It sounds ridiculous but love is often ridiculous to those on the outside. Take the elevator down to the street and wait five minutes for a ridiculous couple to walk by, what are they wearing, something ridiculous, mismatched socks, you might have a little chuckle but you will envy with all your heart the inarguable adoration in their smiles. I am coming around to my point: I have never done a town before, sir, and I would love to. To give the world your light.

"What I want to do is establish the brand superiority of Talcott for all things Talcott-related. The name of your town, Talcott, Tallll-cott, it rolls off the tongue and that's half the battle. The sound of things is half my job. Egon. 'A coffee table is not a coffee table unless it is an Egon coffee table.' How many times have you heard this phrase? Sounds so good and right you might think it's Solomon that said it, it's something from the Bible and handed down. I didn't make it up, wish I had, but this is not an advertising agency I run here, those offices and cubicles you passed out there are not the offices and cubicles of an advertising agency, but I helped to get out the truth of Egon coffee tables to the people and now you know this simple truth about coffee tables as well as you know your wife's maiden name. Her maiden name is what she was before. Now she is something else. Do you ever think about that? I'm talking about the lines that divide you from one stage to another. The natural image is the cocoon. Light bulbs, cocoons, I'm coming back to light bulbs, don't fret. What I'm really talking about is the exact moment between the cocoon and the butterfly, the moment of change, the exact instant when the potential is released into light because that is what we are discussing at the moment. This is where we are now with your town. Would you like some water?

"A coffee table is not a coffee table . . . I didn't make that up. I'm not that clever. But I did my humble effort to urge Egon coffee tables into deserving living rooms across the country. They are stark and scratch-proof and fit easily into any preexisting design motif or lack thereof, they do not stick out, are unobtrusive, but they have their own subtle radiance. They shine in their own right. I don't know you. I can't describe your life, but I know the world. The world is full of undiscovered treasures waiting to reveal their true light. Are you a kind man? Are you a forgiving man? I don't know, I've just met you, sir. I have picked up on a few things. You cross your legs and uncross your legs and you have that thing you do with your chin. I have learned that you are an attentive listener, but if I said I knew you I would be lying so I'm not going to insult you by saying that I do. But I know the world, and it is full of light. Here and there, it leaks out, and this is where I come in. Lumens and lumens. Talcott is full of light. It is a silent star. It is a superheated solar furnace that is dark and waiting to become light. You have plans and ideas. I will give them to the world. All I ever do is release radiance. This is light bulbs, sir, and this is why I say I am in the light bulb business. This is light bulbs."

Steven C. Lo

FULLY UTILIZED

Steven C. Lo *(1949–) was born in Taipei, Taiwan, and educated there and at Texas Tech and Northwestern University. He has lived in the United States since 1978 and is currently the president of Asiatic International, Inc., a business consulting firm based in Dallas. He wrote* The Incorporation of Eric Chung *(1989), his first novel, in his spare time, often using his laptop computer in airports and on airplanes. In the chapter reprinted below, Eric Chung telescopes the tale of how the fast-talking Roger Holton met a certain Texas rich man named Malcolm Coldwell and sold him on a truly Texas-sized idea.*

If there was one person who changed my life in America—I am skipping way ahead in my story—it was Roger Holton. Roger Holton got me in Mr. Coldwell's business. *The* Mr. *Malcolm* Coldwell. Chances are you already know how big Mr. Coldwell is, and you know, too, how much it means to be *in* Mr. Coldwell's business. It's not like I was just an employee. It's much more.

First, Roger introduced himself to Mr. Coldwell at a party. Then he got Mr. Coldwell interested in a business idea. Then he talked Mr. Coldwell into investing in this idea. Then he had both him and me hired in this business, with me working under him. And, on top of all that, Mr. Coldwell agreed that as soon as the business began to make money, Roger and I would be made partners of the business, Roger a bigger partner than I. Roger pulled the whole thing off. One miracle after another. Your average man on the street couldn't even get second glances from Mr. Coldwell's secretaries. The world was full of people who "only needed five minutes" of Mr. Coldwell's "valuable time." I don't know how exactly Roger did it. That Roger, he was something else.

* * *

Roger first told me about Mr. Coldwell in the spring of 1979 when we were at the Jojo's on Spring Valley. For me the place was only five minutes' walk from where I was working at the time, Taltex's main building in north Dallas. Roger worked downtown; he had to drive thirty minutes on that day "in the worst traffic," he said, just so that we could "meet and lunch." I was then in my seventh year in the States, things were generally slow for me, and a little boring. But I had a quiet feeling that, somehow, my life was *improving*, that I'd seen my worst days in America.

I'd recently been promoted to Systems Programmer/Analyst Two at Taltex. My boss, the Systems Programming Manager, was beginning to realize, after two and a half years, that I might have "long-term potentials" because everybody else in my department either had quit or was quitting. So now I was kind of looking forward to becoming a Senior Systems Programmer/Analyst in twelve months (as a "fast-track rising star"), or, at most, in three years (if I didn't make a lot of mistakes). Things were not bad for me at the time; I was taking more long lunches than ever. I was also using bigger words in my memos. Like "accordingly," "corresponding to," "retrospective," and so on.

Roger was with Taltex too, in the Corporate Marketing Group. His title was Market Communications Manager. Basically, what he did was to set up Taltex booths and displays at the large electronics conventions you sometimes read about in the newspapers. Taltex always sent an army of salesmen to these conventions. They used the booths and displays to give customers the sales talk. Roger had three people working for him, and he traveled a lot to be wherever the conventions were. He had hired Darth Vader once to sign posters by the booth. Since then he'd carried a picture of him and Darth Vader together, before a bright Taltex sign. Roger's job grade at Taltex was 28, mine was 26. Roger had been with Taltex for seventeen years when we had our talk at Jojo's.

"Eric, I'm leaving Taltex," Roger said, as soon as we sat down at a table by the window. From where we were, we could see the top part of the glass Taltex buildings shining under the sun. Roger was in a suit, which was unusual for a Taltex employee of his job grade. Only Department Managers (job grade: 36 or 38), Division Vice Presidents (job grade: 40), and the President (no job grade) wore suits at Taltex. Branch Managers (job grade: 34) put on ties now and then but never coats or suits. People ranking lower, Roger and I included, should be in "casual, but decent" clothes of some kind (meaning shirt-and-pants for most of us). The company originally banned formal clothes altogether to "encourage a hard-working and friendly culture." Sometime back the rule bent, but only for the top guys because of their "customer-related functions." Roger, however, was always formal with a dark suit, white shirt, and expensive silk tie. Add to that his short hair, his clean-shaven red face, his six-foot-two height, and his broad shoulders, he looked, to me, as important as any executive.

"I gave Ron and Henry my resignation this morning," Roger continued. Ron was Roger's boss; and Henry, a Branch Manager, was Ron's boss. I never did learn Ron's last name. Or Henry's. Another big thing at Taltex, other than what to wear, was that all employees were to be addressed by their first names only. To this there were no exceptions, not even the President, Fred.

"Why?" I gave him a raised voice out of politeness. I was more interested in why he wanted to talk to me. You couldn't possibly be surprised about anybody's quitting. There were over seventy thousand employees at Taltex, and at least half of them talked about quitting on a daily basis. Not that there was anything seriously wrong with the company. Considering only a handful would eventually make it to the top, a great majority of the seventy thousand were bound to feel, one way or the other, not "fully utilized." Roger, after seventeen years, was unlikely an exception.

Roger had asked me to do some translation work for him once. That had been my only dealing with him. He was expecting a delegation from China to come through his booths at the Consumer Electronics Show in Las Vegas, and he wanted some brochures in Chinese. He had paid me well for the job. And I wanted to know, quitting or no quitting, if he was going to ask me again. "Well," Roger said, mysteriously, "I have been offered a very good opportunity."

"Oh, that's great!" I said, again out of politeness. People always told you they quit Taltex to work for a company "that really cared about its people" and all that.

"Yeah, and that's why I want to talk to you."

"Yeah?"

"Yeah. You know those brochures you helped me translate for the Las Vegas show?"

"Yes?"

"You did great. That was a wonderful job you did. People liked it a lot."

"You mean the Chinese?"

"Yes, we've had very good comments about them. And that's what I want to talk to you about."

"You mean you want to make more Chinese brochures?" I said with delight.

"No . . . Well, what I am about to do is much more." Roger looked me straight in the eyes. He moved his elbows forward on the table. Bright light from outside picked up the calm, elegant colors of his suit. I could see he had great confidence, that he was about to impress the hell out of me. "I might as well tell you. But please, please, this is only between you and me."

"Sure, Roger, sure."

"Well, Eric, I have been asked to develop business in China for the wealthiest man in the United States."

"You, you mean . . . Rockefeller?"

"No, Eric. But this man is just as wealthy. And he knows the Rocke-fellers too. His name is Malcolm Coldwell. Mr. Coldwell."

"Who is he?" I said quickly. I felt the conversation was becoming more than I could handle.

"He is . . . I'm sure you've heard of him." Roger sounded disap-pointed. He turned toward the window. "You see these buildings around us? Mr. Coldwell owns most of them. If you ask around, you'll know."

"Oh." I saw outside a couple of children playing on the sidewalk. The top parts of the Taltex buildings were too bright to look at.

"Anyway, he's one of the most influential men in the United States. Certainly the most influential in Texas. He wants to develop a relation-ship with China. He believes in it. A big business. We're talking big in-vestment." Roger look satisfied. He leaned back and crossed his arms. "It's like Armand Hammer. Have you heard of Armand Hammer?"

"No . . ." My voice lowered.

"Armand Hammer developed a relationship with the Russian government from way back. He was the one who got the Russians to give him an exclusive franchise for selling arms to them. Now he is probably the richest man in the world."

"You mean . . . richer than Malc . . . Malc . . . richer than the guy you told me about?"

"I wouldn't say so, but they are all very important, you know." Roger was becoming impatient. "You know these are people who really run this country. You don't see them in the newspapers every day. But they are the ones that really count."

"Oh."

"And Mr. Coldwell, who's widowed and childless, is well known for surrounding himself with sharp young men and giving them the complete authority to run his business."

"Oh."

"Getting back to the point, Mr. Coldwell wants me to see what he can do with China. He commissioned me to do some work. I've been to China twice already to talk to the government." Roger slowly stirred his coffee.

"Yeah?" Roger must have seen how I suddenly brightened up. I was beginning to feel a pure sense of respect for the man. It was 1979. Nobody went to China in the 1970s. Nobody but Nixon and Kissinger. There I was, a Chinese by birth and education, fluent only in Chinese, but knowing as much about China as any good old boy from Seminole, Texas, population 236. I must admit I was *awed*. This man, Roger Holton, Market Communication Manager, job grade 28, could easily become my hero. He only had to convince me what he had said was true. And the way things were going, it was not going to be hard either. It was now important to find out as much as I could. "Well," I muttered, "what do you want me to do?"

"I need your help," Roger replied. He was very much at ease with himself. "I can't do all this by myself. I need all kinds of people to help me. We are building a big business, from the ground up. We must draw the best talents into this." Roger spoke evenly and thoughtfully; he squinted at the Taltex buildings. Outside the lunch traffic was thinning out, now even the streets were shiny under the sun. "That is," he turned to me, "if you are interested. You have the language and cultural skills. You have a good head. From what I can see, you are a quick-study also. This is going to be a tough business—no one has done what we are about to do. And we, Mr. Coldwell and I, need people who can really contribute. People like you."

"Well . . . Thank you, Roger . . ."

The rest of the conversation was fairly straightforward. Every word Roger had to say was music to my ears. I remember mumbling a lot, about what a "tremendous career challenge" it was to be in the China business with him, and how I saw myself devoting the "rest of my life" to it. Basically, what came out in the end was that I agreed to help him put a plan together, without pay. He'd then present the plan to Mr. Coldwell. There was to be a meeting two months later of Mr. Coldwell, his top advisers, and Roger. Once the plan was approved, I was to quit Taltex and join him as "one of the first employees" of this business. And that would be the beginning of our being able to "forget all our worries."

When I returned to work, a good one and a half hours after the lunch break, the computer terminal, the desk, the thick technical books and everything within fifty yards of my seat looked just about the most miserable things I had ever seen. My life as a Programmer/Analyst Two, job grade 26, had turned most seriously dull. I felt very happy about the future, and very lucky. I felt bad for my fellow Systems Programmer/ Analysts, all of them six to eight job grades away from wearing a tie, and a good twelve to fourteen job grades away, if they could ever make it, from a suit. I also felt a sense of warmth, for the first time in two and a half years, for my boss, the Systems Programming Manager.

In the next few years I was able to gather, piece by piece, the general truth about how Roger had gotten started with Mr. Coldwell and with the China business. Roger had never been to China like he told me at Jojo's. He never went to China, period, until much later, when he went with me. He had all the Chinese brochures in Las Vegas, and nobody ever showed up to look at them, except a man who called himself Professor Zhang. Roger ended up spending a long time talking to this Professor Zhang, you know, just to shoot the breeze. Professor Zhang later wrote Roger a letter from China, telling Roger that he was "welcomed to come to China" some day. And that was it, in total, the entire "China connection" for Roger—Professor Zhang, a nice chat, and one letter.

A few months after the Las Vegas show, Roger was at a fund-raising party as a volunteer worker representing Taltex. He was walking through the crowd, delivering a drink to his boss Ron's wife, when he overheard a man talking about China. The man, sixtyish, white-haired, and raspy-voiced, did not have much to say about China other than his niece had been trying to get invited to the Canton Fair. He had the un-divided attention, though, from the expensively-dressed younger men and women around him. Roger stopped to listen, and before you knew it, he made himself heard.

"Excuse the interruption, sir, but I had some dealings with China," Roger said. He went directly up to the man and volunteered more: "And the key to dealing with the Chinese is to have proper introduc-tions. It's very important, *most* important—having proper introduc-tions." Good old Roger. He stopped briefly, allowing the man a good look at him, and continued with a raised voice to address the whole group. "Speaking from experience, I do believe a good relationship, or connection, with certain high ranking Communist party officials can open doors, many kinds of doors."

The man was apparently intrigued by Roger. None of his followers, the good-looking men and women, turned away. So Roger proceeded to tell all he knew about China, which was very little. But everyone listened—for about twenty minutes. Roger didn't forget to mention Professor Zhang. He called Professor's letter "an official invitation to visit China for business discussions." And that it was "extremely rare," this invitation, because nobody else had ever gotten one. "I've worked hard at getting my invitation," Roger said to the man before leaving the group, "for a long, long time."

The man turned out to be Mr. Coldwell, the sponsor of the party.

Anyway, Mr. Coldwell and Roger exchanged business cards. When Roger tried later to find out about Mr. Coldwell, he must have gotten the same treatment as he was to give me, from whomever he asked.

But Roger saw a possibility. He saw an opening in his life. And he went for it, with everything he had. He called up Mr. Coldwell a few days later and said the Chinese had contacted him again, "through official channels," and that he felt Mr. Coldwell might be interested in the "content of this communication." When everything was said and done, before Roger came to talk to me at Jojo's, there had only been a couple of meetings between him and Mr. Coldwell. In the second meeting, there were also Mr. Coldwell's lawyers and consultants. And, this time, did Roger put on a show. I mean really. Roger himself described it to me later in glorious details. Everybody saw the *scenario*. Roger's *scenario*. Nothing but Roger's *scenario*. It went like this:

The Chinese trusted Roger. The Chinese did not trust too many Americans because the United States had been hostile for over thirty years. The Chinese government now wanted to do business. Big business. They wanted to "modernize." They wanted relationships with important American businessmen, and they didn't know how to go about it. But they trusted Roger. And they also knew he, as a "senior executive" in an American corporation, had contacts with important American businessmen. Through him they wanted to do business with important American businessmen. Enter Mr. Coldwell, the important American businessman.

Anyway, at the end of the second meeting a deal was struck. Roger was to find out exactly what the Chinese wanted, then put "the numbers" together for Mr. Coldwell. They agreed to meet again in two months. In the meantime, Mr. Coldwell gave Roger a check, 1500 dollars, for "interim expenses." Fifteen hundred lousy dollars. And Roger was on the way to the biggest game in his life. He was ready to quit Taltex right there and then. You couldn't help but respect him. He had the right stuff. He wanted to begin living *his* life, bad.

I also found out later that one of Mr. Coldwell's men had been smart enough to ask, in the second meeting, how Roger planned to overcome his "unfamiliarity" with the Chinese language, culture, and all that. Roger first responded bravely that he'd studied Chinese at Yale. Then he admitted the need for a "native Chinese speaker." He told Mr. Cold-well the Chinese contingency in Washington, D.C., was so interested in the project they had recommended an "overseas Chinese" to him.

That's how I came into the picture.

I remember well what Roger said as we walked out of Jojo's. "Eric," he said. "I want you to be there in the next meeting with the Coldwell people. This time you and I are going to blow them away with our op-erational plans. We are going to get the whole business going, right there and then. We are going to ask for about thirty million." I remem-ber how he opened his car door and then raised his head to look at a flock of high-flying birds. I remember how he shook my hand and pat-ted my shoulder as we were parting. There was no room for any doubt from me. Or from himself. He, Roger Holton, was in command. Noth-ing could possibly stand in his way. He'd let you know it, too. By the way he spoke his words, the way he inspected the things around us as we walked. A totally realized master of the situations—his, and possibly mine. The great Roger Holton himself. The one and only. You couldn't *deny* him.

Herman Wouk

from *YOUNGBLOOD HAWKE*

Herman Wouk *(1915–) was born in New York and attended Columbia University. His father was a Russian-Jewish immigrant who built a success-ful career in the laundry business. Wouk is best known for his World War II epics—*The Caine Mutiny *(1951), which won a Pulitzer Prize, and* The Winds of War *(1971) and its sequel,* War and Remembrance *(1978)—but he also has a knack for breezy comedy. Early in his career he wrote gags for ra-dio comedians including, notably, Fred Allen. He created a larger-than-life protagonist in* Youngblood Hawke *(1962), and in this memorable opener Hawke jumps to life as a hick, a hack, an unpolished upstart whose drawl be-lies a deft negotiator. Wouk marvelously captures the antics of a publisher's of-fices in this send-up, which made it to the silver screen in 1969 with James Franciscus in the title role.*

Have you ever known a famous man before he became famous? It may be an irritating thing to remember, because chances are he seemed like anybody else to you.

The manuscript loomed on the desk between the two men, a high pile of torn and dented blue typing-paper cartons. The yellow labels on the boxes had been scrawled over with thick red crayon, *Alms for Oblivion*, *Part 1, Part 2, Part 3.* Two of the boxes, overstuffed with manuscript, had split open. Dog-eared dirty sheets of typewritten manuscript showed through, mostly white, with sprinklings of yellow and green. Waldo Fipps had never seen a larger or more untidy manuscript—or for that matter, a larger and more untidy author.

He stared at the young man with peculiarly stirred feelings. The young man, who looked more like a truck driver than a writer, stared back. He had big piercing brown eyes, and the lower lip of his full wide mouth was curled and pressed tight over the upper, as though to say, "Try and stop me!" This part of Hawke's attitude was unconscious. He presented the usual agitated surface of the new author, bashfulness and fear struggling with pride, hope, and greed for praise, all this covered by stammering modesty and awkward shifts in the hard yellow chair. Young authors were all afraid of Fipps. Under the business-like smiles of the editor lay the fishy chill of a man who had read too many novels, and criticized too many. The odd thing was that Fipps felt a little afraid of Hawke, this hulking sloven of twenty-six who had written an ugly bellowing dinosaur of a novel, amateurish as it could be, full of imitation, crude, slopped-over, a horror of an editing task, the kind of writing Fipps least admired.

"Cigarette?" Fipps leaned toward Hawke, offering him the pack.

"Mand ef Ah smoke uh see-gaw?" said Hawke. It was the thickest Southern accent Fipps had ever heard.

He said, "Not at all. I'm sorry I don't have any. But I think Mr. Prince—" he broke off, seeing Hawke draw a glossy leather cigar case from the breast pocket of his shabby wrinkled blue suit.

"Ma one vass," said Hawke. It took Fipps a few seconds to realize that what Hawke had said was, "My one vice." Removing the cedar wrapping from an enormous cocoa-brown cigar, Hawke held a flaming match to the end until it was well scorched, then lit it up with expert puffs. A wisp of blue drifted to the nostrils of Fipps, reminding him unpleasantly of his employer, Jason Prince. This preposterous pauper, this scribbling hillbilly, smokes dollar cigars, he thought. He decided then and there that he did not like Youngblood Hawke. "Well, first things first," Fipps said amiably. "Everybody in the house likes the book. Or at least is impressed."

Hawke's attempt to be impassive was pitiable. The big cigar shook in his fingers. The joy that crossed his face was like a wave of powerful heat; Fipps almost felt it. Perhaps it was real animal heat given off by the blood that rushed into the broad thick-featured rustic face. Hawke stammered a little, trying to say lightly, "It's a—a little too long, isn't it?"

Fipps said, "Well, you are a very exuberant writer. I'm reminded of Dickens, of Dreiser. Perhaps a bit of Dostoevsky?" He paused, smiling.

Gloom, joy, fear, uncertainty: Hawke's look changed almost with every word Fipps uttered. "Mr. Fipps, you've nailed me. My three gods. The three D's."

"Yes. Well," Fipps said in a dry cutting tone, stabbing two fingers at the manuscript, "I think possibly we want a good strong dose of Flaubert. The art of leaving out, you know! From the first page to the last. Practically in every paragraph. Whole sections would have to go."

He savored the quenched, the staggered look of Hawke. No determination in the big mouth now; the open hanging pain of a man punched in the stomach. Fipps' mood improved, and he was ready to forgive this big, possibly profitable oaf for his power of tumbling out exciting scenes and vivid portraits in a muddy torrent of verbiage, full of recognizable flotsam and jetsam from standard authors. "We want to publish your book, Mr. Hawke," he said. "We're really enthusiastic. Providing, of course, that you'll meet us in the matter of revising."

Hawke stood. "You—you want to *publish* mah book? You *goin'* to publish it?"

Fipps was drawn to his feet by the fierce excitement in the young man's voice. "Of course we want to publish it. We expect to have a lot of fun with it, and we think—"

Youngblood Hawke put down his cigar, strode around the desk, and folded the elegant Waldo Fipps in a crushing hug. He bawled like a bull, pounding the editor's back. "Mr. Fipps, god damn it, you're a brilliant goddamn bastard. I've read about you, heard about you, read your books, you know everything about novels, everything, and you want to publish *mah novel!*" Fipps was astonished and not at all pleased to find himself being hugged and pounded, his face jammed against rough blue serge reeking of cigar smoke. Hawke was half a head taller than Fipps, and half again as broad. He was pasty-faced, he needed a haircut; there were flecks of dandruff on his suit; he had cut himself near his ear shaving, and dried blood stood in the gash. Fipps was skinny, brown, his suit was tweedy brown, he was immaculate to the last hair of his sandy little mustache.

"My dear fellow—" murmured Fipps.

Hawke shook him like a doll. "I'll write forty books, Mr. Fipps, forty goddamn wonderful truthful books and every one better than the last, and you'll publish them all. And we'll make millions. You'll see. I'm not just talking. I'm a goddamn genius, Mr. Fipps, or I'm nothing. God, I'm so happy! *ee*-yowww!"

Throughout the busy halls of Prince House, stenographers looked up from their typing, and shipping clerks halted in their tracks, and editors glanced at their secretaries, as the male bellow echoed down the sound-proofed corridors.

Fipps disengaged himself from Hawke with a thin embarrassed smile. "Well, I'm glad you're pleased. I'd like to take you to lunch. We have a lot to talk about. First come and meet Jason." He added, at Hawke's puzzled look, in a humorous tone, "Mister Prince."

"Mr. Prince? I get to meet Mr. Prince?" said Hawke, retrieving his cigar and following Fipps humbly into the corridor. Fipps led the big clumsy young man through corridors and offices full of talk and typing clatter, a cut-up maze of partitions and desks, to a heavy door made of pearly wood, the only closed door Hawke had seen in the place. A girl at a desk by the door said to Fipps, "Mr. Prince is waiting for you."

Fipps opened the pearly door.

Take an ostrich egg, color it fleshy-gray, ink small shrewd features on it, attach a pair of large ears, and you have a fair likeness of what confronted Youngblood Hawke from behind the desk of Jason Prince. The egg hung between broad gray-clad shoulders, peering suspiciously upward. Very long powerful arms clutched a typewritten contract on an otherwise empty desk, the more strikingly empty because the desk top was a slab of glass, allowing a view of a huge empty leather wastebasket underneath, and of Mr. Prince's lolling legs. The office was very long and very wide. The windows were open, and the air was cold. Bare bleak modern furniture, and bookshelves too-smoothly lined with too-clean books from ceiling to floor on two walls, added to the cold emptiness. The other walls were mostly glass, looking out on downtown New York, the jagged skyscrapers in a gray midday haze under a low black sky that threatened snow, and the far muddy rivers, sloshing away the great city's dirt.

"This is Youngblood Hawke, Jay," said Fipps.

The suspicious egg changed into the face of a warm friendly man of fifty or so who happened to be very bald, whose pale blue eyes were not at all shrewd and veiled, but gay and candid. "*Alms for Oblivion*, eh?" he said in a strong throaty voice, all different from Fipps' controlled pipe. He stood and offered his hand. "No oblivion for you, my young friend. Quite an explosion of talent, that book. And only the beginning."

The long arms of the two men—Hawke's was a little longer—met in a powerful clasp over the desk; the two tall men looked straight into each other's eyes. There was a silence. To Fipps it seemed a long silence, and he was a bit surprised at the way Hawke met the glance of Prince. Then a blush spread over the young author's face, he shuffled his feet, and awkwardly dropped Prince's hand.

"Hope you get back the price of the printing job, sir," he said. "It's my first try."

"We'll get back more than that," said Prince. "And we're going to do a lot of printing, too." He pressed a button, and said into a voice box, "Bring me a box of cigars and the Hawke contract." He pulled a chair beside his desk, and motioned Hawke into it, ignoring Fipps, who lounged into a settee behind the publisher. "Long experience with artists," Prince said, "has convinced me that I can best minister to your sensitive spirits by discussing dough." Hawke laughed uproariously. The publisher smiled and went on, "Advances for a first novel generally run about five hundred to a thousand dollars. I've advanced fifteen hundred for a sure-fire first book." He named a best-seller of a few years back. "Turned out to be right. Been spectacularly wrong on occasion. Right often enough to stay in this chair and keep the rent paid. Why haven't you got an agent?"

"Should I have one?" Hawke said. "I don't know anything about all this."

Prince shrugged. "I can't advise you to give away ten percent of your bloodstained earnings to an agent. I can't advise you to trust yourself to my tender mercies, either." A girl came in with a box of cigars and a contract, put them on the publisher's desk, and left. Prince thrust the cigars toward Hawke. "I get these sent up to me from Havana. Try them."

Hawke opened the plain wooden box, and saw an array of unbanded brownish-green cigars, longer and thicker than his Romeos. He took one, slid the box to Prince, and found it abruptly pushed back at him. "All for you," Prince said. "The contract's ready. It's our standard form.

The only blank in it is the amount of the advance. Take it away with you and have a lawyer or an agent look over the fine print. Or sign it and take our check away instead. Suit yourself. It's a good contract."

Hawke looked at the publisher for a long moment, his lower lip pressed over the upper one. Then he pursed his mouth like an old lady, and shrugged. "I'll sign it. Your business isn't to skin authors."

"No it isn't. Our business is to make them rich and pay our bills in the process. How about the advance?"

"I'd like five thousand dollars," Hawke said.

The suspicious egg briefly reappeared where Prince's affable head had been. It turned and glanced at Fipps, but by the time the glance came back to Hawke the egg was gone and there was a pleasant face again, wryly surprised.

"I'm sure you would like five thousand dollars," Prince said. "But it's ten times the going advance for a first novel. The chances against your earning that much in royalties are slim, in fact prohibitive. You'd better get an agent. He'll explain all that to you."

The young man said, "The thing is, Mr. Prince, I'm halfway into my second novel, a war book. It's called *Chain of Command*. It's much better than *Alms for Oblivion*. But I'm wasting time working on a construction job by day. I only get to write a few hours at night, and I'm tired." He spoke reasonably and winningly, with no hesitation, the soft Southern cadences giving his speech almost the beat of poetry. (Ah only git to *rat* a few ahrs at *nat*, an' Ah'm *tahd*.) "I figure I can finish it and start on a third—which I've got all blocked out in my head, a political novel— inside of a year if I do nothing else. You feel like gambling on me, fine. Otherwise let me try another publisher. Though I sure would like my first book coming out with the imprint of Prince House. To me that's always been a magic name."

Prince looked over his shoulder at Fipps again, his glance uncertain and amused. "Waldo, move around here where I don't have to break my neck to talk to you."

Fipps picked up a chair, brought it forward of the desk, and sat. Prince said, "What do you make of all this?"

The editor pressed his fingertips together, appraising Hawke like a dean looking at a delinquent college boy. "If I understand Mr. Hawke, he's actually asking for an advance on three books. But even at that the figure is absurd, Jay." He turned to Hawke. "Look here, it's always better to be candid. Mr. Prince cast the deciding vote for your novel. Several of us had strong reservations, though we all of us, myself included, admire your promise. You'll get your book published elsewhere—though they'll want you to work on it just as we do—but I very much doubt that anyone else will give you a bigger advance than a thousand, if that much. We're not the movies."

Hawke said with sudden boyish good humor, odd in a big man with such an intense look, "Well, look, Mr. Fipps, why don't I just try another publisher? I'm mighty encouraged by your interest, and grateful to you, and there's no reason to—"

Jason Prince had been sitting hunched over his desk, large knobby fingers interlaced, the knuckles blue-white. Now he sat up. "Hawke, five-thousand advance against three novels. Is that what you want?"

"I want five thousand advanced against this one."

"Suppose this one doesn't earn back the advance? If it does it'll be a real freak of a first novel. Do you want us to lose money on you? Your price is fantastic. You wouldn't ask for it if you weren't so inexperienced. Now look here. I'll give you five hundred dollars a month for the next ten months. That's meeting your terms. But for that I want the second novel delivered and an outline of the third before the period is up."

"Okay," said Youngblood Hawke, as casually as if he were agreeing to go for a walk.

Fipps said severely, "You'll sign a contract to that effect?"

"Sure."

"But what is this optimism based on?" the editor said. "Can you show us the outlines of your next two novels?"

"I don't work from outlines, Mr. Fipps, I just sort of go along."

"Well, can we see what you've written so far on this war book?"

Hawke said, "The thing is it's in a big mess and it's simpler just to finish it."

Fipps rolled his eyes at the publisher in exasperation.

Prince said, "All right, Waldo." He pressed a button, and through the voice box asked for a check book. "The usual thing, Hawke," he said, "is for the check to be handed over when the contract is signed, but this contract will have to be revised. Meantime would you like to see the color of our money? Sort of an earnest of good faith? If you take the check you're tying up three novels."

"I'll take it."

The book came. Prince wrote a check for five hundred dollars, and handed it to Hawke. "The first of ten," he said.

Hawke stared at the stiff orange slip of paper. "Well, doggone. I've been paid for writing prose," he said. "I've been paid for English prose."

Fipps said, "Haven't you sold anything before?"

"Nothing."

"The wrong kind of prose isn't worth the paper it's written on," said Prince. "The right kind is worth its weight in diamonds. Remember that, as you pound the typewriter. It's a great era for writers. There has never been such an era."

"Dickens and Balzac did all right," Hawke said. "Adjust your currency and I bet Dickens did better than Sinclair Lewis. No taxes. I'd like to phone my mother. My mother's in Kentucky. Can I use the phone in your office?" he said to Fipps.

Fipps, who was having a little trouble catching his breath, nodded. Hawke walked out. He came back instantly, picked up the box of cigars Prince had given him, grinned at the two men, and left.

The editor and the publisher stared at each other. Waldo Fipps, in a lifetime of writing, had never received five thousand dollars, or half that much, for a piece of work. At forty-five, at the top of his reputation, he had once drawn an advance of twenty-five hundred dollars for a clever but tenuous play which had remained unproduced. He said testily, "What on earth is this, Jay? So far as I'm concerned the main thing this man has is enormous energy. He has no style, no wit, just coarse humor, he's crude, imitative, in fact he frequently shades off into plagiarism. Possibly he has a good narrative sense, and a serviceable knack of caricature. You're being strangely generous with him."

Prince leaned back, cradling his head against interlocked fingers, his elbows spread out, one long leg crooked over a knee. "The thing is, Waldo," he said, "I think Youngbood Hawke is money."

* * *

The cigar box under his arm, Hawke stroke happily down the long narrow corridor to Fipps' office, peeking into each open door that he passed, taking automatic note of what he saw. He had been keeping this mental inventory of every passing detail around him all his life, and was scarcely aware of the habit. It was the reason for his strange obtuseness to some things and his overkeen awareness of others. He had noticed, for instance, Waldo Fipps' way of blinking his eyes half a dozen times and then opening them wide before saying anything to Prince. But he was unaware that he himself had just scored a historic victory over one of the closest bargainers in the publishing trade.

Jay Prince was notorious for his meager advances. The most hard-bitten literary agent in New York in 1946 would not have tried to extract five thousand dollars from Prince for a first book, with a wild story of a second big novel coming in September and a third one the following year. But Hawke had experienced few business interviews. The entire process of testing for pressure, interest and advantage, the cautious hard game of words by which men of affairs came to grips over money, was unknown to him. While talking to Prince he had gone on with his inventory, noting the coldness of the room, the whiteness of Prince's knuckles as he clasped them on the desk, Waldo Fipps' quick change in attitude from acidly confident critic to hangdog employee, marked by an apprehensive stare at his boss and a wary tightness of the mouth. He had made the offer to go to another publisher in all innocence, not realizing that this was the shot across the bow. Prince had scornfully told agents dozens of times to go down the street by all means, when they had ventured this warning shot. But to Youngblood Hawke he had meekly run up the white flag. Such is sometimes the power, or the luck, of ignorance.

William H. Whyte

GIVE THE DEVILS NO MERCY

William H. Whyte *(1917–1999) was raised in West Chester, Pennsylvania, and graduated with honors from Princeton in 1939. He joined the U.S. Marine Corps as an intelligence officer in 1941 and saw service at Guadalcanal. In 1946, he went to work at* Fortune *magazine, where he was soon writing features about the emerging postwar corporate culture, among other things. His book* The Organization Man *(1956), which began as a series of articles about a new residential development in the outlying suburbs of Chicago, hit a nerve, added a new term to the language, and was a worldwide bestseller; he began the book by admonishing young workers to "fight The Organization" (or at least the feeling of belonging to it). He followed his own advice and left* Fortune *in 1958 to become a freelance writer and never held another corporate position. "Give the Devils No Mercy," which ran in* Fortune *in 1955, is a reminiscence of Whyte's first job after college, in particular the training program that preceded it at the Vicks Chemical Company's School of Applied Merchandising: a grueling eleven-month program of selling VapoRub and other remedies to small-town pharmacists. Whyte's apprenticeship came at the end of what he styled "the heroic years of commerce, when the customer was the acknowledged enemy to be conquered and only the fittest predators survived."*

Over the last several years I have had occasion to talk with several groups of college seniors about business life, and invariably they ask about junior-executive training programs. Well, it so happens, I explain, that I was a graduate of one of the pioneer training schools, that of Vick Chemical Co., maker of such cold remedies as VapoRub chest salve and Va-tro-nol nose drops. I proceed to tell them of my own experiences and dwell with some relish on the sales techniques taught us by that hardheaded company.

The seniors begin to grin broadly. Plainly, they don't believe me, or if they do believe me, they look shocked. Was business really like that? As I describe the "double clincher," the "sign trick," and other such skills, the seniors imply clearly that I ought to be ashamed of myself. I begin to feel like a relic from some dark age of commercial depravity. My experience hadn't been so very long ago—1939, to be exact—but to judge from the incredulous faces before me it might as well have been 1890.

For what historical interest it may hold, accordingly, I shall set down some brief notes on what it was like to be a trainee in one company back in the 1930s. I intend to draw no great moral. True enough, when measured against managerial practices that young men now consider progressive, the Vick experience illustrates the direct opposite. But the comparisons need not be invidious.

As veterans of other organizations will recall, the basic approach used by Vick's was by no means peculiar to that company. Even our little alumni group, furthermore, is of two minds about the experience. We shudder at the recollection of some of the things we had to do, yet we feel grateful for having been given so concentrated a dose of reality so early. They really separated the men from the boys in those days, we assure each other; yes, indeed, they don't make them like us any more.

Back in 1939, when corporations, and not college seniors, were in the drivers' seats, a chance to join Vick's was something special. It wasn't just a job we were going off to; it was a *school*—the Vick School of Applied Merchandising. Out of hundreds of applicants, we explained to our less fortunate classmates, some thirty men from different colleges were going to be rewarded with a year's postgraduate training under a farseeing and enlightened management. There would be classroom work in New York, a continuing course in advertising, and then eleven months of field study under veteran practitioners of merchandising and distribution. True, the work was connected with sales, and then as now, seniors were apprehensive lest they be required to do something so vulgar as direct selling. At Vick's, however, we would not be selling so much as learning merchandising, which, of course, would be quite different.

Furthermore, we would be paid for all this. By all rights, we actually should pay tuition for this training, for though we would do some work in connection with our studies, the company let us understand that the incidental services we would perform would be far outweighed by the heavy investment in us. Nevertheless, the company was going to pay us $75 a month and traveling expenses. In addition, it was going to credit us with an extra $25 a month that, for reasons we were soon to appreciate, would be paid only if we stuck to the end of the year.

In the summer of 1939, about thirty of us—brisk, well-groomed, confident, egos unbruised—gathered in New York and the schooling began. We were indoctrinated in the history of the company, told of Lunsford Richardson's discovery of VapoRub, and we spent a day at the Philadelphia plant watching VapoRub being mixed.

One thing became quickly apparent: we were not being trained to be executives. Vick did assert that the program would help produce the leaders of tomorrow, and very prominent in many Vick offices was a framed picture of a sea captain at the wheel, beneath which was a signed statement by the chairman of the company, Mr. H. S. Richardson, that the foremost duty of management was to bring along younger men. At the same time, it was made clear that the question whether any of us would one day be executives could easily be deferred a long time.

Our training was what would now be called job-centered. We were required to memorize list prices, sales spiels, rebuttals to possible objections, and the prices and techniques of Plough, Inc., whose Penetro line was frequently to give us trouble. There was no talk that I can remember about the social responsibilities of business, and I am sure the term "human relations" never came up at all.

But the company did have a philosophy, and it was put to us with considerable force. Shortly before the month in New York ended, Mr. Richardson assembled us for lunch at the Cloud Club atop the Chrysler Building. Through the windows of this executive eyrie, we saw stretched out before us the spires of the Graybar Building, the Chanin Building, and a magnificent sweep of Park Avenue. Certainly, here was Golconda. Were we up to it? Some would make it. Some would not. The race would be to the swiftest.

Over coffee Mr. Richadson drove home to us the kind of philosophy that might get some of us back up to the Cloud Club for keeps. He posed a hypothetical problem. Suppose, he said, that you are a manufacturer and for years a small firm has been making paper cartons for your product. This supplier has specialized so much to service you that he has become utterly dependent on your business. But one day another man walks in and says he will make the boxes for you cheaper. What do you do? He bade each one of us in turn to answer.

But *how much* cheaper, we asked? How much time could we give the old supplier to match the new bid? Mr. Richardson became impatient. Either you were a businessman or you were not a businessman. The new man, obviously, should get the contract. Mr. Richardson advised us strongly against letting sentimentality obscure fundamentals. Business was survival of the fittest, he indicated, and we would soon learn the fact.

He was as good as his word. The Vick School was just that—survival of the fittest. Of the thirty who sat there in the Cloud Club, the rules of the game dictated that only six or seven would be asked to stay with Vick's. The rest would "graduate" to make way for another batch.

Within a few days of our glimpse of the Cloud Club, we were deployed through the hinterland—in my case, the mountain counties of eastern Kentucky. We were each given a panel truck, a load of signs, a ladder, a stock of cough-drop and nose-drop samples, and an order pad. After a few days under the eye of a senior salesman, we were on our own.

To take a typical day of any one of us, we would rise at six or six-thirty in some bleak boardinghouse or broken-down hotel and, after a greasy breakfast, set out to squeeze in some advertising study. This consisted of stapling a supply of large fiber signs on barns and clamping smaller metal ones to telephone poles and trees. By eight we would have arrived at a general store for our first exercise in merchandising. Our assignment was to persuade the dealer to order a year's supply of Vick goods all at once, or preferable, more than a year's supply. After the sale, or no sale, we would turn to market research—i.e., count the storekeeper's shelf stock, estimate his annual sales of Vick's and competitive lines. Next we would do some introductory work on new products. Nose drops being unknown in the mountains, we would suddenly instruct the dealer to tilt his head back and, before he could recover his senses, squirt up his nostrils a whopping dropperful of Va-tro-nol.

Wiping the tears from his eyes, the dealer would delightedly tell the loungers by the stove to let the Vick drummer shoot some of that stuff up their noses. After this messy job was done, we plastered the place with cardboard signs, and left. Then, some more signposting in the barnyards, and ten or twelve miles of mud road to the next call. So, on through the day, the routine was repeated until at length, long after dark, we would get back to our lodgings in time for dinner—and two hours' work on our report forms.

The acquisition of a proper frame of mind toward all this was a slow process. The faded yellow second sheets of our daily report book tell the story. At first, utter demoralization. Day after day, the number of calls would be a skimpy eight or nine, and the number of sales sometimes zero. But it was never our fault. In the large space left for explanations, we would affect a cheerful humor—the gay adventurer in the provinces—but this pathetic bravado could not mask a recurrent note of despair. I quote some entries from my own daily report forms:

"They use 'dry' creek beds for roads in this country. 'Dry!' Ha! Ha! . . . Sorry about making only four calls today, but I had to go over to Ervine to pick up a drop shipment of ¾ tins and my clutch broke down. . . . Everybody's on WPA in this county. Met only one dealer who sold more than a couple dozen VR a year. Ah, well, it's all in the game! . . . Bostitched my left thumb to a barn this morning and couldn't pick up my first call until after lunch. . . . The local brick plant here is shut down and nobody's buying anything . . . Five, count 'em, *five* absent dealers in a row. Seems they're having a fishing derby in these parts today. Could I wring Isaac Walton's neck! . . . Sorry about the $20.85 but the clutch broke down again. . . . The Penetro man was through here last week and are the dealers loaded! . . . They use railroad tracks for roads in this county!"

By all these bids for sympathy, the people in the home office were unmoved; they let us understand it was *they* who were being put upon. The weekly letter written to each trainee would start with some perfunctory remarks that it was too bad about the clutch breaking down, the hurt thumb, and so on. But this spurious sympathy was only a prelude to some sharp comments on the torpor, lack of aggressiveness, and slipshod work revealed between the lines of our daily reports. We too are sorry about those absent dealers, the office would say, but we note that in the very same area McClure, Youst, and Coyle don't seem to be running into this trouble. Perhaps if you got up earlier in the morning?

But it was the *attitude* of the student that concerned the home-office people most. As they sensed quite correctly from my daily reports, I was growing sorry for myself; I used to read timetables at night, and often in the evening I would somehow find myself by the C.&O. tracks when the eastbound George Washington swept by, its shining windows a fleeting reminder of civilization left behind. I was also sorry for many of the country storekeepers, most of whom existed on a precarious credit relationship with wholesalers, and as a consequence I sold them very little of anything.

The company sent its head training supervisor to see if anything could be salvaged. After several days with me, this old veteran of the road told me he knew what was the matter. It wasn't so much my routine, wretched as this was; it was my state of mind. "Fella," he told me, "you will never sell anybody anything until you learn one simple thing. The man on the other side of the counter is the *enemy*."

It was a gladiators' school we were in. Selling may be no less competitive now, but in the Vick program, strife was honored far more openly than today's climate would permit. Combat was the ideal—combat with the dealer, combat with the "chiseling competitors" (characteristically, the company had an entry blank on its daily report forms for "chiseling competitors" but no blank for any other kind), and combat with each other. There was some talk about "the team," but it was highly abstract. Our success depended on beating our fellow students.

Slowly, as our sales-to-calls ratios crept up, we gained in rapacity. Somewhere along the line, by accident or skill, each of us finally manipulated a person into doing what we wanted him to do. Innocence was lost, and by the end of six months, with the pack down to about twenty-three men, we were fairly ravening for the homestretch back to the Cloud Club. At this point, our motivations brought to peak strength, we were taken off general-store and grocery work and turned loose on the rich drugstore territory.

The advice of the old salesman now became invaluable. While he had a distaste for any kind of dealer, with druggists he was implacably combative. He was one of the most decent and kindly men I have ever met, but when he gave us pep talks about this enemy ahead of us, he spoke with great intensity. Some druggists were good enough fellows, he told us (i.e., big, successful ones who bought big deals), but the tough ones were a mean, servile crew; they would insult you, keep you waiting while they pretended to fill prescriptions, lie to you about their inventory, whine at anything less than a 300 percent markup, and switch their customers to chiseling competitors.

The old salesman would bring us together in batches, like Fagin's brood, for several days of demonstration. It was a tremendous experience for us, for though he seemed outwardly a phlegmatic man, we knew him for the artist he was. Outside the store he was apt to be jumpy and nervous, but once inside, he was composed to the point of apparent boredom. He rarely smiled, and almost never opened up with a joke. His demeanor seemed to say, I am a busy man and you are damn lucky I have stopped by your miserable store. Sometimes, if the druggist was unusually insolent, he would blow cigar smoke at his face. "Can't sell it if you don't have it," he would say condescendingly, and then, rather pleased with himself, glance back at us, loitering in the wings, to see if we had marked that.

Only old pros like himself could get away with that, he told us in the postmortem sessions, but there were lots of little tricks we could pick up. As we gathered around him, he would demonstrate how to watch for the victim's shoulders to relax before throwing the clincher; how to pick up the one-size jar of a competitive line that had an especially thick glass bottom and chuckle knowingly; how to feign suppressed worry that maybe the deal was too big for "the smaller druggist like yourself" to take; how to disarm the nervous druggist by fumbling and dropping a pencil. No mercy, he would tell us; give the devils no mercy.

Now came the acid test of our gall. One of the gauges by which we were next to be judged was the number of drugstores in which we managed to erect "flange" signs. By all the standards of the trade this sign-posting should have been an impossible task. Almost every chiseling competitor would give the druggist at least $5 to let him put up a sign; we could not offer this druggist a nickel. Our signs, furthermore, were not the usual cardboard kind the druggist could throw away after we had left. They were hideous plates of metal, and they were screwed to the druggists' cherished oak cabinets.

The trick was in the timing. When we were in peak form the procedure went like this. Just after the druggist had signed the order, his shoulders would subside, and this would signal a momentary period of mutual bonhomie. "New fella, aren't you?" The druggist was likely to say, relaxing. This was his mistake. As soon as we judged the good will to be at full flood, we would ask him if he had a ladder. (There was a ladder out in the car, but the fuss of fetching it would have broken the mood.) The druggist's train of thought would not at that moment connect the request with what was to follow, and he would good-naturedly dispatch someone to bring out a ladder. After another moment of chatter, we would make way for the waiting customer who would soon engage the druggist's attention. Then, forthrightly, we would slap the ladder up against a spot we had previously reconnoitered. "Just going to get this sign up for you," we would say, as if doing him the greatest favor in the world. A few quick turns of the awl, place the bracket in position, and then the automatic screwdriver. Bang! Bang! On with the sign. Then down with the ladder, shift it over to the second spot, and up again.

About this time the druggist would start looking up a little unhappily, but he was constrained from action. He didn't want to hurt our feelings. Ineffectually, he would mumble something about not being keen on the signs. We would hold up the second one. It bore a picture of a woman getting a nose dropper in position. We would leer fatuously at it. "Just going to lay this blonde on the top of the cabinet for you, Mr. Jones," we would say, winking.

I shudder to tell the rest. We were beyond shame now, and in our final month in Brooklyn, in the very shadow of the Cloud Club, we were knocking over some 95 percent of the stores—with what jokes and techniques I shall not describe.

But this was the end of the heroic years. No longer is there a Vick School of Applied Merchandising. Several classes followed us in much the same fashion, but Vick's has changed with the times, too. Trainees are no longer eliminated by "graduation"; they are exposed to many more aspects of management, and they don't have to badger dealers with metal signs. They are enrolled in the Vick "Executive Development Program."

PART 2

The Office

Joseph Heller

THE OFFICE IN WHICH I WORK

Joseph Heller *(1923–1999) was born in Brooklyn and, like Herman Wouk (see page 43), was of Russian-Jewish decent, attended Columbia University, was best known as a novelist of World War II (his* Catch-22 *was a worldwide bestseller), and was a wry observer of the social comedy of modern life. In this excerpt from his novel* Something Happened *(1974), Heller presumably drew heavily on his own experience as a corporate employee of Time Inc. and elsewhere in devising the character of Bob Slocum, whose mordant musings on office life amount to a kind of existentialist shtick.*

In the office in which I work there are five people of whom I am afraid. Each of these five people is afraid of four people (excluding overlaps), for a total of twenty, and each of these twenty people is afraid of six people, making a total of one hundred and twenty people who are feared by at least one person. Each of these one hundred and twenty people is afraid of the other one hundred and nineteen, and all of these one hundred and forty-five people are afraid of the twelve men at the top who helped found and build the company and now own and direct it.

All these twelve men are elderly now and drained by time and success of energy and ambition. Many have spent their whole lives here. They seem friendly, slow, and content when I come upon them in the halls (they seem dead) and are always courteous and mute when they ride with others in the public elevators. They no longer work hard. They hold meetings, make promotions, and allow their names to be used on announcements that are prepared and issued by somebody else. Nobody is sure anymore who really runs the company (not even the people who are credited with running it), but the company does run.

Sometimes these twelve men at the top work for the government for a little while. They don't seem interested in doing much more. Two of them know what I do and recognize me, because I have helped them in the past, and they have been kind enough to remember me, although not, I'm sure, by name. They inevitably smile when they see me and say: "How are you?" (I inevitably nod and respond: "Fine.") Since I have little contact with these twelve men at the top and see them seldom, I am not really afraid of them. But most of the people I am afraid of in the company are.

Just about everybody in the company is afraid of somebody else in the company, and I sometimes think I am a cowering boy back in the automobile casualty insurance company for which I used to work very long ago, sorting and filing automobile accident reports after Mrs. Yerger was placed in charge of the file room and kept threatening daily to fire us all. She was a positive, large woman of overbearing confidence and nasty amiability who never doubted the wisdom of her biases. A witty older girl named Virginia sat under a big Western Union clock in that office and traded dirty jokes with me ("My name's Virginia— Virgin for short, but not for long, ha, ha.") ; she was peppy and direct, always laughing and teasing (with me, anyway), and I was too young and dumb then to see that she wasn't just joking. (Good God—she used to ask me to get a room for us somewhere, and I didn't even know how! She was extremely pretty, I think now, although I'm not sure I thought so then, but I did like her, and she got me hot. Her father had killed himself a few years before.) Much went on there in that company too that I didn't know about. (Virginia herself had told me that one of the married claims adjusters had taken her out in his car one night, turned insistent, and threatened to rape her or put her out near a cemetery, until she pretended to start to cry.) I was afraid to open doors in that company too, I remember, even when I had been sent for by one of the lawyers or adjusters to bring in an important file or a sandwich. I was never sure whether to knock or walk right in, to tap deferentially or rap loudly enough to be heard at once and command admission. Either way, I would often encounter expressions of annoyance and impatience (or feel I did. I had arrived too soon or arrived too late).

Mrs. Yerger bullied us all. In a little while, nearly all of the file clerks quit, a few of the older ones to go into the army or navy, the rest of us for better jobs. I left for a job that turned out to be worse. It took nerve to give notice I was quitting, and it always has. (I rehearsed my resignation speech for days, building up the courage to deliver it, and formulated earnest, self-righteous answers to accusing questions about my reasons for leaving that neither Mrs. Yerger nor anyone else even bothered to ask.) I have this thing about authority, about walking right up to it and looking it squarely in the eye, about speaking right out to it bravely and defiantly, even when I know I am right and safe. (I can never make myself believe I *am* safe.) I just don't trust it.

That was my first job after graduating (or being graduated *from*) high school. I was seventeen then—that "older," witty, flirting girl under the Western Union clock, Virginia, was only twenty-one (too young now by at least a year or two, even for me)—and in every job I've had since, I've always been afraid I was about to be fired. Actually, I have never been fired from a job; instead, I receive generous raises and rapid promotions, because I am usually very alert (at the beginning) and grasp things quickly. But this feeling of failure, this depressing sense of imminent catastrophe and public shame, persists even here, where I do good work steadily and try to make no enemies. It's just that I find it impossible to know exactly what is going on behind the closed doors of all the offices on all the floors occupied by all the people in this and all the other companies in the whole world who might say or do something, intentionally or circumstantially, that could bring me to ruin. I even torture myself at times with the ominous speculation that the CIA, FBI, or Internal Revenue Service has been investigating me surreptitiously for years and is about to close in and arrest me, for no other reason than that I have some secret liberal sympathies and usually vote Democratic.

I have a feeling that someone nearby is soon going to find out something about me that will mean the end, although I can't imagine what that something is.

In the normal course of a business day, I fear Green and Green fears me. I am afraid of Jack Green because my department is part of his department and Jack Green is my boss; Green is afraid of me because most of the work in my department is done for the Sales Department,

which is more important than his department, and I am much closer to
Andy Kagle and the other people in the Sales Department than he is.

Green distrusts me fitfully. He makes it clear to me every now and
then that he wishes to see everything coming out of my department before it is shown to other departments. I know he does not really mean
this: he is too busy with his own work to pay that much attention to all
of mine, and I will bypass him on most of our assignments rather than
take up his time and delay their delivery to people who have (or think
they have) an immediate need for them. Most of the work we do in my
department is, in the long run, trivial. But Green always grows alarmed
when someone from another department praises something that has
come from my department. He turns scarlet with rage and embarrassment if he has not seen or heard of it. (He is no less splenetic if he *has*
seen it and fails to remember it.)

The men in the Sales Department like me (or pretend to). They
don't like Green. He knows this. They complain about him to me and
make uncomplimentary remarks, and he knows this too. He pretends
he doesn't. He feigns indifference, since he doesn't really like the men
in the Sales Department. I don't really like them, either (but I pretend
I do). Generally, Green makes no effort to get along with the men in
the Sales Department and is pointedly aloof and disdainful. He worries,
though, about the enmity he creates there. Green worries painfully that
someday soon the Corporate-Operations Department will take my department away from his department and give it to the Sales Department. Green has been worrying about this for eighteen years.

In my department, there are six people who are afraid of me, and one
small secretary who is afraid of all of us. I have one other person working for me who is not afraid of anyone, not even me, and I would fire
him quickly, but I'm afraid of him.

[. . .]

The people in the company who are most afraid of most people are the
salesmen. They live and work under pressure that is extraordinary. (I
would not be able to stand it.) When things are bad, they are worse for
the salesmen; when things are good, they are not much better.

They are always on trial, always on the verge of failure, collectively and individually. They strain, even the most secure and self-assured of them, to look good on paper; and there is much paper for them to look good on. Each week, for example, a record of the sales results of the preceding week for each sales office and for the Sales Department as a whole for each division of the company is kept and compared to the sales results for the corresponding week of the year before; the figures are photocopied on the latest photocopying machines and distributed throughout the company to all the people and departments whose work is related to selling. In addition to this, the sales record for each sales office for each quarter of each year for each division of the company and for the company as a whole is tabulated and compared to the sales record for the corresponding quarter of the year before; along with this, cumulative quarterly sales totals are also kept, and all these quarterly sales totals are photocopied and distributed too. In addition to this, quarterly and cumulative sales totals are compared with quarterly and cumulative sales totals* (*estimated) of other companies in the same field, and these figures are photocopied and distributed too. The figures are tabulated in stacks and layers of parallel lines and columns for snap comparisons and judgments by anyone whose eyes fall upon them. The result of all this photocopying and distributing is that there is almost continuous public scrutiny and discussion throughout the company of how well or poorly the salesmen in each sales office of each division of the company are doing at any given time.

When salesmen are doing well, there is pressure upon them to begin doing better, for fear they may start doing worse. When they are doing poorly, they are doing terribly. When a salesman lands a large order or brings in an important new account, his elation is brief, for there is danger he might lose that large order or important new account to a salesman from a competing company (or from a competing division of this company, which shows how complex and orderly the company has become) the next time around. It might even be canceled before it is filled, in which case no one is certain if anything was gained or lost. So there is crisis and alarm even in their triumphs.

Nevertheless, the salesmen love their work and would not choose any other kind. They are a vigorous, fun-loving bunch when they are not suffering abdominal cramps or brooding miserably about the future; on the other hand, they often turn cranky without warning and complain and bicker a lot. Some sulk, some bully; some bully and then sulk. All of them drink heavily until they get hepatitis or heart attacks or are warned away from heavy drinking for some other reason, and all of them, sooner or later, begin to feel they are being picked on and blamed unfairly. Each of them can name at least one superior in the company who he feels has a grudge against him and is determined to wreck his career.

The salesmen work hard and earn big salaries, with large personal expense accounts that they squander generously on other people in and out of the company, including me. They own good houses in good communities and play good games of golf on good private golf courses. The company encourages this. The company, in fact, will pay for their country club membership and all charges they incur there, if the club they get into is a good one. The company seeks and rewards salesmen who make a good impression on the golf course.

Unmarried men are not wanted in the Sales Department, not even widowers, for the company has learned from experience that it is difficult and dangerous for unmarried salesmen to mix socially with prominent executives and their wives or participate with them in responsible civic affairs. (Too many of the wives of these prominent and very successful men are no more satisfied with their marital situation than are their husbands.) If a salesman's wife dies and he is not ready to remarry, he is usually moved into an administrative position after several months of mourning. Bachelors are never hired for the sales force, and salesmen who get divorced, or whose wives die, know they had better remarry or begin looking ahead toward a different job.

(Red Parker has been a widower too long and is getting into trouble for that and for his excessive drinking. He is having too good a time.)

Strangely enough, the salesmen, who are aggressive, egotistical, and individualistic by nature, react very well to the constant pressure and rigid supervision to which they are subjected. They are stimulated and motivated by discipline and direction. They thrive on explicit guidance toward clear objectives. (This may be one reason golf appeals to them.) For the most part, they are cheerful, confident, and gregarious when they are not irritable, anxious, and depressed. There must be something in the makeup of a man that enables him not only to *be* a salesman, but to *want* to be one. Ours actually *enjoy* selling, although there seem to be many among them who suffer from colitis, hernia, hemorrhoids, and chronic diarrhea (I have one hemorrhoid, and that one comes and goes as it pleases and is no bother to me at all, now that I've been to a doctor and made sure it isn't cancer), not to mention the frequent breakdowns from tension and overwork that occur in the Sales Department as well as in other departments, and the occasional suicide that pops up among the salesmen about once every two years.

The salesmen are proud of their position and of the status and importance they enjoy within the company, for the function of my department, and of most other departments, is to help the salesmen sell. The company exists to sell. That's the reason we were hired, and the reason we are paid.

[. . .]

Green now thinks I am conspiring to undermine him. He is wrong. For one thing, I don't have the initiative; for another, I don't have the nerve; and for still another thing, I guess I really like and admire Green in many respects (even though I also hate and resent him in many others), and I know I am probably safer working for him than I would be working for anyone else—even for Andy Kagle in the Sales Department if they did decide to move me and my department from Green's department to Kagle's department.

In many ways and on many occasions Green and I are friends and allies and do helpful, sometimes considerate things for each other. Often, I protect and defend him when he is late or forgetful with work of his own, and I frequently give him credit for good work from my department that he does not deserve. But I never tell him I do this; and I never let him know when I hear anything favorable about him. I enjoy seeing Green apprehensive. I'm pleased he distrusts me (it does wonders for my self-esteem), and I do no more than necessary to reassure him.

And I am the best friend he has here.

Franz Kafka

MY NEIGHBOR

Franz Kafka *(1883–1924) was born in Prague. His father was a strong-willed merchant who was often absent on business. Kafka is a most revered ancestor of all writers who concern themselves with the awful absurdities of modern institutional life, be it in government, business, or religion. "My Neighbor" was collected in* The Great Wall of China and Other Pieces *(1946), which, like most of Kafka's work, was published posthumously, and against his express wishes, courtesy of his friend Max Brod. This extremely short story will resonate with anyone who has tried to start a small business and worried—if not, as here, to the point of paranoia—about the competition. The translation from the German is by Willa and Edwin Muir.*

My business rests entirely on my own shoulders. Two girl clerks with typewriters and ledgers in the front office, my own room with writing-desk, safe, consulting-table, easy chair, and telephone: such is my entire working apparatus. So simple to control, so easy to direct. I'm quite young, and lots of business comes my way. I don't complain, I don't complain.

At the beginning of the year a young man snapped up the empty premises next to mine, which very foolishly I hesitated to close with until too late. They also consist of a room and a front room, with a kitchen, however, thrown in—a room and a front room I would certainly have found some use for, my two girl clerks feel somewhat over-driven as it is—but what use would a kitchen have been to me? This petty consideration was solely responsible for my allowing the premises to be snatched from under my nose. Now that young man sits there. Harras, his name is. What he actually does there I have no idea. On the door there is a plate: "Harras Bureau." I have made enquiries and I am told it is a business similar to mine. One can't exactly warn people against giving the fellow credit, for after all he is a young and pushing man who probably has a future; yet one can't advise people to trust him either, for by all appearances he has no assets so far. The usual thing said by people who don't know.

Sometimes I meet Harras on the stairs; he seems always to be in an extraordinary hurry, for he literally shoots past me. I have never got a good look at him yet, for his office key is always in his hand when he passes me. In a tick he has the door open. Like the tail of a rat he has slipped through and I'm left standing again before the plate "Harras Bureau," which I have read already far oftener than it deserves.

The wretchedly thin walls betray the honorable and capable man, but shield the dishonest. My telephone is fixed to the wall that separates me from my neighbor. But I single that out merely as a particularly ironical circumstance. For even if it hung on the opposite wall, everything could be heard in the next room. I have accustomed myself to refrain from naming the names of my customers when speaking on the telephone to them. But of course it does not need much skill to guess the names from characteristic but unavoidable turns of the conversation. Sometimes I absolutely dance with apprehension round the telephone, the receiver at my ear, and yet can't help divulging the secret.

Because of all this my business decisions have naturally become unsure, my voice nervous. What is Harras doing while I am telephoning? If I wanted to exaggerate—and one must often do that so as to make things clear in one's mind—I might assert that Harras does not require a telephone, he uses mine, he pushes his sofa against the wall and listens; while I at the other side must fly to the telephone, listen to all the requests of my customers, come to difficult and grave decisions, carry out long calculations—but worst of all, during all this time, involuntarily give Harras valuable information through the wall.

Perhaps he doesn't wait even for the end of the conversation, but gets up at the point where the matter has become clear to him, flies through the town with his usual haste and, before I have hung up the receiver, is already at his goal working against me.

Jill Nelson

from *VOLUNTEER SLAVERY*

Jill Nelson *(1952–) here describes her experience in an all-day series of job interviews at the* Washington Post; *her worries that day, though mixed with excitement, were not unfounded, as she tells it in her memoir* Volunteer Slavery: My Authentic Negro Experience *(1993), from which this excerpt is reprinted. Jill Nelson is the author of several other books, including* Straight, No Chaser: How I Became a Grown-up Black Woman *(1997),* Sexual Healing *(2003), and* Finding Martha's Vineyard: African Americans at Home on an Island *(2005). She lives in New York City.*

"Well, this is the final stage of the *Washington Post* interview procedure," says the editor of the newspaper's Sunday magazine. "Talking to Ben."

Jay Lovinger and I walk through the cavernous newsroom toward executive editor Ben Bradlee's glassed-in office on the north wall. Around me, hundreds of reporters sit at computer terminals, banging away. A few sneak surreptitious glances at me. No one makes eye contact except the two sisters at the switchboard. I feel like a side of beef hooked on a pulley in a meat refrigerator, circling for the buyer's inspection. It is April, 1986.

"Everyone hired at the *Post* talks to Ben. He is an incredible interviewer," Lovinger says.

"Oh really?" I say. I almost say "Ow really," as a needle of excruciating pain shoots up from the cramped space between my little toe and the one next to it. My feet, in three-inch heels, are killing me.

"So far, everyone really likes you."

"Great," I say. What I really want to say is, "Likes me? Who gives a damn if they like me? This is a writing job, not a personality contest, isn't it?"

"The Metro editors even want you for their staff," he says, as if conferring some much coveted status. "They were intrigued by your perspective."

I'm not surprised. Two white males running the Metropolitan desk in a 70-percent-black city that is also the nation's capital are probably in a constant state of intrigue. Mostly involving how to parlay that job into a better, whiter one.

"If everything goes well with Ben, then we'll talk money," he says as we near the glass office, guarded by a fierce-looking redhead. "Just be yourself," he cautions.

I turn to look at him to see if he's trying to be funny, but of course he's dead serious. I decide not to ask him who else but myself he imagines I am, or could be. Instead, I smooth the folds of my turquoise ultrasuede dress, lick my lips, and wiggle my feet, trying to get the wad of Dr. Scholl's lambswool between my toes—the only thing standing between me and triple minority status: black, female, and handicapped—back into a more functional position.

But by now I am tired of being on. For me, the notion of coming to work at the *Washington Post* is mostly about money, but that's a black thing, which these people wouldn't understand. For twelve years, I have lived happily in New York as a successful yet poor freelance writer. I never thought about working for anyone but myself. Then one night the phone rang, and it was the man who's now escorting me to Bradlee's office.

"Hello," he said. "I'm the new editor of the new *Washington Post* magazine, and we'd like to talk to you about working with us."

After the obligatory yah-yah about purpose, art, and objectives, I cut to the chase: "What salary range are you offering?" The figure, twice what I earned the year before, gets me on a plane to this interview.

"What's Bradlee's interview technique like?" I ask.

"Fascinating. Absolutely fascinating. Don't be surprised if he does most of the talking, he usually does. He'll tell you about himself to find out about you. Even though you may not say much, Ben is incredibly insightful about people. He's an amazing judge of character."

"That's interesting," I say, and relax. This I can definitely deal with. White boy interview technique 101, in which he talks about himself in order to see if I can deal with him, which means he can deal with me. I didn't go to prep school and Columbia Journalism for nothing. My parents will be happy their money wasn't wasted.

"This is Jill Nelson. She's here to see Ben," Lovinger says to the secretary/sentinel.

"Go right in," she says, and smiles.

"Good luck," says Lovinger.

"Thank you," I say, smiling, wondering what I'm getting into. Then I remember that I'm just a piece of meat, dark meat at that. And after all, the blacker the berry, the sweeter the juice. It wasn't until years later that Daisy, one of the few friends I made in Washington, pointed out, "Yeah, but who wants sugar diabetes?" She ought to know. Short and olive-shaped, Daisy is Washington's smallest P.R. maven, a native of Boston who escaped via the East Village of the 1960s and ended up in D.C. Smart, acerbic, and outspoken, she pays homage to no one and has everyone's ear.

I am momentarily stunned when I enter Bradlee's office. I'm expecting Jason Robards from *All the President's Men*, tall, gray, and handsome. Instead I'm greeted by a short, gray, wrinkled gnome.

"Ben Bradlee. Nice to meet you. Sit down," he booms. Well, at least he has Jason Robards' voice. I sit.

"Tell me something about yourself."

Temporarily, my mind is null and void. All I can think to tell him is that my feet are killing me and that, in a static-cling war with my dress, my slip has risen up to encircle my waist. Then an ancient Temptations song pops into my head—"Papa Was a Rollin' Stone." For years the words to this song, which I didn't particularly like when it was a hit in 1972, spring into mind when I'm queried about myself by white folks. I suspect many think the song defines the authentic Negro experience.

But truthfully, Papa wasn't a rolling stone, he was a dentist, Mommy was a businesswoman and librarian, we were solidly upper-middle-class. Besides, I remind myself, this is the 1980s. The day of the glorification of the stereotypical poor, pathological Negro is over. Just like the South, it is time for the black bourgeoisie to rise again. I am a foot soldier in that army. So I tell Bradlee, briefly, about my educational and journalistic background. Am I imagining it, or is he really impatient for me to shut up?

"Let me tell you about my magazine," Bradlee says, almost before my lips have closed over my last word.

"I want it to have an identity of its own, but at the same time be a mixture of *Esquire*, *New York* magazine, and *The New York Times Magazine*. I want it to be provocative, insightful, funny, and controversial . . ." He goes on.

I sit there looking at him, halfway listening as he talks and talks, struck by the notion of defining a new magazine by old ones, and old tired ones at that. I try to imagine myself, an African-American female, working and thriving at a publication that's an amalgam of white man at his best, a celebration of yuppie-dom, and all the news that fits, we print. I come up blank.

"I want the fashions to be exciting, new, to portray women who dress with style, like my wife," Bradlee is saying when I tune in again. I know he's married to Sally Quinn, but I'll be damned if I know what she wears. I don't remember reading her name in *W* or the fashion columns. What am I doing here?

"I want it to illuminate what really goes on in this city, to get under Washington's skin . . ."

It's when he says *skin* that I remember why I'm here. I'm black and female. The magazine, to debut in a few months, has no black or female writers. In 1986, I'm about to realize my destiny—or pay off some terrible karmic debt—and become a first. Hallelujah!

"So, have you always lived in New York?"

Again, I snap back. "Yes. Except for three years at prep school in Pennsylvania and a year I lived on Martha's Vineyard."

"Martha's Vineyard. How'd you wind up there?" It is the first time he has seemed sincerely interested in anything I've said. After all, only the best people wind up on the Vineyard.

"My parents have a home there. I've spent summers on the Vineyard since I was a child and just decided to spend a year there and write," I say.

He grins. It's as if he's suddenly recognized that the slightly threatening black guy asking for a hand-out on the street is actually a Harvard classmate fallen on hard times. The bond of the Vineyard makes me safe, a person like him.

"Ahhh," he says, "So you're part of that whole black bourgeoisie scene with the Bullocks and the Washingtons?"

"I guess you could say that," I say, and chuckle. So does he. I don't know what he's grinning about, but the notion of myself as part of the black socialite scene I've spent a lifetime avoiding on and off the Vineyard strikes me as laughable. So does his evocation of the Bullocks, old Washingtonians, and former Mayor Walter Washington, who is married to a Bullock. The Washingtons, after all, don't own, they visit—an important distinction in Vineyard society.

Our eyes meet, our chuckle ends, and I know I'm over. The job is mine. Simply by evoking residence on Martha's Vineyard, I have separated wheat from chaff, belongers from aspirers, rebellious chip-on-the-shoulder Negroes from middle-class, responsible ones.

Vanquished is the leftist ghost of my years writing for the *Village Voice*. Gone are the fears he might have had about my fitting in after a life as a freelance writer, an advocacy journalist, a free black. By dint of summers spent on Martha's Vineyard, I am, in his eyes, safe. I may be the darker sister, but I'm still a sister. I will fit into the *Washington Post* family.

Bradlee launches into a story about his house on the Vineyard, traded in for one in the more social media enclave of the Hamptons. I relax, stop listening, and start counting dollars. Unfortunately, there aren't enough of them to last the length of Bradlee's story. He keeps on talking and I just sit there, smiling. A feeling of foreboding expands geometrically around me. I shake it off and concentrate on willing my brain and feet into numbness.

By the time my day of infamy, er, interviews is over, Ben has communicated his feelings to the editors—probably by talking about himself—and I've been offered a job on the Sunday magazine, I have no feeling left in my feet, and I'm just about brain dead.

I feel as if thousands of cornea-sized holes have been burned into the back of my dress from the discreet scrutiny of the voiceless reporters who may soon become my colleagues.

Lovinger walks me to the elevator.

"Well, what do you think? We'd really like you to be a part of the magazine."

"I'm interested, but I'd like a few days to think about the offer and talk to my daughter," I say.

"Why? Is there a problem?" He looks at me with a mixture of surprise, annoyance, and panic, as if the thought that I might not want to join this particular family is heretical. He needs me, black and breasted, to complete his staff.

A Jew who grew up in the housing projects of Manhattan, Jay Lovinger's come to the *Post* via *People* magazine and is desperate to make the magazine work, and to prove himself—poor, Jewish, a college dropout—worthy of membership in the *real* white boys club, the WASP one. It isn't enough that he's making big money and working for the number-two newspaper in the country (after *The New York Times*) without benefit of even the most mediocre college education. No, he wants to truly belong. Doesn't he know that without Harvard his efforts are futile?

Belonging isn't what I crave; I'm after money and a larger audience. But as we used to say in the 1960s, I don't like the vibes around here. No one makes eye contact, no one speaks, everyone watches. In nearly eight hours, the only people who've said squat to me besides editors are Joyce and Margo, the sisters at the switchboard. I am not optimistic about the future.

I am so whipped after being on all day that I don't even have the energy to smile superficially. Since ten in the morning I've hobbled from cubicle to cubicle, white male to white male, being interrogated. I feel like a felon up for parole trying to cop a plea with the commissioners.

I've also been doing the standard Negro balancing act when it comes to dealing with white folks, which involves sufficiently blurring the edges of my being so that they don't feel intimidated, while simultaneously holding on to my integrity. There is a thin line between Uncle Tomming and Mau-Mauing. To fall off that line can mean disaster. On one side lies employment and self-hatred: on the other, the equally dubious honor of unemployment with integrity. Walking that line as if it were a tightrope results in something like employment with honor, although I'm not sure exactly how that works.

I keep getting this creepy feeling that the *Washington Post* is doing me some kind of favor. It's as if, as an African-American, female, freelance writer, I'm a handicapped person they've decided to mainstream. The words to "Look at Me I'm Walking," the theme song of the annual Jerry Lewis Muscular Dystrophy Telethon, pop into my head.

The thought of all those bills being pledged to a good cause makes me think about my favorite cause—me—and my interview with Tom Wilkinson, the money man. As far as I can tell, all he does is talk to people about money and deliver bad news.

"There're not many reporters here who've just been freelancers. This is a tough institution. Most of our people have worked their way up from smaller papers. Do you think you'll be able to fit in, handle the demands of working for a daily newspaper?" he asks me.

"I think freelancers, people who work for themselves, work harder than people who have job-jobs," I say, trying not to sound as exhausted and borderline sullen as I am. My college friend Adrienne, who went off to teach in St. Thomas and never came back, coined the term "job-job." We met in a class on black women writers at City College and first connected when the teacher, an African-American woman, announced that she didn't know what racism was until she was twenty-five. Adrienne and I found this statement both hilarious and outrageous, and said so. We've been tight ever since. "Job-job" is the phrase Adrienne used to differentiate working for someone else from working for yourself. "Have you ever noticed," she'd say, "how the 'J' in job looks just like a hook?"

"We hope you'll come and work here. Everyone liked you," Wilkinson says. Here we go again with the popularity contest. I'm glad I wore the turquoise dress. I smile, cross my legs. Then I recross them.

"Now. Let's talk about salary. How much money did you make last year?" I stare at him. He sits, a thin, intense man in his forties with a weasel-like face, waiting for a response. I do what everyone does in salary negotiations. I lie.

"About $40,000."

"We can offer you $42,500," he spits out.

"Well, the editor mentioned a salary of—"

"$45,000," he interrupts. I feel like a damaged urn under bid at a Sotheby's auction. Get me off the block fast and maybe no one will notice the cracks.

"I was thinking more in terms of—"

"Without newspaper experience, I think that is a good starting salary. Of course, if things work out well, there'll be raises and that sort of thing."

"I understand that," I say, "But I'll be moving both myself and my daughter from New York, she has to go to school and—"

He looks at me with what I think is exasperation, then glances at his wrist. Clearly, I am taking up too much time. I feel myself slipping off that tightrope. I also feel like a troublemaker, a subversive for not being properly grateful for the chance to work at the *Washington Post*, whatever the salary. I also feel out of my league. Mommy and Daddy never fully explained to me that I'd have to support myself when I grew up. They certainly never mentioned salary negotiations.

I have the feeling that even though I'm doing the right thing, I'm also somehow in bad taste, a familiar feeling for African-Americans. It's like I'm the first black woman to become Miss America and instead of feeling thankful I refuse to put on the tiara because the rhinestones are of such lousy quality. Instead of being happy I'm an ingrate.

"All right, $50,000," he snaps. I can almost hear a voice saying, "Going once, going twice, gone." I'm not sure anymore which way is which.

"Fine. But I need a few days to think about it." Now he looks really annoyed, but what the hell? Last year I made about $20,000, so $50,000 would be a hefty raise. So why do I have a feeling of impending doom? I try to talk myself out of it, but I can't think of what to say.

Then I hear my mother's voice from the day before.

"I think it's a great opportunity even though if you move I'll miss you and Misu you'll be making good money and the *Post* is a good liberal newspaper after all they brought down Nixon that son of a bitch you're getting older and have to start thinking about college for your daughter and retirement some security you can't be a vagabond all your life what about health insurance . . ."

Enough. I shut her off. My mind begins to wander to boutiques, malls, bookstores, liposuctionists, all the places I can spend the *Post*'s money. I don't notice Wilkinson standing by the door waiting to usher me out until he says, "Nice meeting you." I want to ask him, "But do you like me, really *like* me?" Instead, I leave.

"Please let me know your decision as soon as possible," Lovinger says as I leave, sticking his long neck and nearly bald head inside the elevator doors. "We'd like you to be a part of what we're trying to do." It's as if I'm being recruited to join a crusade, but no one will tell me its objective.

"I will," I say. The doors close. I fall back against the wall and do some deep yogic breathing. What I'd really like to do is scream. My pantyhose feels like a girdle, slowly cutting off the circulation from feet to waist. I barely manage to cross the street to The Madison Hotel, where my daughter Misu, age thirteen, awaits me.

As I am soon to discover is true of much of Washington, The Madison Hotel is a warped facsimile, an unknowing parody of something that probably never was real. It has cachet because Washington is a city of pretension and nostalgia. Whites yearn for the time when the city was run by a cabal of presidentially appointed commissioners and not a black mayor; for the good old days when D.C. was a cultural backwater but there were no traffic jams; for the bygone era when there was no race problem because genteel segregation reigned. Black people yearn for the 1960s, before the riots, when it really did seem things would change. They yearn for Marion Barry in his first two—sober—terms, for D.C.B.C., before crack. Organizations have their own specific nostalgia; at the *Post*, it is for the boom days of Richard Nixon and Watergate.

The Madison, with its faux tapestry-upholstered loveseats, neo-Japanese flower arrangements, bad food, and obsequious Central American waiters, is a wannabee's vision of the life of the powerful WASP. Aspiring yuppies, brought to Washington by a job in corporate or political middle-management, lunch at The Madison and declare themselves important, in the know, powerbrokers. This is a town where importance and longevity are connoted by having a capital "The" in front of everything.

"Hi, Misu. I'm back." My daughter sits propped up on one of the two double beds, watching television. She is brown, thin, wears braces. The debris of room service—trays, frilly paper things, silverware, and the smell of grease—surrounds her.

"Sorry I took so long." My daughter, a hotel abuser from way back, shrugs. Being left alone in a room she doesn't have to clean up, with television and room service, is a significant element in her vision of nirvana.

"That's okay, Mom. How'd it go?"

"Okay. But really weird," I say, yanking off my shoes and stockings in one effective but less than fluid movement. I walk into the bathroom, turn on the water, and begin scraping mascara and eyeliner from my face before I'm blinded.

"I don't really think the *Washington Post* is the place for me—" I begin, shouting to be heard above the roar of Madison water.

"I like it here, Mom. I think we should move here," my daughter says.

"Why?" I ask, drying my face. "What do you like about it here?" I try to keep my tone neutral.

"The buildings are small. The people are nice. And it's clean," she says. "If we lived here, we'd live in a house, right? Then we could have a car and lots of cats and a dog and all that stuff, like the Cosbys, couldn't we?"

I open my mouth to point out that the Cosbys don't have cats or dogs, that they have a father, that they live in New York. Then I look at the dreamy expression on my daughter's face, and close my mouth again. Abruptly, it all becomes clear to me.

My daughter is tired of being a leftist. She is tried of eccentric clothes, artists, vegetarian diets, the New York subway, and living in an apartment. The culturally rich and genteel poverty in which she was raised is played out. Deep in her little African-American heart, she yearns to be Vanessa Huxtable, her age cohort in the television Cosby clan. With a perfect room, in a perfect house, with perfect parents and lots of perfectly hip clothes in the closet. She is sick of my Sixties class-suicide trip, of middle-class Mommy's vow of poverty in pursuit of the authentic Negro experience. She is tired, simply, of hanging in there with my trip.

She's got a point. I'm tired, too. Taking the job would not only fulfill some of her fantasies, it would provide me with a ready-made escape from New York, Ed Koch and his soul mate, subway gunman Bernhard Goetz, not to mention my life there. Let's face it. I'm burnt out and dread answering the telephone. I'm dating a mortician who's about to lose his business, which is located in the heart of the area with the most liquor stores and highest death rate in the city. At thirty-four, post-divorce, I am again living with my own Mommy. How much worse could Washington be? Still, I have a stress stomachache and the feeling that I'm about to make the wrong decision for all the right reasons. I had the same feeling the night before I got married.

"It might be fun to live here for a while, Mom. Not forever. What do you think?"

"We'll see," I say, falling back on every parent's favorite meaningless expression in a desperate bid for time. "What'd you do today?"

"Watched television and ordered lunch. You know what I like about Washington? When I ordered my lunch they didn't have shakes on the menu. So when I called I asked the lady, 'Do you have milkshakes?' And the woman said, 'My dear, this is The Madison. We have everything.' Having everything. Isn't that great?"

My fate is sealed. We will move to Washington. I will go to work for the *Washington Post*. We will live the life of the Cosbys, sans Daddy. I feel I owe my daughter stability, bourgeoisdom, charge accounts at Woodies, a chance to join the mainstream. I will be the Cosmo mom, the queen of having it all, and my daughter a Cosby clone. For $50,000 smackeroos, how bad could it be?

Three months later we move to Washington. In the four and a half years I work at the *Post*, my daughter never has another milkshake at The Madison.

Gwendolyn M. Parker

UPPITY BUPPIE

Gwendolyn M. Parker *(1950–) is the author of a novel,* These Same Long Bones *(1994), and the memoir* Trespassing: My Sojourn in the Halls of Privilege *(1997), from which this excerpt is reprinted. Parker's trials as the only black woman at a Wall Street law firm, and her later stint as an attorney at American Express, brought her—and now us—face-to-face with the entrenched "white shoe" baggage of corporate business.*

I left Cadwalader, Wickersham & Taft less than a year after the Christmas party. I had accepted a new position as a tax attorney at the American Express Company. My leave-taking was more a bolt than a considered career move, but even as I ran, I slowed down to consider the change. After all, two years at a place like Cadwalader could be put down to experience. This new job was a real commitment to a career in mainstream corporate America. I was twenty-eight at the time, old enough, I told myself, to have a more solid sense of direction. I had lunch with my old professor and friend from NYU, and when I told him of the new job I'd accepted, he asked me why I hadn't chosen to clerk for a judge instead. "Or think about politics or government service," he said. "You could make a real contribution."

Contribution. It was indeed a reverberant word. It was all that I had heard growing up, but it was a word I found increasingly confusing. I thought about my ancestors, living in a much more circumscribed world, and not by choice. How much easier it must have been for them to make a contribution, with every achievement redounding to their credit. How was a contribution going to be defined or measured in this much wider world?

"Well, business people make a contribution," I said, giving the answer I'd been practicing for a while. "Most of my family were businessmen."

"Really?" my professor asked.

I gave him the litany: my father, my grandfather, my great-grandfather.

"Back in Durham?" he asked, and I nodded. He took another bite of his lunch. "That's not exactly the same as American Express."

I shrugged in response. He was so sure of himself, and in this, he reminded me of my great-grandfather. I knew he was right, and at the same time his sureness frightened me. It seemed to call me to a task I wasn't ready to do. In the last few years I had gone through the motions, as if my real life were waiting for me in the wings. But now, for just a second, in my professor's eyes I saw that this life I was leading was real. And it was also a life, I could tell, that he found lacking. In my honest moments, I found it lacking as well. But the alternatives appeared just as daunting, as if the life that he led, like the one my great-grandfather had led, was too ardent and real. They stood on life's stage naked of props.

"Well, isn't this what we've been marching and protesting about?" I asked. "Making it possible for black people to go anywhere they choose?"

Now it was my professor's turn to shrug. "Is that what we've been struggling to do?" he quietly asked. I gave him my now commonplace rationalizations, and he accepted them. And in place of any sureness about my decision, I focused instead on the sheer relief I felt to be leaving the firm.

I started at American Express in the fall of 1978. From a world that was stultifying and oppressively male, I was suddenly in a company that prided itself on its youthfulness and its energy, and whose ranks, at least at the middle-management level, were filling with women. Jim Robinson, the chairman and chief executive officer, was in his early forties, and the company's new hires, like me, bore faces that reflected the growing diversity of the American workforce. Where I'd had no delusions that a place like Cadwalader was about to change, hopeful signs of transformation were everywhere at American Express.

The first was in the look of the workplace at the start of the day. The firm had been all hushed, narrow hallways, but Amex Plaza was all marble and light. The headquarters overlooked the Hudson, at the very tip of Manhattan, a short lunchtime stroll to the Staten Island ferry and the Circle Line to the Statue of Liberty. I remember how it felt those first few weeks when I arrived at work each morning: the lobby abuzz with messengers and mailroom sorters and secretaries and junior managers and lawyers and senior executives, people from all over the city and from all over the world. Among the large workforce there were Hispanics and Asians and blacks, Pakistanis and Frenchmen, Barbadians, and Italians—everywhere faces that bespoke difference. It was easy, particularly in contrast with the strangled conformity of the firm, to imagine that this was truly a microcosm of America, that we were, in fact, creating the new American community.

Of course, at the upper reaches of the company, the faces were as nearly uniformly white and male as they had been at the firm. Still, the sheer number of us at the bottom and the middle who were different was cause for hope. Surely this diversity was not just happenstance; in our growing numbers there must have been a purposeful design. Perhaps all of our female and brown, black, tan, pink, umber faces were included not with reluctance but with real dedication to change.

Having my first female boss only accelerated and strengthened this fantasy. Finally I was working for someone I could not only learn from in a narrow, technical way, but for whom I had a large measure of personal respect. My new boss, Diane, was smart, professional, perfectionist in her approach to problems, and incredibly hard-working. She was also sweet, unfailingly polite, and easy to get along with. We worked well together, and when we had lunch together, as we often did, we could easily turn from business and relax.

My first few months at American Express were like a powerful antidote to my nearly two years at the firm. This, I hoped, was the real face of American business—no evildoers plotting the exploitation of the masses; instead, nice people, fun people even, pleasantly and for the most part respectfully doing their jobs. For the better part of a year, simple politeness was a welcome tonic.

Toward the end of my first year, Diane had scheduled a trip to Guatemala that she was unable to make because of a lingering ailment.

Though I had not worked on the launch of the new credit card that was the occasion for the trip, Diane passed all of the files on to me and asked that I take her place on the trip. I eagerly took on the assignment. It was a challenge to get up to speed quickly on the issues, and I felt that this was the first time I would be doing a major task all on my own. The last-minute preparations and phone calls were exciting, and it was a heady feeling to jet off to a foreign country as one half of the legal team responsible for supervising the foreign counsel working on the launch.

When I arrived at the airport in Guatemala, I was met by the Mexican and Guatemalan attorneys and accountants who would be working with us. They had been told that another attorney was coming in Diane's place, and when they realized that I was she, there were the usual looks of surprise, not dissimilar to the looks I had grown accustomed to whenever I traveled on business for Cadwalader. The other attorney, handling the nontax issues, was also a woman, and our hosts did not disguise the fact that they found two women attorneys on one trip to be quite unexpected. "Both of you are women," they kept exclaiming.

"And both so tall!" another added. The fact that I was black was surely a second shock, but they did not comment on this. Instead, my height apparently became the surrogate. They all looked google-eyed at me. "You are really, really tall," they would each say when I caught them staring.

We proceeded from there to an all-day meeting. At first I was too engrossed in the task to notice the careful attentiveness when I had something to say, the solicitousness for my comfort, the smiles set on High, the casual deference. But midway through the meeting it dawned on me that there was a significant shift from the position I had occupied within Cadwalader. I was no longer solely defined by my race and my sex; I had now attained a stature inflated by the weight of the company I represented. My opinion mattered to these men: if they were charming and efficient and apparently competent, they wanted me to take note of those facts. For that would mean a positive assessment of them, and that in turn would mean that dollars from the company would continue to flow to them. It was a simple equation, but it represented my first experience of the power that accrues by virtue of position. At Cadwalader, no one had been beholden to me. I was at the bottom of the heap, and my opinions held no sway. Here I already possessed a certain status.

It was not an instantaneous transformation, but I was slowly seduced by the pleasant feeling of being treated as if I were somebody special. Not just smart or competent, but special at the core, as if formed from fine building material. I liked being in charge, liked having my awkwardness interpreted as judicious reserve. I discovered, in fact, that there were clear merits to me in this system that valued power above personality. As the tax attorney from American Express, I rose above being merely Gwen.

Concomitant with this shift in my status, there was a subtle shift in my attitude toward my job. I began to enjoy telling people what I did for a living. I liked the nods of approval that followed. I liked the expense-account dinners when I worked late, calling cabs to take me home, the company élan that rubbed off on me. I especially liked the new status I held within my family. Though my parents had been proud of my job at Cadwalader, it was a pride I could take no joy in because I found the workplace itself so depressing. Here I could bask in the pride without penalty. At family gatherings my father made sure everyone knew about my title and responsibilities, and with his encouragement I added tidbits about my business travels. Though I sometimes felt overwhelmed by the workload, and Diane and I often groused to each other about it, the hours were nothing like the ones I had been expected to work at the firm. I even had time now to spend the good money I was earning. I began to believe that I had discovered a life I could settle into and enjoy.

During my second year with American Express I was placed in a program for preparing minority employees, both women and blacks, for senior-management positions. There were about ten of us in my group, all identified as "high-potential" minority employees. The course supposedly cost the company nearly ten thousand dollars per employee, and we were all encouraged to feel important by virtue of this investment.

We met once a month or so and were given assignments, such as to make a contact in a new area of the company we wanted to learn more about or to call up a senior manager and ask him or her to lunch.

Afterward we wrote up our thoughts and impressions and shared them with the rest of the group, and the senior managers gave us feedback on our completed assignments. The program's purpose was to give us a better understanding of the culture we were part of, and point out when we did not understand its mores and rules.

I learned very quickly, for example, that my tendency to base relationships on whether I liked someone or not was wholly at odds with the culture. Relationships, I was led to understand, should be built around mutual goals and requirements and power. By contrast, outside day-to-day projects, I rarely approached people for whom I had no natural feeling of sympathy. This reticence on my part, I learned, was interpreted as a lack of ambition.

An example of this lack of ambition was an incident cited by my boss's boss in which I had ridden the elevator with him one day and not taken the opportunity such access afforded. I had merely made small talk with him and then fallen silent. I had mistakenly seen the encounter as a purely personal one, and on a personal level, I had nothing much to say to him. I was later told that a white male who was ambitious would have seen this as a chance to ingratiate and impress, perhaps the time to regale the boss's boss with news of his work and his progress.

When an upcoming party was planned, we were asked to define our goals for the event. Not really believing that others went to a party with business objectives in mind, I asked three of my white male colleagues what their expectations were and was surprised when I received very specific answers from all three of them.

The course was an eye opener, but I found it vaguely depressing as well. Each month we sat and took copious notes on how to act like an ambitious white male. It apparently never occurred to anyone that we might have something to offer by acting out of our own traditions and backgrounds, and no one offered that as an alternative. Though I never expressed it, deep down I resisted the course. I did the assignments, expressed an understanding of the new concepts that were revealed, but despite my seeming acquiescence I assumed that I would be able to make my way in the company playing by my own set of rules. I learned to be more forthcoming with my superiors, relied less on my personal likes and dislikes, but continued to believe that if I merely did an excellent job, I would eventually be rewarded for that work.

Two years after I joined Amex, I transferred to the Office of Corporate Strategic Planning. I had learned in the management development program and through my experiences in the company that there was a major difference between staff and line employees. Those of us in the Legal Department were considered staff, well paid but essentially only helpers. Though my position brought me a certain status with outside vendors and outside lawyers, within the company the pecking order still placed me at the low end. Line positions were those with responsibility for making money for the company. I was advised by numerous people that if I was serious about moving up, I needed to shift to the business side.

I did indeed want to move up. During the spring of my first year at American Express, a small article on me appeared in *Mademoiselle* magazine. It was part of a regular feature that insiders at the magazine called "Real Girls," showing young career women on the way up, our photographs accompanied by brief comments about our goals along with details of where readers could buy the clothes and accessories we wore. In the picture I was suited for power, standing on a windy New York City street with my briefcase open and ready for action. My comments fit the image: I was a woman on the move, an ambitious corporate go-getter. If I had felt at the time that I was only pretending to be this person, by now my Real Girl ambitions had become quite real. I was growing fond of the treatment that said I was due a certain esteem and respect.

The Office of Corporate Strategic Planning was a perfect segue from the law to the more prestigious business side. The office was the brainchild of Harry Freeman, a brilliant and somewhat eccentric man whose mind was forever in motion. Harry had spawned the idea of "cause marketing," the marriage of art, commerce, and philanthropy, a clever marketing device that linked using the American Express card with donations to charity and with an overall feeling of doing good. It took someone like Harry to carry off the idea of forming a cadre of thinkers for senior managers—their own little think tank that would explore the viability of new business ideas.

We were an eclectic crew, drawn from a variety of backgrounds and disciplines, all dedicated to that precious eighties notion of synergy—that out of the combination of disparate things would emerge something greater than the whole. There were several Ivy League M.B.A.ers, a line manager from Marketing, a former engineer, and me, a lawyer with a tax specialty, like Harry himself. My strengths—I had an analytical mind and approach to problem-solving, and had had training that could be turned to any number of challenges—were tailor-made for someone like Harry, a generalist who felt he could solve any problem that he unleashed his intellect and imagination upon. So I was selected. The employee newsletter trumpeted that this was the first director-level job ever to be filled through job posting. My career as an erstwhile businesswoman was born.

With this job came an intense camaraderie, a new experience for me. Harry believed in brainstorming, and almost daily he held staff meetings where we all sat around the conference table, throwing out ideas and endlessly debating their merits and demerits. We each had our special area of expertise. Because Harry was brilliant, we were supposedly all brilliant too, and there were indeed some certifiable geniuses among us. Kimberly, a young woman from Yale, was the uncontested brain of the group. She was quiet, unassuming, and there was nothing she did not know. Any question that Harry might ask—and he had a penchant for asking questions constantly on anything and everything—Kimberly knew the answer to it: the trading price of the stock of some start-up company, the uses of fiber optics, the latest price-earnings differential of a competitor. She never seemed to go home—at 7 A.M. she was there and at 11 P.M. she was there. If she hadn't been so nice, her brilliance might have caused a great deal of envy, but she simply knew everything there was to know, and that was that. Because she so firmly occupied that spot, we all sought other ways to distinguish ourselves.

A young line manager who briefly shared an office with me was the one with the practical information of our ongoing smaller-scale marketing efforts. One of the Ivy League M.B.A.s was always impressing everyone with her command of strategic buzzwords and charts of analysis. My forte was synthesis and creativity. I knew almost nothing about business per se, and even less about balance sheets and the like, but I had a knack for recombining things into a hitherto unconsidered new whole. It meant I was quiet for long stretches of time, but every once in a while I had something to say to which others wanted to listen.

Equally exciting to me was how the sphere I was operating in had expanded. As a lawyer, I had been a kind of technician, responsible for a range of issues but ones that covered only a narrow field. Here in Strategic Planning, however, we were led to believe that we were helping to chart the future of the company, and in that future lay the destinies of thousands of people. My great-grandfather, Dr. Moore, had been concerned with several things in his work at the Mutual. But most important, he made sure that the institution provided a needed service for blacks who may otherwise have been deprived of such service, since it was a practice at the time for mainstream insurance companies to temporarily suspend the coverage of Negroes or not to provide coverage at all. He also wanted to provide jobs and the means of a dignified livelihood for many Negroes who had few opportunities to rise to management positions. And he wanted to illustrate to Negroes themselves what they were truly capable of achieving. Similarly, in Strategic Planning I felt I was being shown the grand design of the company: what the world of integrated financial services might mean to the average consumer, the thousands of back-office jobs that future expansion would create, the promise of quality service that the company strove to uphold.

It was in Strategic Planning that I began to fall completely for the lure of the company. It was not at all dissimilar to falling in love. Suddenly words like "synergy" and "future trends" and "the global village" took on a new hue: they were the harbingers of a new world order, based not on the hegemony of old, outmoded distinctions among people, but on a true meritocracy that would span the world. I now wanted to advance not only for personal reasons, but because I believed I was helping to usher in a wave of change that was sweeping the company and all of American business. Much of the optimism about this purported future was due to Harry Freeman's influence. In addition to his job as cochair of the Office of Corporate Strategic Planning, Harry was also the head of Corporate Affairs and Community Relations, and in this role he was a master at finding the intersections of the company's interests and those of the larger community. Amex sponsored art exhibits and musical performances, funded soup kitchens and programs to develop minority interns. It was easy, under Harry's sway, to imagine that these dual interests of profit and community service were of equal importance. This farsightedness also extended to his personal style. As a manager, Harry was indifferent to color and gender—in fact, he was indifferent to most things that other people paid attention to. I never once, in his presence, felt like "the black woman" or "the black director," though I was the only black director in the group. All that appeared to matter to Harry were ideas, and if you had a good one, he wouldn't have noticed if you'd presented it in the nude.

His style was infectious, and these were exhilarating times for all of us. We had access to senior management in the form of early morning meetings. We went on countless retreats, where we brainstormed from six o'clock breakfast until long after dinner, sometimes as late as midnight. Our heads began to nod while Harry, as indefatigable physically as he was intellectually, still held court, throwing out ideas, assigning topics that someone would read up on for the next day.

As my allegiance to the company deepened, I couldn't help but hearken again and again to my great-grandfather. When I joined American Express, I halfheartedly wondered if I would uncover the zeal he had brought to the many business ventures he encouraged. Now I thought I had discovered the secret that lay behind his passion. My great-grandfather had been sure that he could combine an entrepreneurial mission with a collective social mission, and in the zest that Harry brought to his work, I perceived the same kind of passion. That's the kind of business person I want to be, I decided, and with this decision my larger ambition was born. Already the novelty of being treated with deference was starting to pale, and I needed a new reason to work. Finally I'd found it. My job was no longer just a place to pump up my somewhat bruised ego from the Cadwalader days, a place to hang out and do interesting work for which I was well paid. I now wanted seriously to get ahead, as far as I could go, in the company.

On one of our many retreats, I remember sitting at breakfast one morning bleary-eyed, not so much from lack of sleep as from constant togetherness. Harry was reading the *Wall Street Journal*, as was everyone else at the table, and he talked aloud as he read, commenting cryptically on those things he found of interest, giving us random assignments to follow up on something or other. As usual, his interest ranged widely. To me he mentioned a regulatory change that he thought might have significance for the company.

Harry's remarks were not new to me. In my days as a lawyer, I had often followed legislative trends to see what effect laws would have on the company's interests, so that we could try to influence the outcome in our favor. But now I saw for the first time the single-mindedness with which he approached his work. We were discussing an issue of general public interest, and though we were exchanging different arguments that could be made to support a particular position, it was apparent that the underlying public interest, in Harry's mind, was a poor relation: he gave it only secondary importance, if that. Instead, all of Harry's far-ranging interests, from art to politics to social policy to legislation, were subsumed to the one goal that counted within the company—namely, how to increase the bottom line. And why shouldn't that be so? Wasn't that what American business was about? Nevertheless, the absurd simplicity of his preoccupation shocked me. Unknowingly, I had so thoroughly absorbed the ethics of the business world I knew as a youth that I had grafted those beliefs onto this new environment, even as the evidence of major differences between the two rose before me.

Sitting there with my peers, I felt as if the skin of a common perspective that had bound us as a group had been unceremoniously ripped from me. Did anyone else feel as I did? At Cadwalader I had been set apart by the obvious differences of my race and my gender, but here I saw that something else set me apart: the values I'd been bequeathed in my youth.

Through the window I could see that it was a beautiful day, green and springlike. The landscape was lovely, with rolling hills and mature trees off in the distance. As I looked at Harry, so wholly immersed in this game of business, I saw that he was as oblivious of the physical surroundings as he was of any personal details about us. That he was truly, thoroughly engrossed in this discussion and its central aim. And more important, that this was a genuine passion for him. That where he was was exactly where he wished to be.

And I knew that none of this was true for me. Not once in the two-plus years I had been with American Express had I awakened with the company's fundamental purpose in mind—to make more money. In fact, the quarterly earnings was a figure I had trouble remembering at all. I would memorize it for an upcoming meeting, then forget it as soon as the meeting was over. I wasn't in the least interested in growth curves and quarterly earnings and price-earning differentials and all the other buzzwords I labored to keep straight in my head. Instead, I enjoyed the people I worked with, I worked on interesting problems that captured my attention, and I particularly enjoyed the places where the company's mission intersected with that of the larger community. But about the money Amex earned per se, I realized I really didn't care.

Walker Percy

from *THE MOVIEGOER*

Walker Percy *(1916–1990) was a member of the Fellowship of Southern Writers, and William Faulkner was an occasional visitor to his childhood home; but he did his best to transcend the label of Southern writer. The Moviegoer (1961), his first published novel, earned him a lasting reputation and a National Book Award. In the excerpt below, he introduces Binx Bolling, a New Orleans stockbroker whose favored form of escape is the silver screen. Slyly imposing philosophical sublimity upon the mundaneness of the everday, Percy here offers up a true hero in the American grain: a mind straining (with every imaginative ounce at his disposal) against letting his seemingly benign workaday surroundings hem him in.*

Life in Gentilly is very peaceful. I manage a small branch office of my uncle's brokerage firm. My home is the basement apartment of a raised bungalow belonging to Mrs. Schexnaydre, the widow of a fireman. I am a model tenant and a model citizen and take pleasure in doing all that is expected of me. My wallet is full of identity cards, library cards, credit cards. Last year I purchased a flat olive-drab strongbox, very smooth and heavily built with double walls for fire protection, in which I placed my birth certificate, college diploma, honorable discharge, G.I. insurance, a few stock certificates, and my inheritance: a deed to ten acres of a defunct duck club down in St. Bernard Parish, the only relic of my father's many enthusiasms. It is a pleasure to carry out the duties of a citizen and to receive in return a receipt or a neat styrene card with one's name on it certifying, so to speak, one's right to exist. What satisfaction I take in appearing the first day to get my auto tag and brake sticker! I subscribe to *Consumer Reports* and as a consequence I own a first-class television set, an all but silent air conditioner and a very long lasting deodorant. My armpits never stink. I pay attention to all spot announcements on the radio about mental health, the seven signs of cancer, and safe driving—though, as I say, I usually prefer to ride the bus. Yesterday a favorite of mine, William Holden, delivered a radio announcement on litterbugs. "Let's face it," said Holden. "Nobody can do anything about it—but you and me." This is true. I have been careful ever since.

In the evenings I usually watch television or go to the movies. Weekends I often spend on the Gulf Coast. Our neighborhood theater in Gentilly has permanent lettering on the front of the marquee reading: Where Happiness Costs So Little. The fact is I am quite happy in a movie, even a bad movie. Other people, so I have read, treasure memorable moments in their lives: the time one climbed the Parthenon at sunrise, the summer night one met a lonely girl in Central Park and achieved with her a sweet and natural relationship, as they say in books. I too once met a girl in Central Park, but it is not much to remember. What I remember is the time John Wayne killed three men with a carbine as he was falling to the dusty street in *Stagecoach*, and the time the kitten found Orson Welles in the doorway in *The Third Man*.

My companion on these evening outings and weekend trips is usually my secretary. I have had three secretaries, girls named Marcia, Linda, and now Sharon. Twenty years ago, practically every other girl born in Gentilly must have been named Marcia. A year or so later it was Linda. Then Sharon. In recent years I have noticed that the name Stephanie has come into fashion. Three of my acquaintances in Gentilly have daughters named Stephanie. Last night I saw a TV play about a nuclear test explosion. Keenan Wynn played a troubled physicist who had many a bad moment with his conscience. He took solitary walks in the desert. But you could tell that in his heart of hearts he was having a very good time with his soul-searching. "What right have we to do what we are doing?" he would ask his colleagues in a bitter voice. "It's my four-year-old daughter I'm really thinking of," he told another colleague and took out a snapshot. "What kind of future are we building for her?" "What is your daughter's name?" asked the colleague, looking at the picture. "Stephanie," said Keenan Wynn in a gruff voice. Hearing the name produced a sharp tingling sensation on the back of my neck. Twenty years from now I shall perhaps have a rosy young Stephanie perched at my typewriter.

Naturally I would like to say that I had made conquests of these splendid girls, my secretaries, casting them off one after the other like old gloves, but it would not be strictly true. They could be called love affairs, I suppose. They started off as love affairs anyway, fine careless raptures in which Marcia or Linda (but not yet Sharon) and I would go spinning along the Gulf Coast, lie embracing in a deserted cove of Ship Island, and hardly believe our good fortune, hardly believe that the world could contain such happiness. Yet in the case of Marcia and Linda the affair ended just when I thought our relationship was coming into its best place. The air in the office would begin to grow thick with silent reproaches. It would become impossible to exchange a single word or glance that was not freighted with a thousand hidden meanings. Telephone conversations would take place at all hours of the night, conversations made up mostly of long silences during which I would rack my brain for something to say while on the other end you could hear little else but breathing and sighs. When these long telephone silences come, it is a sure sign that love is over. No, they were not conquests. For in the end my Lindas and I were so sick of each other that we were delighted to say good-by.

I am a stock and bond broker. It is true that my family was somewhat disappointed in my choice of a profession. Once I thought of going into law or medicine or even pure science. I even dreamed of doing something great. But there is much to be said for giving up such grand ambitions and living the most ordinary life imaginable, a life without the old longings; selling stocks and bonds and mutual funds; quitting work at five o'clock like everyone else; having a girl and perhaps one day settling down and raising a flock of Marcias and Sandras and Lindas of my own. Nor is the brokerage business as uninteresting as you might think. It is not a bad life at all.

We live, Mrs. Schexnaydre and I, on Elysian Fields, the main thoroughfare of Faubourg Marigny. Though it was planned to be, like its namesake, the grandest boulevard of the city, something went amiss, and now it runs an undistinguished course from river to lake through shopping centers and blocks of duplexes and bungalows and raised cottages. But it is very spacious and airy and seems truly to stretch out like a field under the sky. Next door to Mrs. Schexnaydre is a brand new school. It is my custom on summer evenings after work to take a shower, put on shirt and pants and stroll over to the deserted playground and there sit on the ocean wave, spread out the movie page of the *Times-Picayune* on one side, phone book on the other, and a city map in my lap. After I have made my choice, plotted a route—often to some remote neighborhood like Algiers or St. Bernard—I stroll around the schoolyard in the last golden light of day and admire the building. Everything is so spick-and-span: the aluminum sashes fitted into the brick wall and gilded in the sunset, the pretty terrazzo floors and the desks molded like wings. Suspended by wires above the door is a schematic sort of bird, the Holy Ghost I suppose. It gives me a pleasant sense of the goodness of creation to think of the brick and the glass and the aluminum being extracted from common dirt—though no doubt it is less a religious sentiment than a financial one, since I own a few shares of Alcoa. How smooth and well-fitted and thrifty the aluminum feels!

But things have suddenly changed. My peaceful existence in Gentilly has been complicated. This morning, for the first time in years, there occurred to me the possibility of a search. I dreamed of the war, no, not quite dreamed but woke with the taste of it in my mouth, the queasy-quince taste of 1951 and the Orient. I remembered the first time the search occurred to me. I came to myself under a chindolea bush. Everything is upside-down for me, as I shall explain later. What are generally considered to be the best times are for me the worst times, and that worst of times was one of the best. My shoulder didn't hurt but it was pressed hard against the ground as if somebody sat on me. Six inches from my nose a dung beetle was scratching around under the leaves. As I watched, there awoke in me an immense curiosity. I was onto something. I vowed that if I ever got out of this fix, I would pursue the search. Naturally, as soon as I recovered and got home, I forgot all about it. But this morning when I got up, I dressed as usual and began as usual to put my belongings into my pockets: wallet, notebook (for writing down occasional thoughts), pencil, keys, handkerchief, pocket slide rule (for calculating percentage returns on principal). They looked both unfamiliar and at the same time full of clues. I stood in the center of the room and gazed at the little pile, sighting through a hole made by thumb and forefinger. What was unfamiliar about them was that I could see them. They might have belonged to someone else. A man can look at this little pile on his bureau for thirty years and never once see it. It is as invisible as his own hand. Once I saw it, however, the search became possible. I bathed, shaved, dressed carefully, and sat at my desk and poked through the little pile in search of a clue just as the detective on television pokes through the dead man's possessions, using his pencil as a poker.

The idea of a search comes to me again as I am on my way to my aunt's house, riding the Gentilly bus down Elysian Fields. The truth is I dislike cars. Whenever I drive a car, I have the feeling I have become invisible. People on the street cannot see you; they only watch your rear fender until it is out of their way. Elysian Fields is not the shortest route to my aunt's house. But I have my reasons for going through the Quarter. William Holden, I read in the paper this morning, is in New Orleans shooting a few scenes in the Place d'Armes. It would be interesting to catch a glimpse of him.

It is a gloomy March day. The swamps are still burning at Chef Menteur and the sky over Gentilly is the color of ashes. The bus is crowded with shoppers, nearly all women. The windows are steamed. I sit on the lengthwise seat in front. Women sit beside me and stand above me. On the long back seat are five Negresses so black that the whole rear of the bus seems darkened. Directly next to me, on the first cross seat, is a very fine-looking girl. She is a strapping girl but by no means too big, done up head to toe in cellophane, the hood pushed back to show a helmet of glossy black hair. She is magnificent with her split tooth and her Prince Val bangs split on her forehead. Gray eyes and wide black brows, a good arm and a fine swell of calf above her cellophane boot. One of those solitary Amazons one sees on Fifty-seventh Street in New York or in Nieman Marcus in Dallas. Our eyes meet. Am I mistaken or does the corner of her mouth tuck in ever so slightly and the petal of her lower lip curl out ever so richly? She is smiling—at me! My mind hits upon half a dozen schemes to circumvent the terrible moment of separation. No doubt she is a Texan. They are nearly always bad judges of men, these splendid Amazons. Most men are afraid of them and so they fall victim to the first little Mickey Rooney that comes along. In a better world I should be able to speak to her: come, darling, you can see that I love you. If you are planning to meet some little Mickey, think better of it. What a tragedy it is that I do not know her, will probably never see her again. What good times we could have! This very afternoon we could go spinning along the Gulf Coast. What consideration and tenderness I could show her! If it were a movie, I would have only to wait. The bus would get lost or the city would be bombed and she and I would tend the wounded. As it is, I may as well stop thinking about her.

Then it is that the idea of the search occurs to me. I become absorbed and for a minute or so forget about the girl.

What is the nature of the search? you ask.

Really it is very simple, at least for a fellow like me; so simple that it is easily overlooked.

The search is what anyone would undertake if he were not sunk in the everydayness of his own life. This morning, for example, I felt as if I had come to myself on a strange island. And what does such a castaway do? Why, he pokes around the neighborhood and he doesn't miss a trick.

To become aware of the possibility of the search is to be onto something. Not to be onto something is to be in despair.

The movies are onto the search, but they screw it up. The search always ends in despair. They like to show a fellow coming to himself in a strange place—but what does he do? He takes up with the local librarian, sets about proving to the local children what a nice fellow he is, and settles down with a vengeance. In two weeks time he is so sunk in everydayness that he might just as well be dead.

What do you seek—God? you ask with a smile.

I hesitate to answer, since all other Americans have settled the matter for themselves and to give such an answer would amount to setting myself a goal which everyone else has reached—and therefore raising a question in which no one has the slightest interest. Who wants to be dead last among one hundred and eighty million Americans? For, as everyone knows, the polls report that 98 percent of Americans believe in God and the remaining 2 percent are atheists and agnostics—which leaves not a single percentage point for a seeker. For myself, I enjoy answering polls as much as anyone and take pleasure in giving intelligent replies to all questions.

Truthfully, it is the fear of exposing my own ignorance which constrains me from mentioning the object of my search. For, to begin with, I cannot even answer this, the simplest and most basic of all questions: Am I, in my search, a hundred miles ahead of my fellow Americans or a hundred miles behind them? That is to say: Have 98 percent of Americans already found what I seek or are they so sunk in everydayness that not even the possibility of a search has occurred to them?

On my honor, I do not know the answer.

PART 3

The Rich Man's House

John Cheever

THE HOUSEBREAKER
OF SHADY HILL

John Cheever *(1912–1982) was born in Quincy, Massachusetts. He pub-*
lished his first story in the New Republic *in 1930, when he wasn't yet twenty*
years old. Malcolm Cowley, who edited that first story, recounted in 1983: "At
the time, his only dependable income was $10 a week from his brother Fred,
who had kept his job during the Depression and believed in John's talent. His
only capital was a typewriter for which he couldn't often buy a new ribbon.
That first winter in New York he lived—so he reported—mostly on stale bread
and buttermilk. . . . The New Republic couldn't help him much except by
giving him unreviewed books for sale; it was a 'journal of opinion,' mostly po-
litical, and John wasn't given to expressing opinions; by instinct he was a sto-
ryteller. He kept writing stories and they began to be printed, always in little
magazines that didn't pay for contributions." A couple of years later, Cowley
handed Cheever along to Katharine White at the New Yorker, *which over*
the years published 119 of his stories. The Stories of John Cheever appeared
in 1978 and won the Pulitzer Prize and the National Book Critics Circle
Award. Cheever also wrote novels; his first, The Wapshot Chronicle
(1957), won the National Book Award. The territory of Cheever's fiction was
often what Malcolm Cowley characterized as "the middle-aged nightmare of
moral or financial collapse." Johnny Hake, the spirited protagonist of "The
Housebreaker of Shady Hill," is in the throes of such a nightmare, and he
flounders in his efforts to right himself.

My name is Johnny Hake. I'm thirty-six years old, stand five feet eleven
in my socks, weigh one hundred and forty-two pounds stripped, and

am, so to speak, naked at the moment and talking into the dark. I was conceived in the Hotel St. Regis, born in the Presbyterian Hospital, raised on Sutton Place, christened and confirmed in St. Bartholomew's, and I drilled with the Knickerbocker Greys, played football and base-ball in Central Park, learned to chin myself on the framework of East Side apartment-house canopies, and met my wife (Christina Lewis) at one of those big cotillions at the Waldorf. I served four years in the Navy, have four kids now, and live in a *banlieue* called Shady Hill. We have a nice house with a garden and a place outside for cooking meat, and on summer nights, sitting there with the kids and looking into the front of Christina's dress as she bends over to salt the steaks, or just gaz-ing at the lights in heaven, I am as thrilled as I am thrilled by more hardy and dangerous pursuits, and I guess this is what is meant by the pain and sweetness of life.

I went to work right after the war for a parablendeum manufacturer, and seemed on the way to making this my life. The firm was patriarchal; that is, the old man would start you on one thing and then switch you to another, and he had his finger in every pie—the Jersey mill and the pro-cessing plant in Nashville—and behaved as if he had wool-gathered the whole firm during a catnap. I stayed out of the old man's way as nimbly as I could, and behaved in his presence as if he had shaped me out of clay with his own hands and breathed the fire of life into me. He was the kind of despot who needed a front, and this was Gil Bucknam's job. He was the old man's right hand, front, and peacemaker, and he could garnish any deal with the humanity the old man lacked, but he started staying out of the office—at first for a day or two, then for two weeks, and then for longer. When he returned, he would complain about stomach trouble or eyestrain, although anyone could see that he was looped. This was not so strange, since hard drinking was one of the things he had to do for the firm. The old man stood it for a year and then came into my office one morning and told me to get up to Buck-nam's apartment and give him the sack.

This was as devious and dirty as sending an office boy to can the chairman of the board. Bucknam was my superior and my senior by many years, a man who condescended to do so whenever he bought me a drink, but this was the way the old man operated, and I knew what I had to do. I called the Bucknam apartment, and Mrs. Bucknam said that I could see Gil that afternoon. I had lunch alone and hung around the office until about three, when I *walked* from our midtown office to the Bucknams' apartment, in the East Seventies. It was early in the fall— the World Series was being played—and a thunderstorm was entering the city. I could hear the noise of big guns and smell the rain when I got to the Bucknams' place. Mrs. Bucknam let me in, and all the troubles of that past year seemed to be in her face, hastily concealed by a thick coat of powder. I've never seen such burned-out eyes, and she was wearing one of those old-fashioned garden-party dresses with big flowers on it. (They had three kids in college, I knew, and a schooner with a hired hand, and many other expenses.) Gil was in bed, and Mrs. Bucknam let me into the bedroom. The storm was about to break now, and everything stood in a gentle half darkness so much like dawn that it seemed as if we should be sleeping and dreaming, and not bringing one another bad news.

Gil was jolly and lovable and condescending, and said that he was *so* glad to see me; he had bought a lot of presents for my children when he was last in Bermuda and had forgotten to mail them. "Would you get those things, darling?" he asked. "Do you remember where we put them?" Then she came back into the room with five or six large and expensive-looking packages and unloaded them into my lap.

I think of my children mostly with delight, and I love to give them presents. I was charmed. It was a ruse, of course—hers, I guessed—and one of many that she must have thought up over the last year to hold their world together. (The wrappings were not fresh, I could see, and when I got home and found in them some old cashmere sweaters that Gil's daughters had not taken to college and a Scotch cap with a soiled sweatband, it only deepened my feeling of sympathy for the Bucknams in their trouble.) With a lap full of presents for my kiddies and sympathy leaking out of every joint, I couldn't give him the ax. We talked about the World Series and about some small matters at the office, and when the rain and the wind began, I helped Mrs. Bucknam shut the windows in the apartment, and then I left and took an early train home through the storm. Five days later, Gil Bucknam went on the wagon for good, and came back to the office to sit again at the right hand of the old man, and my skin was one of the first he went after. It seemed to me that if it had been my destiny to be a Russian ballet dancer, or to make art jewelry, or to paint *Schuhplattler* dancers on bureau drawers and landscapes on clamshells and live in some very low-tide place like Provincetown, I wouldn't have known a queerer bunch of men and women than I knew in the parablendeum industry, and I decided to strike out on my own.

My mother taught me never to speak about money when there was a shirtful, and I've always been very reluctant to speak about it when there was any scarcity, so I cannot paint much of a picture of what ensued in the next six months. I rented office space—a cubicle with a desk and a phone was what it amounted to—and sent out letters, but the letters were seldom answered and the telephone might just as well have been disconnected, and when it came time to borrow money, I had nowhere to turn. My mother hated Christina, and I don't think she can have much money, in any case, because she never bought me an overcoat or a cheese sandwich when I was a kid without telling me that it came out of her principal. I had plenty of friends, but if my life depended on it I couldn't ask a man for a drink and touch him for five hundred—and I needed more. The worst of it was that I hadn't painted anything like an adequate picture to my wife.

I thought about this one night when we were dressing to go to dinner up the road at the Warburtons'. Christina was sitting at her dressing table putting on earrings. She is a pretty woman in the prime of life, and her ignorance of financial necessity is complete. Her neck is graceful, her breasts gleamed as they rose in the cloth of her dress, and, seeing the decent and healthy delight she took in her own image, I could not tell her that we were broke. She had sweetened much of my life, and to watch her seemed to freshen the wellsprings of some clear energy in me that made the room and the pictures on the wall and the moon that I could see outside the window all vivid and cheerful. The truth would make her cry and ruin her make-up and the Warburtons' dinner party for her, and she would sleep in the guest room. There seemed to be as much truth in her beauty and the power she exerted over my senses as there was in the fact that we were overdrawn at the bank.

The Warburtons are rich, but they don't mix; they may not even care.

She is an aging mouse, and he is the kind of man that you wouldn't have liked at school. He has a bad skin and rasping voice and a fixed idea—lechery. The Warburtons are always spending money, and that's what you talk about with them. The floor of their front hall is black-and-white marble from the old Ritz, and their cabanas at Sea Island are being winterized, and they are flying to Davos for ten days, and buying a pair of saddle horses, and building a new wing. We were late that night, and the Meserves and the Chesneys were already there, but Carl Warburton hadn't come home, and Sheila was worried. "Carl has to walk through a terrible slum to get to the station," she said, "and he carries thousands of dollars on him, and I'm so afraid he'll be *victimized*. . . ." Then Carl came home and told a dirty story to the mixed company, and we went in to dinner. It was the kind of party where everybody has taken a shower and put on their best clothes, and where some old cook has been peeling mushrooms or picking the meat out of crab shells since daybreak. I wanted to have a good time. That was my wish, but my wishes could not get me off the ground that night. I felt as if I was at some god-awful birthday party of my childhood that my mother had brought me to with threats and promises. The party broke up at about half past eleven, and we went home. I stayed out in the garden finishing one of Carl Warburton's cigars. It was a Thursday night, and my checks wouldn't bounce until Tuesday, but I had to do something soon. When I went upstairs, Christina was asleep, and I fell asleep myself, but I woke again at about three.

I had been dreaming about wrapping bread in colored parablendeum Filmex. I had dreamed a full-page spread in a national magazine: BRING SOME COLOR INTO YOUR BREADBOX! The page was covered with jewel-toned loaves of bread—turquoise bread, ruby bread, and bread the color of emeralds. In my sleep the idea had seemed to me like a good one; it had cheered me, and it was a letdown to find myself in the dark bedroom. Feeling sad then, I thought about all the loose ends of my life, and this brought me around to my old mother, who lives alone in a hotel in Cleveland. I saw her getting dressed to go down and have dinner in the hotel dining room. She seemed pitiable, as I imagined her—lonely and among strangers. And yet, when she turned her head, I saw that she still had some biting teeth left in her gums.

She sent me through college, arranged for me to spend my vacations in pleasant landscapes, and fired my ambitions, such as they are, but she bitterly opposed my marriage, and our relations have been strained ever since. I've often invited her to come and live with us, but she always refuses, and always with bad feeling. I send her flowers and presents, and write her every week, but these attentions only seem to fortify her conviction that my marriage was a disaster for her and for me. Then I thought about her apron strings, for when I was a kid, she seemed to be a woman whose apron strings were thrown across the Atlantic and the Pacific oceans; they seemed to be looped, like vapor trails, across the very drum of heaven. I thought of her now without rebellion or anxiety—only with sorrow that all our exertions should have been rewarded with so little clear emotion, and that we could not drink a cup of tea together without stirring up all kinds of bitter feeling. I longed to correct this, to reenact the whole relationship with my mother against a more simple and human background, where the cost of my education would not have come so high in morbid emotion. I wanted to do it all over again in some emotional Arcadia, and have us both behave differently, so that I could think of her at three in the morning without guilt, and so that she would be spared loneliness and neglect in her old age.

I moved a little closer to Christina and, coming into the area of her warmth, suddenly felt all kindly and delighted with everything, but she moved in her sleep, away from me. Then I coughed. I coughed again. I coughed loudly. I couldn't stop coughing, and I got out of bed and went into the dark bathroom and drank a glass of water. I stood at the bathroom window and looked down into the garden. There was a little wind. It seemed to be changing its quarter. It sounded like a dawn wind—the air was filled with a showery sound—and felt good on my face. There were some cigarettes on the back of the toilet, and I lit one in order to get back to sleep. But when I inhaled the smoke, it hurt my lungs, and I was suddenly convinced that I was dying of bronchial cancer.

I have experienced all kinds of foolish melancholy—I've been homesick for countries I've never seen, and longed to be what I couldn't be— but all these moods were trivial compared to my premonition of death. I tossed my cigarette into the toilet (ping) and straightened my back, but the pain in my chest was only sharper, and I was convinced that the corruption had begun. I had friends who would think of me kindly, I knew, and Christina and the children would surely keep alive an affectionate memory. But then I thought about money again, and the Warburtons, and my rubber checks approaching the clearinghouse, and it seemed to me that money had it all over love. I had yearned for some women—turned green, in fact—but it seemed to me that I had never yearned for anyone the way I yearned that night for money. I went to the closet in our bedroom and put on some old blue sneakers and a pair of pants and a dark pullover. Then I went downstairs and out of the house. The moon had set, and there were not many stars, but the air above the trees and hedges was full of dim light. I went around the Trenholmes' garden then, gumshoeing over the grass, and down the lawn to the Warburtons' house. I listened for sounds from the open windows, and all I heard was the ticking of a clock. I went up the front steps and opened the screen door and started across the floor from the old Ritz. In the dim night light that came in at the windows, the house looked like a shell, a nautilus, shaped to contain itself.

I heard the noise of a dog's license tag, and Sheila's old cocker came trotting down the hall. I rubbed him behind the ears, and then he went back to wherever his bed was, grunted, and fell asleep. I knew the plan of the Warburtons' house as well as I knew the plan of my own. The staircase was carpeted, but I first put my foot on one of the treads to see if it creaked. Then I started up the stairs. All the bedroom doors stood open, and from Carl and Sheila's bedroom, where I had often left my coat at big cocktail parties, I could hear the sound of deep breathing. I stood in the doorway for a second to take my bearings. In the dimness I could see the bed, and a pair of pants and a jacket hung over the back of a chair. Moving swiftly, I stepped into the room and took a big billfold from the inside pocket of the coat and started back to the hall. The violence of my emotions may have made me clumsy, because Sheila woke. I heard her say, "Did you hear that noise, darling?" "S'wind," he mumbled, and then they were quiet again. I was safe in the hall—safe from everything but myself. I seemed to be having a nervous breakdown out there. All my saliva was gone, the lubricants seemed to drain out of my heart, and whatever the juices were that kept my legs upright were going. It was only by holding on to the wall that I could make any progress at all. I clung to the banister on my way down the stairs, and staggered out of the house.

Back in my own dark kitchen, I drank three or four glasses of water. I must have stood by the kitchen sink for a half hour or longer before I thought of looking in Carl's wallet. I went into the cellarway and shut the cellar door before I turned the light on. There was a little over nine hundred dollars. I turned the light off and went back into the dark kitchen. Oh, I never knew that a man could be so miserable and that the mind could open up so many chambers and fill them with self-reproach! Where were the trout streams of my youth, and other innocent pleasures? The wet-leather smell of the loud waters and the keen woods after a smashing rain; or at opening day the summer breezes smelling like the grassy breath of Holsteins—your head would swim—and all the brooks full then (or so I imagined, in the dark kitchen) of trout, our sunken treasure. I was crying.

Shady Hill, as I say, a *banlieue* and open to criticism by city planners, adventurers, and lyric poets, but if you work in the city and have children to raise, I can't think of a better place. My neighbors are rich, it is true, but riches in this case mean leisure, and they use their time wisely. They travel around the world, listen to good music, and given a choice of paper books at an airport, will pick Thucydides, and sometimes Aquinas. Urged to build bomb shelters, they plant trees and roses, and their gardens are splendid and bright. Had I looked, the next morning, from my bathroom window into the evil-smelling ruin of some great city, the shock of recalling what I had done might not have been so violent, but the moral bottom had dropped out of my world without changing a mote of sunlight. I dressed stealthily—for what child of darkness would want to hear the merry voices of his family?—and caught an early train. My gabardine suit was meant to express cleanliness and probity, but I was a miserable creature whose footsteps had been mistaken for the noise of the wind. I looked at the paper. There had been a thirty-thousand-dollar payroll robbery in the Bronx. A White Plains matron had come home from a party to find her furs and jewelry gone. Sixty thousand dollars' worth of medicine had been taken

from a warehouse in Brooklyn. I felt better at discovering how common
the thing I had done was. But only a little better, and only for a short
while. Then I was faced once more with the realization that I was a
common thief and an imposter, and that I had done something so rep-
rehensible that it violated the tenets of every known religion. I had
stolen, and what's more, I had criminally entered the house of a friend
and broken all the unwritten laws that held the community together.
My conscience worked so on my spirits—like the hard beak of a carniv-
orous bird—that my left eye began to twitch, and again I seemed on the
brink of a general nervous collapse. When the train reached the city, I
went to the bank. Leaving the bank, I was nearly hit by a taxi. My anxiety
was not for my bones but for the fact that Carl Warburton's wallet might
be found in my pocket. When I thought no one was looking, I wiped the
wallet on my trousers (to remove the fingerprints) and dropped it into
the ash can.

I thought that coffee might make me feel better, and went into a
restaurant, and sat down at a table with a stranger. The soiled lace-
paper doilies and half-empty glasses of water had not been taken away,
and at the stranger's place there was a thirty-five-cent tip, left by an earlier customer. I looked at the menu, but out of the corner of my eye I
saw the stranger pocket the thirty-five-cent tip. What a crook! I got up
and left the restaurant.

I walked into my cubicle, hung up my hat and coat, sat down at my
desk, shot my cuffs, sighed, and looked into space, as if a day full of
challenge and decision were about to begin. I hadn't turned on the
light. In a little while, the office beside mine was occupied, and I heard
my neighbor clear his throat, cough, scratch a match, and settle down
to attack the day's business.

The walls were flimsy—part frosted glass and part plywood—and
there was no acoustical privacy in these offices. I reached into my
pocket for a cigarette with as much stealth as I had exercised at the
Warburtons', and waited for the noise of a truck passing on the street
outside before I lit a match. The excitement of eavesdropping took
hold of me. My neighbor was trying to sell uranium stock over the telephone. His line went like this: First he was courteous. Then he was
nasty. "What's the matter, Mr. X? Don't you want to make any money?"

Then he was *very* scornful. "I'm sorry to have bothered you. Mr. X. I thought you *had* sixty-five dollars to invest." He called twelve numbers without any takers. I was as quiet as a mouse. Then he telephoned the information desk at Idlewild, checking the arrival of planes from Europe. London was on time. Rome and Paris were late. "No, he ain't in yet," I heard him say to someone over the phone. "It's dark in there." My heart was beating fast. Then my telephone began to ring, and I counted twelve rings before it stopped. "I'm positive, I'm positive," the man in the next office said. "I can hear his telephone ringing, and he ain't answering it, and he's just a lonely son of a bitch looking for a job. Go ahead, go ahead, I tell you. I ain't got time to get over there. Go ahead. . . . Seven, eight, three, five, seven, seven. . . ." When he hung up, I went to the door, opened and closed it, turned the light on, rattled the coat hangers, whistled a tune, sat down heavily at my desk chair, and dialed the first telephone number that came to my mind. It was an old friend—Burt Howe—and he exclaimed when he heard my voice. "Hakie, I been looking for you everywhere! You sure folded up your tents and stole away."

"Yes," I said.

"Stole away," Howe repeated. "Just stole away. But what I wanted to talk with you about is this deal I thought you might be interested in. It's a one-shot, but it won't take you more than three weeks. It's a steal. They're green, and they're dumb, and they're loaded, and it's just like stealing."

"Yes," I said.

"Well, then, can you meet me for lunch at Cardin's at twelve-thirty, and I'll give you the details?" Howe asked.

"O.K.," I said hoarsely. "Thanks a lot, Burt."

"We went out to the shack on Sunday," the man in the next office was saying as I hung up. "Louise got bit by a poisonous spider. The doctor gave her some kind of injection. She'll be all right." He dialed another number and began, "We went out to the shack on Sunday. Louise got bit by a poisonous spider . . ."

It was possible that a man whose wife had been bitten by a spider and who found some time on his hands might call three or four friends and tell them about it, and it was equally possible that the spider might be a code of warning or of assent to some unlawful traffic. What frightened me was that by becoming a thief I seemed to have surrounded myself with thieves and operators. My left eye had begun to twitch again, and the inability of one part of my consciousness to stand up under the reproach that was being heaped into it by another part made me cast around desperately for someone else who could be blamed. I had read often enough in the papers that divorce sometimes led to crime. My parents were divorced when I was about five. This was a good clue and quickly led me on to something better.

My father went to live in France after the divorce, and I didn't see him for ten years. Then he wrote Mother for permission to see me, and she prepared me for this reunion by telling me how drunken, cruel, and lewd the old man was. It was in the summer, and we were on Nantucket, and I took the steamer alone, and went to New York on the train. I met my father at the Plaza early in the evening, but not so early that he hadn't begun to drink. With the long, sensitive nose of an adolescent I smelled the gin on his breath, and I noticed that he bumped into a table and sometimes repeated himself. I realized later that this reunion must have been strenuous for a man of sixty, which he was. We had dinner and then went to see *The Roses of Picardy*. As soon as the chorus came on, Father said that I could have any one of them that I wanted; the arrangements were all made. I could even have one of the specialty dancers. Now, if I'd felt that he had crossed the Atlantic to perform this service for me, it might have been different, but I felt he'd made the trip in order to do a disservice to my mother. I was scared. The show was in one of those old-fashioned theatres that appear to be held together with angels. Brown-gold angels held up the ceiling; they held up the boxes; they even seemed to hold up the balcony with about four hundred people in it. I spent a lot of time looking at those dusty gold angels. If the ceiling of the theatre had fallen on my head, I would have been relieved. After the show, we went back to the hotel to wash before meeting the girls, and the old man stretched out on the bed for a minute and began to snore. I picked his wallet of fifty dollars, spent the night at Grand Central, and took an early morning train to Woods Hole. So the whole thing was explained, including the violence of the emotion I had experienced in the Warburtons' upstairs hall; I had been reliving that scene at the Plaza. It had not been my fault that I had stolen then, and it had not been my fault when I went to the Warburtons'. It was my father's fault! Then I remembered that my father was buried in Fontainebleau fifteen years ago, and could be nothing much more now than dust.

I went into the men's room and washed my hands and face, and combed my hair down with a lot of water. It was time to go out for lunch. I thought anxiously of the lunch ahead of me, and, wondering why, was astonished to realize that it was Burt Howe's free use of the word "steal." I hoped he wouldn't keep on saying it.

Even as the thought floated across my mind in the men's room, the twitching in my eye seemed to spread over my cheek; it seemed as if this verb were embedded in the English language like a poisoned fishhook. I had committed adultery, and the word "adultery" had no force for me; I had been drunk, and the word "drunkenness" had no extraordinary power. It was only "steal" and all its allied nouns, verbs, and adverbs that had the power to tyrannize over my nervous system, as if I had evolved, unconsciously, some doctrine wherein the act of theft took precedence over all the other sins in the Decalogue and was a sign of moral death.

The sky was dark when I came out on the street. Lights were burning everywhere. I looked into the faces of the people that I passed for some encouraging signs of honesty in such a crooked world, and on Third Avenue I saw a young man with a tin cup, holding his eyes shut to impersonate blindness. That seal of blindness, the striking innocence of the upper face, was betrayed by the frown and the crow's-feet of a man who could see his drinks on the bar. There was another blind beggar on Forty-first Street, but I didn't examine his eye sockets, realizing that I couldn't assess the legitimacy of every beggar in the city.

Cardin's is a men's restaurant in the Forties. The stir and bustle in the vestibule only made me feel retiring, and the hat-check girl, noticing, I suppose, the twitch in my eye, gave me a very jaded look.

Burt was at the bar, and when we had ordered our drinks, we got down to business. "For a deal like this, we ought to meet in some back alley," he said, "but a fool and his money *and* so forth. It's three kids. P. J. Burdette is one of them, and they've got a cool million between them to throw away. Someone's bound to steal from them, so it may as well be you." I put my hand over the left side of my face to cover the tic. When I tried to raise my glass to my mouth, I spilled gin all over my suit. "They're all three of them just out of college," Burt said. "And they've all three of them got so much in the kitty that even if you picked them clean they wouldn't feel any pain. Now, in order to participate in this burglary, all you have to do . . ."

The toilet was at the other end of the restaurant, but I got there. Then I drew a basin of cold water and stuck my head and face into it. Burt had followed me to the washroom. As I was drying myself with a paper towel, he said, "You know, Hakie, I wasn't going to mention it, but now that you've been sick, I may as well tell you that you look awful. I mean, from the minute I saw you I knew something was wrong. I just want to tell you that whatever it is—sauce or dope or trouble at home—it's a lot later than you think, and maybe you should be doing something about it. No hard feelings?" I said that I was sick, and waited in the toilet long enough for Burt to make a getaway. Then I got my hat and another jaded look from the hat-check girl, and saw in the afternoon paper on a chair by the check-room that some bank robbers in Brooklyn had got away with eighteen thousand dollars.

I walked around the streets, wondering how I would shape up as a pickpocket and bag snatcher, and all the arches and spires of St. Patrick's only reminded me of poor boxes. I took the regular train home, looking out of the window at a peaceable landscape and a spring evening, and it seemed to me fishermen and lone bathers and grade-crossing watchmen and sand-lot ball players and lovers unashamed of their sport and the owners of small sailing craft and old men playing pinochle in firehouses were the people who stitched up the big holes in the world that were made by men like me.

Now Christina is the kind of woman who, when she is asked by the alumnae secretary of her college to describe her status, gets dizzy thinking about the variety of her activities and interests. And what, on a given day, stretching a point here and there, does she have to do? Drive me to the train. Have the skis repaired. Book a tennis court. Buy the wine and groceries for the monthly dinner of the Société Gastronomique du

Westchester Nord. Look up some definitions in Larousse. Attend a League of Women Voters symposium on sewers. Go to a full-dress lunch for Bobsie Neil's aunt. Weed the garden. Iron a uniform for the part-time maid. Type two and half pages of her paper on the early novels of Henry James. Empty the wastebaskets. Help Tabitha prepare the children's supper. Give Ronnie some batting practice. Put her hair in pin curls. Get the cook. Meet the train. Bathe. Dress. Greet her guests in French at half past seven. Say *bon soir* at eleven. Lie in my arms until twelve. Eureka! You might say that she is prideful, but I think only that she is a woman enjoying herself in a country that is prosperous and young. Still, when she met me at the train that night, it was difficult for me to rise to all this vitality.

It was my bad luck to have to take the collection at early Communion on Sunday, although I was in no condition. I answered the pious looks of my friends with a very crooked smile and then knelt by a lancet-shaped stained-glass window that seemed to be made from the butts of vermouth and Burgundy bottles. I knelt on an imitation-leather hassock that had been given by some guild or auxiliary to replace one of the old, snuff-colored hassocks, which had begun to split at the seams and show bits of straw, and made the whole place smell like an old manger. The smell of straw and flowers, and the vigil light, and the candles flickering in the rector's breath, and the damp of this poorly heated stone building were all as familiar to me and belonged as much to my early life as the sounds and smells of a kitchen or a nursery, and yet they seemed, that morning, to be so potent that I felt dizzy. Then I heard, in the baseboard on my right, a rat's tooth working like an auger in the hard oak. "Holy, Holy, Holy," I said very loudly, hoping to freighten the rat. "Lord God of hosts, Heaven and earth are FULL of Thy Glory!" The small congregation muttered its amens with a sound like a footstep, and the rat went on scraping away at the baseboard. And then—perhaps because I was absorbed in the noise of the rat's tooth, or because the smell of dampness and straw was soporific—when I looked up from the shelter I had made of my hands, I saw the rector drinking from the chalice and realized that I had missed Communion.

At home, I looked through the Sunday paper for other thefts, and there were plenty. Banks had been looted, hotel safes had been emptied of jewelry, maids and butlers had been tied to kitchen chairs, furs and industrial diamonds had been stolen in job lots, delicatessens, cigar stores, and pawnshops had been broken into, and someone had stolen a painting from the Cleveland Institute of Art. Late in the afternoon, I raked leaves. What could be more contrite than cleaning the lawn of the autumn's dark rubbish under the streaked, pale skies of spring?

While I was raking leaves, my sons walked by. "The Toblers are having a softball game," Ronnie said. "*Everybody's* there."

"Why don't you play?" I asked.

"You can't play unless you've been invited," Ronnie said over his shoulder, and then they were gone. Then I noticed that I could hear the cheering from the softball game to which we had not been invited. The Toblers lived down the block. The spirited voices seemed to sound clearer and clearer as the night came on; I could even hear the noise of ice in glasses, and the voices of the ladies raised in a feeble cheer.

Why hadn't I been asked to play softball at the Toblers'? I wondered. Why had we been excluded from these simple pleasures, this light-hearted gathering, the fading laughter and voices and slammed doors of which seemed to gleam in the darkness as they were withdrawn from my possession? Why wasn't *I* asked to play softball at the Toblers'? Why should social aggrandizement—*climbing*, really—exclude a nice guy like me from a softball game? What kind of a world was that? Why should I be left alone with my dead leaves in the twilight—as I was—feeling so forsaken, lonely, and forlorn that I was chilled?

If there is anybody I detest, it is weak-minded sentimentalists—all those melancholy people who, out of an excess of sympathy for others, miss the thrill of their own essence and drift through life without identity, like a human fog, feeling sorry for everyone. The legless beggar in Times Square with his poor display of pencils, the rouged old lady in the subway who talks to herself, the exhibitionist in the public toilet, the drunk who has dropped on the subway stairs, do more than excite their pity; they are at a glance transformed into these unfortunates. Derelict humanity seems to trample over their unrealized souls, leaving them at twilight in a condition closely resembling the scene of a prison riot. Disappointed in themselves, they are always ready to be disappointed for the rest of us, and they will build whole cities, whole creations, firmaments and principalities, of tear-wet disappointment. Lying in bed at night, they will think tenderly of the big winner who lost his pari-mutuel ticket, of the great novelist whose magnum opus was burned mistakenly for trash, and of Samuel Tilden, who lost the Presidency of the United States through the shenanigans of the electoral college. Detesting this company, then, it was doubly painful for me to find myself in it. And, seeing a bare dogwood tree in the starlight, I thought, How sad everything is!

Wednesday was my birthday. I recalled this fact in the middle of the afternoon, at the office, and the thought that Christina might be planning a surprise party brought me in one second from a sitting to a standing position, breathless. Then I decided that she wouldn't. But just the preparations the children would make presented an emotional problem; I didn't see how I could face it.

I left the office early and had two drinks before I took the train. Christina looked pleased with everything when she met me at the station, and I put a very good face on my anxiety. The children had changed into clean clothes, and wished me a happy birthday so fervently that I felt awful. At the table there was a pile of small presents, mostly things the children had made—cuff links out of buttons, and a memo pad, and so forth. I thought I was very bright, considering the circumstances, and pulled my snapper, put on my silly hat, blew out the candles on the cake, and thanked them all, but then it seemed that there was another present—my *big* present—and after dinner I was made to stay inside while Christina and the children went outside, and then Juney came in and led me outdoors and around in back of the house, where they all were. Leaning against the house was an aluminum extension ladder with a card and a ribbon tied to it, and I said, as if I'd been hit, "What in *hell* is the meaning of this?"

"We thought you'd need it, Daddy," Juney said.

"What would I ever need a ladder for? What do you think I am—a second-story worker?"

"Storm windows," Juney said. "Screens—"

I turned to Christina. "Have I been talking in my sleep?"

"No," Christina said. "You haven't been talking in your sleep."

Juney began to cry.

"You could take the leaves out of the rain gutters," Ronnie said. Both of the boys were looking at me with long faces.

"Well, you must admit it's a very unusual present," I said to Christina.

"*God!*" Christina said. "Come on, children. Come on." She herded them in at the terrace door.

I kicked around the garden until after dark. The lights went on upstairs. Juney was still crying, and Christina was singing to her. Then she was quiet. I waited until the lights went on in our bedroom, and after a little while I climbed the stairs. Christina was in a nightgown, sitting at her dressing table, and there were heavy tears in her eyes.

"You'll have to try and understand," I said.

"I couldn't possibly. The children have been saving for months to buy you that damned-fool contraption."

"You don't know what I've been through," I said.

"If you'd been through hell, I wouldn't forgive you," she said. "You haven't been through anything that would justify your behavior. They've had it hidden in the garage for a week. They're so *sweet.*"

"I haven't felt like myself," I said.

"Don't tell *me* that you haven't felt like yourself," she said. "I've looked forward to having you leave in the morning, and I've dreaded having you come home at night."

"I can't have been all that bad," I said.

"It's been hell," she said. "You've been sharp with the children, nasty to me, rude to your friends, and malicious behind their backs. It's been hideous."

"Would you like me to go?"

"Oh, Lord, would I like you to go! Then I could breathe."

"What about the children?"

"Ask my lawyer."

"I'll go, then."

I went down the hall to the closet where we keep the bags. When I took out my suitcase, I found that the children's puppy had chewed the leather binding loose all along one side. Trying to find another suitcase, I brought the whole pile down on top of me, boxing my ears. I carried my bag with this long strip of leather trailing behind me back into our bedroom. *"Look,"* I said. "Look at this, Christina. The dog has chewed the binding off my suitcase." She didn't even raise her head. "I've poured twenty thousand dollars a year into this establishment for ten years," I shouted, "and when the time comes for me to go, I don't even have a decent suitcase! Everybody else has a suitcase. Even the cat has a nice traveling bag." I threw open my shirt drawer, and there were only four clean shirts. "I don't have enough clean shirts to last a week!" I shouted. Then I got a few things together, clapped my hat on my head, and marched out. I even thought, for a minute, of taking the car, and I went into the garage and looked it over. Then I saw the FOR SALE sign that had been hanging on the house when we bought it long, long ago. I wiped the dirt off the sign and got a nail and a rock and went around to the front of the house and nailed the FOR SALE sign onto a maple tree. Then I walked to the station. It's about a mile. The long strip of leather was trailing along behind me, and I stopped and tried to rip it off the suitcase, but it wouldn't come. When I got down to the station, I found there wasn't another train until four in the morning. I decided I would wait. I sat down on my suitcase and waited five minutes. Then I marched home again. Halfway there I saw Christina coming down the street, in a sweater and a skirt and sneakers—the quickest things to put on, but summery things—and we walked home together and went to bed.

On Saturday, I played golf, and although the game finished late, I wanted to take a swim in the club pool before I went home. There was no one at the pool but Tom Maitland. He is a dark-skinned and nice-looking man, very rich, but quiet. He seems withdrawn. His wife is the fattest woman in Shady Hill, and nobody much likes his children, and I think he is the kind of man whose parties and friendship and affairs in love and business all rest like an intricate superstructure—a tower of matchsticks—on the melancholy of his early youth. A breath could bring the whole thing down. It was nearly dark when I had finished swimming; the clubhouse was lighted and you could hear the sounds of dinner on the porch. Maitland was sitting at the edge of the pool dabbling his feet in the bright-blue water, with its Dead Sea smell of chlorine. I was drying myself off, and as I passed him, I asked if he wasn't going in. "I don't know how to swim," he said. He smiled and looked away from me then to the still, polished water of the pool, in the dark landscape. "We used to have a pool at home," he said, "but I never got a chance to swim in it. I was always studying the violin." There he was, forty-five years old and at least a millionaire, and he couldn't even float, and I don't suppose he had many occasions to speak as honestly as he had just spoken. While I was getting dressed, the idea settled in my head—with no help from me—that the Maitlands would be my next victims.

A few nights later, I woke up at three. I thought over the loose ends in my life—Mother in Cleveland, and parablendeum—and then I went into the bathroom to light a cigarette before I remembered that I was dying of bronchial cancer and leaving my widow and orphans penniless. I put on my blue sneakers and the rest of the outfit, looked in at the open doors of the children's rooms, and then went out. It was cloudy. I walked through back gardens to the corner. Then I crossed the street and turned up the Maitlands' driveway, walking on the grass at the edge of the gravel. The door was open, and I went in, just as excited and frightened as I had been at the Warburtons' and feeling insubstantial in the dim light—a ghost. I followed my nose up the stairs to where I knew their bedroom was, and, hearing heavy breathing and seeing a jacket and some pants on a chair, I reached for the pocket of the jacket, but there wasn't one. It wasn't a suit coat at all; it was one of those bright satin jackets that kids wear. There was no sense in looking for a wallet in *his* trousers. He couldn't make that much cutting the Maitlands' grass. I got out of there in a hurry.

I did not sleep any more that night but sat in the dark thinking about Tom Maitland, and Gracie Maitland, and the Warburtons, and Christina, and my own sordid destiny, and how different Shady Hill looked at night than in the light of day.

But I went out the next night—this time to the Pewters', who were not only rich but booze fighters, and who drank so much that I didn't see how they could hear thunder after the lights were turned out. I left, as usual, a little after three.

I was thinking sadly about my beginnings—about how I was made by a riggish couple in a midtown hotel after a six-course dinner with wines, and my mother had told me so many times that if she hadn't drunk so many Old-Fashioneds before that famous dinner I would still be unborn on a star. And I thought about my old man and that night at the Plaza and the bruised thighs of the peasant women of Picardy and all the brown-gold angels that held the theatre together and my terrible destiny. While I was walking toward the Pewters', there was a harsh stirring in all the trees and gardens, like a draft on a bed of fire, and I wondered what it was until I felt the rain on my hands and face, and then I began to laugh.

I wish I could say that a kindly lion had set me straight, or an innocent child, or the strains of distant music from some church, but it was no more than the rain on my head—the smell of it flying up to my nose—that showed me the extent of my freedom from the bones in Fontainebleau and the works of a thief. There were ways out of my trouble if I cared to make use of them. I was not trapped. I was here on earth because I chose to be. And it was no skin off my elbow how I had been given the gifts of life so long as I possessed them, and I possessed them then—the tie between the wet grass roots and the hair that grew out of my body, the thrill of my mortality that I had known on summer nights, loving the children, and looking down the front of Christina's dress. I was standing in front of the Pewters' by this time, and I looked up at the dark house and then turned and walked away. I went back to bed and had pleasant dreams. I dreamed I was sailing a boat on the Mediterranean. I saw some worn marble steps leading down into the water, and the water itself—blue, saline, and dirty. I stepped the mast, hoisted the sail, and put my hand on the tiller. But why, I wondered as I sailed away, should I seem to be only seventeen years old? But you can't have everything.

It is not, as somebody once wrote, the smell of corn bread that calls us back from death; it is the lights and signs of love and friendship. Gil Bucknam called me the next day and said that the old man was dying and would I come back to work? I went to see him, and he explained that it was the old man who was after my skin, and, of course, I was glad to come home to parablendeum.

What I did not understand, as I walked down Fifth Avenue that afternoon, was how a world that had seemed so dark could, in a few minutes, become so sweet. The sidewalks seemed to shine, and, going home on the train, I beamed at those foolish girls who advertise girdles on the signboards in the Bronx. I got an advance on my salary the next morning, and, taking some precautions about fingerprints, I put nine hundred dollars into an envelope and walked over to the Warburtons' when the last lights in the neighborhood had been put out. It had been raining, but the rain had let up. The stars were beginning to show. There was no sense in overdoing prudence, and I went around to the back of their house, found the kitchen door open, and put the envelope on a table in the dark room. As I was walking away from the house, a police car drew up beside me, and a patrolman I know cranked down the window and asked, "What are you doing out at this time of night, Mr. Hake?"

"I'm walking the dog," I said cheerfully. There was no dog in sight, but they didn't look. "Here, Toby! Here, Toby! Here, Toby! *Good* dog!" I called, and off I went, whistling merrily in the dark.

Ann Beattie

JANUS

Ann Beattie *(1947–) brings us again into other people's homes in "Janus," in which Anna, a real estate agent, relies on a kind of totem to help her sell houses. She is clever, and business is going well for her. Yet she is anxious, and her anxiety is attributable, at least in part, to this totem, whose secret origin Andrea cannot discuss in her own home, at least not when her husband is around. "Janus" first appeared in the* New Yorker *in 1985. Ann Beattie is the author of the novels* Falling in Place *(1980) and* Picturing Will *(1989), among others; her story collections include* Distortions *(1976),* Secrets and Surprises *(1978),* The Burning House *(1982),* Where You'll Find Me *(1986),* What Was Mine *(1991), and, most recently,* Follies: New Stories *(2005). She lives in Virginia.*

The bowl was perfect. Perhaps it was not what you'd select if you faced a shelf of bowls, and not the sort of thing that would inevitably attract a lot of attention at a crafts fair, yet it had real presence. It was as predictably admired as a mutt who has no reason to suspect he might be funny. Just such a dog, in fact, was often brought out (and in) along with the bowl.

Andrea was a real estate agent, and when she thought that some prospective buyers might be dog lovers, she would drop off her dog at the same time she placed the bowl in the house that was up for sale. She would put a dish of water in the kitchen for Mondo, take his squeaking plastic frog out of her purse and drop it on the floor. He would pounce delightedly, just as he did every day at home, batting around his favorite toy. The bowl usually sat on a coffee table, though recently she had displayed it on top of a pine blanket chest and on a lacquered table. It was once placed on a cherry table beneath a Bonnard still life, where it held its own.

Everyone who has purchased a house or who has wanted to sell a house must be familiar with some of the tricks used to convince a buyer that the house is quite special: a fire in the fireplace in early evening; jonquils in a pitcher on the kitchen counter, where no one ordinarily has space to put flowers; perhaps the slight aroma of spring, made by a single drop of scent vaporizing from a lamp bulb.

The wonderful thing about the bowl, Andrea thought, was that it was both subtle and noticeable—a paradox of a bowl. Its glaze was the color of cream and seemed to glow no matter what light it was placed in. There were a few bits of color in it—tiny geometric flashes—and some of these were tinged with flecks of silver. They were as mysterious as cells seen under a microscope; it was difficult not to study them, because they shimmered, flashing for a split second, and then resumed their shape. Something about the colors and their random placement suggested motion. People who liked country furniture always commented on the bowl, but then it turned out that people who felt comfortable with Biedermeier loved it just as much. But the bowl was not at all ostentatious, or even so noticeable that anyone would suspect that it had been put in place deliberately. They might notice the height of the ceiling on first entering a room, and only when their eye moved down from that, or away from the refraction of sunlight on a pale wall, would they see the bowl. Then they would go immediately to it and comment. Yet they always faltered when they tried to say something. Perhaps it was because they were in the house for a serious reason, not to notice some object.

Once, Andrea got a call from a woman who had not put in an offer on a house she had shown her. That bowl, she said—would it be possible to find out where the owners had bought that beautiful bowl? Andrea pretended that she did not know what the woman was referring to. A bowl, somewhere in the house? Oh, on a table under the window. Yes, she would ask, of course. She let a couple of days pass, then called back to say that the bowl had been a present and the people did not know where it had been purchased.

When the bowl was not being taken from house to house, it sat on Andrea's coffee table at home. She didn't keep it carefully wrapped (although she transported it that way, in a box); she kept it on the table, because she liked to see it. It was large enough so that it didn't seem fragile, or particularly vulnerable if anyone sideswiped the table or Mondo blundered into it at play. She had asked her husband to please not drop his house key in it. It was meant to be empty.

When her husband first noticed the bowl, he had peered into it and smiled briefly. He always urged her to buy things she liked. In recent years, both of them had acquired many things to make up for all the lean years when they were graduate students, but now that they had been comfortable for quite a while, the pleasure of new possessions dwindled. Her husband had pronounced the bowl "pretty," and he had turned away without picking it up to examine it. He had no more interest in the bowl than she had in his new Leica.

She was sure that the bowl brought her luck. Bids were often put in on houses where she had displayed the bowl. Sometimes the owners, who were always asked to be away or to step outside when the house was being shown, didn't even know that the bowl had been in their house. Once—she could not imagine how—she left it behind, and then she was so afraid that something might have happened to it that she rushed back to the house and sighed with relief when the woman owner opened the door. The bowl, Andrea explained—she had purchased a bowl and set it on the chest for safekeeping while she toured the house with the prospective buyers, and she . . . She felt like rushing past the frowning woman and seizing her bowl. The owner stepped aside, and it was only when Andrea ran to the chest that the lady glanced at her a little strangely. In the few seconds before Andrea picked up the bowl, she realized that the owner must have just seen that it had been perfectly placed, that the sunlight struck the bluer part of it. Her pitcher had been moved to the far side of the chest, and the bowl predominated. All the way home, Andrea wondered how she could have left the bowl behind. It was like leaving a friend at an outing—just walking off. Sometimes there were stories in the paper about families forgetting a child somewhere and driving to the next city. Andrea had only gone a mile down the road before she remembered.

In time, she dreamed of the bowl. Twice, in a waking dream—early in the morning, between sleep and a last nap before rising—she had a clear vision of it. It came into sharp focus and startled her for a moment—the same bowl she looked at every day.

She had a very profitable year selling real estate. Word spread, and she had more clients than she felt comfortable with. She had the foolish thought that if only the bowl were an animate object she could thank it. There were times when she wanted to talk to her husband about the bowl. He was a stockbroker, and sometimes told people that he was fortunate to be married to a woman who had such a fine aesthetic sense and yet could also function in the real world. They were a lot alike, really—they had agreed on that. They were both quiet people—reflective, slow to make value judgments, but almost intractable once they had come to a conclusion. They both liked details, but while ironies attracted her, he was more impatient and dismissive when matters became many sided or unclear. But they both knew this; it was the kind of thing they could talk about when they were alone in the car together, coming home from a party or after a weekend with friends. But she never talked to him about the bowl. When they were at dinner, exchanging their news of the day, or while they lay in bed at night listening to the stereo and murmuring sleepy disconnections, she was often tempted to come right out and say that she thought that the bowl in the living room, the cream-colored bowl, was responsible for her success. But she didn't say it. She couldn't begin to explain it. Sometimes in the morning , she would look at him and feel guilty that she had such a constant secret.

Could it be that she had some deeper connection with the bowl—a relationship of some kind? She corrected her thinking: how could she imagine such a thing, when she was a human being and it was a bowl? It was ridiculous. Just think of how people lived together and loved each other . . . But was that always so clear, always a relationship? She was confused by these thoughts, but they remained in her mind. There was something within her now, something real, that she never talked about.

The bowl was a mystery, even to her. It was frustrating, because her involvement with the bowl contained a steady sense of unrequited good fortune; it would have been easier to respond if some sort of demand were made in return. But that only happened in fairy tales. The bowl was just a bowl. She did not believe that for one second. What she believed was that it was something she loved.

In the past, she had sometimes talked to her husband about a new property she was about to buy or sell—confiding some clever strategy she had devised to persuade owners who seemed ready to sell. Now she stopped doing that, for all her strategies involved the bowl. She became more deliberate with the bowl, and more possessive. She put it in houses only when no one was there, and removed it when she left the house. Instead of just moving a pitcher or a dish, she would remove all the other objects from a table. She had to force herself to handle them carefully, because she didn't really care about them. She just wanted them out of sight.

She wondered how the situation would end. As with a lover, there was no exact scenario of how matters would come to a close. Anxiety became the operative force. It would be irrelevant if the lover rushed into someone else's arms, or wrote her a note and departed to another city. The horror was the possibility of the disappearance. That was what mattered.

She would get up at night and look at the bowl. It never occurred to her that she might break it. She washed and dried it without anxiety, and she moved it often, from coffee table to mahogany corner table or wherever, without fearing an accident. It was clear that she would not be the one who would do anything to the bowl. The bowl was only handled by her, set safely on one surface or another; it was not very likely that anyone would break it. A bowl was a poor conductor of electricity: it would not be hit by lightning. Yet the idea of damage persisted. She did not think beyond that—to what her life would be without the bowl. She only continued to fear that some accident would happen. Why not, in a world where people set plants where they did not belong, so that visitors touring a house would be fooled into thinking that dark corners got sunlight—a world full of tricks?

She had first seen the bowl several years earlier, at a crafts fair she had visited half in secret, with her lover. He had urged her to buy the bowl. She didn't *need* any more things, she told him. But she had been drawn to the bowl, and they had lingered near it. Then she went on to the next booth, and he came up behind her, tapping the rim against her shoulder as she ran her fingers over a wood carving. "You're still insisting that I buy that?" she said. "No," he said. "I bought it for you." He had bought her other things before this—things she liked more, at first—the child's ebony-and-turquoise ring that fitted her little finger; the wooden box, long and thin, beautifully dovetailed, that she used to hold paper clips; the soft gray sweater with a pouch pocket. It was his idea that when he could not be there to hold her hand she could hold her own—clasp her hands inside the lone pocket that stretched across the front. But in time she became more attached to the bowl than to any of his other presents. She tried to talk herself out of it. She owned other things that were more striking or valuable. It wasn't an object whose beauty jumped out at you; a lot of people must have passed it by before the two of them saw it that day.

Her lover had said that she was always too slow to know what she really loved. Why continue with her life the way it was? Why be two-faced, he asked her. He had made the first move toward her. When she would not decide in his favor, would not change her life and come to him, he asked her what made her think she could have it both ways. And then he made the last move and left. It was a decision meant to break her will, to shatter her intransigent ideas about honoring previous commitments.

Time passed. Alone in the living room at night, she often looked at the bowl sitting on the table, still and safe, unilluminated. In its way, it was perfect: the world cut in half, deep and smoothly empty. Near the rim, even in dim light, the eye moved toward one small flash of blue, a vanishing point on the horizon.

Sinclair Lewis

BABBITT RISING

Sinclair Lewis *(1883–1951) declined a Pulitzer Prize for his 1924 novel* Arrowsmith *but went on to win (and accept) a Nobel Prize in Literature in 1930 (the first American to be so honored). Lewis was a world traveler who, in his fiction, stayed close to his Minnesota roots: all but six of his twenty-two novels prominently feature the Midwest.* Babbitt *(1922), for which Lewis will always be best remembered, is set in an imaginary state located squarely between Michigan, Indiana, and Ohio. The selection presented here, from early in the novel, recounts a morning in the life of George F. Babbitt, whose bland optimism will be severely tested in the course of this disturbing portrait of a "normal" middle-class businessman.*

The towers of Zenith aspired above the morning mist; austere towers of steel and cement and limestone, sturdy as cliffs and delicate as silver rods. They were neither citadels not churches, but frankly and beautifully office-buildings.

The mist took pity on the fretted structures of earlier generations: the Post Office with its shingle-tortured mansard, the red brick minarets of hulking old houses, factories with stingy and sooted windows, wooden tenements colored like mud. The city was full of such grotesqueries, but the clean towers were thrusting them from the business center, and on the farther hills were shining new houses, homes—they seemed—for laughter and tranquility.

Over a concrete bridge fled a limousine of long sleek hood and noiseless engine. These people in evening clothes were returning from an all-night rehearsal of a Little Theater play, an artistic adventure considerably illuminated by champagne. Below the bridge curved a railroad, a maze of green and crimson lights. The New York Flyer boomed past, and twenty lines of polished steel leaped into the glare.

In one of the skyscrapers the wires of the Associated Press were closing down. The telegraph operators wearily raised their celluloid eyeshades after a night of talking with Paris and Peking. Through the building crawled the scrubwomen, yawning, their old shoes slapping. The dawn mist spun away. Queues of men with lunch-boxes clumped toward the immensity of new factories, sheets of glass and hollow tile, glittering shops where five thousand men worked beneath one roof, pouring out the honest wares that would be sold up the Euphrates and across the veldt. The whistles rolled out in greeting a chorus cheerful as the April dawn; the song of labor in a city built—it seemed—for giants.

There was nothing of the giant in the aspect of the man who was beginning to awaken on the sleeping-porch of a Dutch Colonial house in that residential district of Zenith known as Floral Heights.

His name was George F. Babbitt. He was forty-six years old now, in April, 1920, and he made nothing in particular, neither butter nor shoes nor poetry, but he was nimble in the calling of selling houses for more than people could afford to pay.

His large head was pink, his brown hair thin and dry. His face was babyish in slumber, despite his wrinkles and the red spectacle-dents on the slopes of his nose. He was not fat but he was exceedingly well fed; his cheeks were pads, and the unroughened hand which lay helpless upon the khaki-colored blanket was slightly puffy. He seemed prosperous, extremely married and unromantic; and altogether unromantic appeared this sleeping-porch, which looked on one sizable elm, two respectable grass-plots, a cement driveway, and a corrugated iron garage. Yet Babbitt was again dreaming of the fairy child, a dream more romantic than scarlet pagodas by a silver sea.

For years the fairy child had come to him. Where others saw but Georgie Babbitt, she discerned gallant youth. She waited for him, in the darkness beyond mysterious groves. When at last he could slip away from the crowded house he darted to her. His wife, his clamoring friends, sought to follow, but he escaped, the girl fleet beside him, and they crouched together on a shadowy hillside. She was so slim, so white, so eager! She cried that he was gay and valiant, that she would wait for him, that they would sail—

Rumble and bang of the milk-truck.

Babbitt moaned, turned over, struggled back toward his dream. He could see only her face now, beyond misty waters. The furnace-man slammed the basement door. A dog barked in the next yard. As Babbitt sank blissfully into a dim warm tide, the paper-carrier went by whistling, and the rolled-up *Advocate* thumped the front door. Babbitt roused, his stomach constricted with alarm. As he relaxed, he was pierced by the familiar and irritating rattle of some one cranking a Ford: snap-ah-ah, snap-ah-ah, snap-ah-ah. Himself a pious motorist, Babbitt cranked with the unseen driver, with him waited through taut hours for the roar of the starting engine, with him agonized as the roar ceased and again began the infernal patient snap-ah-ah—a round, flat sound, a shivering cold-morning sound, a sound infuriating and inescapable. Not till the rising voice of the motor told him that the Ford was moving was he released from the panting tension. He glanced once at his favorite tree, elm twigs against the gold patina of sky, and fumbled for sleep as for a drug. He who had been a boy very credulous of life was no longer greatly interested in the possible and improbable adventures of each new day.

He escaped from reality till the alarm-clock rang, at seven-twenty.

It was the best of nationally advertised and quantitatively produced alarm-clocks, with all modern attachments, including cathedral chime, intermittent alarm, and a phosphorescent dial. Babbitt was proud of being awakened by such a rich device. Socially it was almost as creditable as buying expensive cord tires.

He sulkily admitted now that there was no more escape, but he lay and detested the grind of the real-estate business, and disliked his family, and disliked himself for disliking them. The evening before, he had played poker at Vergil Gunch's still midnight, and after such holidays he was irritable before breakfast. It may have been the tremendous home-brewed beer of the prohibition-era and the cigars to which that beer enticed him; it may have been resentment of return from this fine, bold man-world to a restricted region of wives and stenographers, and of suggestions not to smoke so much.

From the bedroom beside the sleeping-porch, his wife's detestably cheerful "Time to get up, Georgie boy," and the itchy sound, the brisk and scratchy sound, of combing hairs out of a stiff brush.

He grunted; he dragged his thick legs, in faded baby-blue pajamas, from under the khaki blanket; he sat on the edge of the cot, running his fingers through his wild hair, while his plump feet mechanically felt for his slippers. He looked regretfully at the blanket—forever a suggestion to him of freedom and heroism. He had bought it for a camping trip which had never come off. It symbolized gorgeous loafing, gorgeous cursing, virile flannel shirts.

He creaked to his feet, groaning at the waves of pain which passed behind his eyeballs. Though he waited for their scorching recurrence, he looked blurrily out at the yard. It delighted him, as always; it was the neat yard of a successful business man of Zenith, that is, it was perfection, and made him also perfect. He regarded the corrugated iron garage. For the three-hundred-and-sixty-fifth time in a year he reflected, "No class to that tin shack. Have to build me a frame garage. But by golly it's the only thing on the place that isn't up-to-date!" While he stared he thought of a community garage for his acreage development, Glen Oriole. He stopped puffing and jiggling. His arms were akimbo. His petulant, sleep-swollen face was set in harder lines. He suddenly seemed capable, an official, a man to contrive, to direct, to get things done.

On the vigor of his idea he was carried down the hard, clean, unused-looking hall into the bathroom.

Though the house was not large it had, like all houses on Floral Heights, an altogether royal bathroom of porcelain and glazed tile and metal sleek as silver. The towel-rack was a rod of clear glass set in nickel. The tub was long enough for a Prussian Guard, and above the set bowl was a sensational exhibit of tooth-brush holder, shaving-brush-holder, soap-dish, sponge-dish, and medicine-cabinet, so glittering and so ingenious that they resembled an electrical instrument-board. But the Babbitt whose god was Modern Appliances was not pleased. The air of the bathroom was thick with the smell of a heathen toothpaste. "Verona been at it again! 'Stead of sticking to Lilidol, like I've re-peat-ed-ly asked her, she's gone, and gotten some confounded stinkum stuff that makes you sick!"

The bath-mat was wrinkled and the floor was wet. (His daughter Verona eccentrically took baths in the morning, now and then.) He slipped on the mat, and slid against the tub. He said "Damn!" Furiously he snatched up his tube of shaving-cream, furiously he lathered, with a belligerent slapping of the unctuous brush, furiously he raked his plump cheeks with a safety-razor. It pulled. The blade was dull. He said, "Damn—oh—oh—damn it!"

He hunted through the medicine-cabinet for a packet of new razor-blades (reflecting, as invariably, "Be cheaper to buy one of these ding-uses and strop your own blades,") and when he discovered the packet, behind the round box of bicarbonate of soda, he thought ill of his wife for putting it there and very well of himself for not saying "Damn." But he did say it, immediately afterward, when with wet and soap-slippery fingers he tried to remove the horrible little envelope and crisp cling-ing oiled paper from the new blade.

Then there was the problem, oft-pondered, never solved, of what to do with the old blade, which might imperil the fingers of his young. As usual, he tossed it on top of the medicine-cabinet, with a mental note that some day he must remove the fifty or sixty other blades that were also temporarily piled up there. He finished his shaving in a growing testiness increased by his spinning headache and by the emptiness in his stomach. When he was done, his round face smooth and streamy and his eyes stinging from soapy water, he reached for a towel. The family towels were wet, wet and clammy and vile, all of them wet, he found, as he blindly snatched them—his own face-towel, his wife's, Verona's, Ted's, Tinka's, and the lone bath-towel with the huge welt of initial. Then George F. Babbitt did a dismaying thing. He wiped his face on the guest-towel! It was a pansy-embroidered trifle which always hung there to indicate that the Babbitts were in the best Floral Heights soci-ety. No one had ever used it. No guest had ever dared to. Guests secre-tively took a corner of the nearest regular towel.

He was raging, "By golly, here they go and use up all the towels, every doggone one of 'em, and they use 'em and get 'em all wet and sopping, and never put out a dry one for me—of course, I'm the goat!—and I want one and—I'm the only person in the doggone house that's got the slightest bit of consideration for other people and thoughtfulness and consider there may be others that may want to use the dog-gone bathroom room after me and consider—"

He was pitching the chill abominations into the bathtub, pleased by the vindictiveness of that desolate flapping sound; and in the midst his wife serenely trotted in, observed serenely, "Why Georgie dear, what are you doing? Are you going to wash out the towels? Why, you needn't wash out the towels. Oh, Georgie, you didn't go and use the guest-towel, did you?"

It is not recorded that he was able to answer.

For the first time in weeks he was sufficiently roused by his wife to look at her.

[. . .]

They had labored, these solid citizens. Twenty years before, the hill on which Floral Heights was spread, with its bright roofs and immaculate turf and amazing comfort, had been a wilderness of rank second-growth elms and oaks and maples. Along the precise streets were still a few wooded vacant lots, and the fragment of an old orchard. It was brilliant to-day; the apple boughs were lit with fresh leaves like torches of green fire. The first white of cherry blossoms flickered down a gully, and robins clamored.

Babbitt sniffed the earth, chuckled at the hysteric robins as he would have chuckled at kittens or at a comic movie. He was, to the eye, the perfect office-going executive—a well-fed man in a correct brown soft hat and frameless spectacles, smoking a large cigar, driving a good motor along a semisuburban parkway. But in him was some genius of authentic love for his neighborhood, his city, his clan. The winter was over; the time was come for the building, the visible growth, which to him was glory. He lost his dawn depression; he was ruddily cheerful when he stopped on Smith Street to leave the brown trousers, and to have the gasoline-tank filled.

The familiarity of the rite fortified him: the sight of the tall red iron gasoline-pump, the hollow-tile and terra-cotta garage, the window full of the most agreeable accessories—shiny casings, spark-plugs with immaculate porcelain jackets, tire-chains of gold and silver. He was flattered by the friendliness with which Sylvester Moon, dirtiest and most skilled of motor mechanics, came out to serve him. "Mornin', Mr. Bab-bitt!" said Moon, and Babbitt felt himself a person of importance, one whose name even busy garagemen remembered—not one of these cheap-sports flying around in flivvers. He admired the ingenuity of the automatic dial, clicking off gallon by gallon; admired the smartness of the sign: "A fill in time saves getting stuck—gas to-day 31 cents"; ad-mired the rhythmic gurgle of the gasoline as it flowed into the tank, and the mechanical regularity with which Moon turned the handle.

"How much we takin' to-day?" asked Moon, in a manner which combined the independence of the great specialist, the friendliness of a familiar gossip, and respect for a man of weight in the community, like George F. Babbitt.

"Fill 'er up."

"Who you rootin' for for Republican candidate, Mr. Babbitt?"

"It's too early to make any predictions yet. After all, there's still a good month and two weeks—no, three weeks—must be almost three weeks,—well, there's more than six weeks in all before the Republican convention, and I feel a fellow ought to keep an open mind and give all the candidates a show—look 'em all over and size 'em up, and then de-cide carefully."

"That's a fact, Mr. Babbitt."

"But I'll tell you—and my stand on this is just the same as it was four years ago, and eight years ago, and it'll be my stand four years from now—yes, and eight years from now! What I tell everybody, and it can't be too generally understood, is that what we need first, last, and all the time is a good, sound business administration!"

"By golly, that's right!"

"How do those front tires look to you?"

"Fine! Fine! Wouldn't be much work for garages if everybody looked after their car the way you do."

"Well, I do try and have some sense about it." Babbitt paid his bill, said adequately, "Oh, keep the change," and drove off in an ecstasy of honest self-appreciation. It was with the manner of a Good Samaritan that he shouted at a respectable-looking man who was waiting for a trolley car, "Have a lift?" As the man climbed in Babbitt condescended, "Going clear down-town? Whenever I see a fellow waiting for a trolley,

I always make it a practice to give him a lift—unless, of course, he looks like a bum."

"Wish there were more folks that were so generous with their machines," dutifully said the victim of benevolence.

"Oh, no, 'tain't a question of generosity, hardly. Fact, I always feel—I was saying to my son just the other night—it's a fellow's duty to share the good things of this world with his neighbors, and it gets my goat when a fellow gets stuck on himself and goes around tooting his horn merely because he's charitable."

The victim seemed unable to find the right answer. Babbitt boomed on:

"Pretty punk service the Company giving us on these car-lines. Nonsense to only run the Portland Road cars once every seven minutes. Fellow gets mighty cold on a winter morning, waiting on a street corner with the wind nipping at his ankles."

"That's right. The Street Car Company don't care a damn what kind of a deal they give us. Something ought to happen to 'em."

Babbitt was alarmed. "But still, of course it won't do to just keep knocking the Traction Company and not realize the difficulties they're operating under, like these cranks that want municipal ownership. The way these workmen hold up the Company for high wages is simply a crime, and of course the burden falls on you and me that have to pay a seven-cent fare! Fact, there's a remarkable service on all their lines—considering."

"Well—" uneasily.

"Darn fine morning," Babbitt explained. "Spring coming along fast."

"Yes, it's real spring now."

The victim had no originality, no wit, and Babbitt fell into a great silence and devoted himself to the game of beating trolley cars to the corner: a spurt, a tail-chase, nervous speeding between the huge yellow side of the trolley and the jagged row of parked motors, shooting past just as the trolley stopped—a rare game and valiant.

And all the while he was conscious of the loveliness of Zenith. For weeks together he noticed nothing but clients and the vexing To Rent signs of rival brokers. To-day, in mysterious malaise, he raged or rejoiced with equal nervous swiftness, and to-day the light of spring was so winsome that he lifted his head and saw.

He admired each district along his familiar route to the office: The bungalows and shrubs and winding irregular driveways of Floral Heights. The one-story shops on Smith Street, a glare of plate-glass and new yellow brick; groceries and laundries and drugstores to supply the more immediate needs of East Side housewives. The market gardens in Dutch Hollow, their shanties patched with corrupted iron and stolen doors. Billboards with crimson goddesses nine feet tall advertising cinema films, pipe tobacco, and talcum powder. The old "mansions" along Ninth Street, S.E., like aged dandies in filthy linen; wooden castles turned into boarding-houses, with muddy walks and rusty, hedges, jostled by fast-intruding garages, cheap apartment-houses, and fruit-stands conducted by bland, sleek Athenians. Across the belt of railroad-tracks, factories with high-perched water-tanks and tall stacks—factories producing condensed milk, paper boxes, lighting-fixtures, motor cars. Then the business center, the thickening darting traffic, the crammed trolleys unloading, and high doorways of marble and polished granite.

It was big—and Babbitt respected bigness in anything; in mountains, jewels, muscles, wealth, or words. He was, for a spring-enchanted moment, the lyric and almost unselfish lover of Zenith. He thought of the outlying factory suburbs; of the Chaloosa River with its strangely eroded banks; of the orchard-dappled Tonawanda Hills to the North, and all the fat dairy land and big barns and comfortable herds. As he dropped his passenger he cried, "Gosh, I feel pretty good this morning!"

Jean Thompson

THE RICH MAN'S HOUSE

Jean Thompson *(1950–) teaches creative writing at the University of Illinois at Urbana-Champaign. Her first story collection,* The Gasoline Wars *(1980), was published to admiring reviews and was followed by two novels and, in 1985, a second collection. But then, like Tillie Olsen and others before her, she was quieted by the midlife demands of parenting and work. Her next book, the story collection* Who Do You Love? *(1999), was a finalist for the National Book Award. In "The Rich Man's House," a neighbor's request to cat-sit becomes an unspoken invitation to probe the life of mysterious fellow-creature, evidently a successful businessman, who, in his absence, leaves tantalizing clues about his personal and professional circumstances.*

It was a rich man's house, designed for expensive recreation and daily luxury, the home of a family with strenuous hobbies and social tastes. But the rich man's wife had left him two years ago, and his children were grown and never visited. The pasture where his daughters had kept their horses was consigned to weeds. No one lobbed balls on the tennis court or showed off on the three-meter diving board. The rich man himself came home late at night and left again at sunrise for his office in the city. I'd see his big smooth car gliding up the driveway, and the wrought-iron gate opening by remote control. Two huge electrified lanterns were set in the stone archways of the entrance. There were nights he didn't come home at all and the lanterns stayed lit, pale filaments burning thinly in the daylight.

Beyond the entrance was a brick courtyard and a fountain (dry), and the triple doors of the enormous garage. Artful landscaping kept the eye from penetrating farther, but there was a suggestion of balconies, verandas, crystal chandeliers suspended in magnificent space. The house was visited regularly by a Mexican maid, by ranks of gardeners, and by workmen engaged to drain and fill and regrout the swimming pool, or pour new cement, or other projects which split the air with saws and drills. Each Tuesday morning a truck from a private water company drove up, carrying plastic water jugs like blue jewels. Each Thursday evening his pristine garbage cans were set out at the curb, and each Friday morning they were whisked back inside. Leaf blowers whined, sprinklers pumped nets of mist onto newly laid sod, panel trucks arrived to disgorge materials, all in the owner's absence. The house made me think of Egyptian pharaohs and the armies that labored building the pyramids.

The rich man's name was Kenneth Dacey. I knew him because I lived next door, the way next door was figured in our rural part of the county. My husband and I had rented a cottage on the parcel of land next to his. My husband had gone away, but I was staying on, at least for now. Kenneth Dacey introduced himself when we moved in, and we waved to each other in passing, and once or twice we'd traded opinions on the weather or marauding deer. But I'd never been inside his house, or he in mine, until the morning he appeared on my front porch, asking if I'd feed his cat.

I peeked at him through the kitchen window before I answered his knock. He was wearing his weekend clothes, a plaid western shirt, sheepskin vest, jeans, boots, a belt with an oversized silver buckle. He was a big bald pink-skinned man, nearly sixty, I guess, with watery blue eyes and a little fair mustache. Those clothes always managed to look like a costume on him. "A banker playing sheriff," my husband used to say.

I opened the door, arranging my face into an expression of surprise and pleasure. I'm one of those people who fall back on niceness when I don't know what else to do. "Good morning," I said to Dacey. I never felt comfortable first-naming him, and I usually avoided calling him anything at all, like an in-law or a repairman.

He said good morning, and then we said it would be a fine fall day once the fog burned off. We turned around to admire the morning, since it was something we both agreed on. The hills of blond grass rose on each side of the valley floor. Oaks and eucalyptus grew on the lower slopes. A ledge of granite and four tall pines crowned the highest hill. The air was milky, and these pines seemed to advance and retreat as the mists shifted. Way overhead was a patch of blue sky, a promise.

When we'd finished with the view we were obliged to turn back to each other again. In a moment more I would have to invite Dacey inside. My husband had been gone for three months, and my house no longer looked as if a man lived there. That's how it seemed to me. It was like my tongue sliding over a row of teeth and coming to rest in an empty space.

But he got down to business then. *Business*; that was what brought him here. He was going away for the weekend, and would I mind feeding his cat? I said I'd be happy to. It seemed like the sort of thing a neighbor ought to do, something social and human, conditions I should aspire to. He said if I had a minute he'd take me up to the house and show me what had to be done.

It was our longest conversation ever, although I'd lived there for a year and a half. We were both people who kept to ourselves, maybe for the same reasons these days, a combination of loneliness and pride. But then I'm always too ready to ascribe my own motives to people and to make assumptions. That's what my husband told me, during that period of our marriage when it was important to him to inventory my flaws. Kenneth Dacey angled his body away from you when he spoke, which could have been from rudeness or shyness or both. His loose pink face was the face of a baby surprised to find itself grown old. An unthinking face that gave no indication of an inner life. It was hard to imagine him deliberately acquiring a family, or maybe he had simply allowed that to happen to him over time.

I grabbed my jacket from the hook and walked with him up the driveway. There was a pickup truck parked just outside the gate, and the usual racket of hammers and shouted instructions. It was curious that with all his gangs of tradesmen and hirelings, he couldn't find one of them to feed a cat. It's possible he meant to make me a kind of employee also, and was the kind of man who was most comfortable with human relationships when they could be mediated with money or obligation. But I didn't think any of this until later.

We reached the wrought-iron gate, and Dacey gave me a key that unlocked a side entrance, a foot passage across the bridge spanning the creekbed. It was the same creek that cut through the back wilderness of my lot, though at the end of this dry season it was only a heap of tumbled gravel and a few patches of soft mud. Once I was inside the gate, I could see that the garden was another kind of construction zone, with heaps of wood chips and black plastic sheeting everywhere. A statue of St. Francis blessed three bare rosebushes.

"All this," said Dacey, waving his hand to indicate the litter of wheelbarrows and rakes and bags of topsoil, "this was supposed to be finished by now." He shook his head, speculating darkly on the wrongs of contractors. I made the appropriate sympathetic noises. But I wondered what was so complicated about the project, when Dacey could, if he chose, arrange for giant palm trees to appear in his yard overnight.

He showed me how to operate the double locks on the front doors, and the code that disarmed the burglar alarm. I was imagining myself ringed by floodlights and sheriff's deputies, with no better alibi than a can of cat food. "All the glass is wired too," said Dacey. "Break a window, they'll get somebody out here in four minutes, guaranteed."

"Really." My voice sounded faint and false. It was oppressive, the effort it took to admire things. We were standing in the entryway, which was two stories high. Suspended overhead was the crystal wedding-cake chandelier you only imagined from the road. It was an odd choice to go with the paneled walls and clay-colored floors, like an argument nobody had won. There was a curving staircase leading up. Dacey climbed it first, and I tried not to watch the elephant-like rolling of his denim hindquarters.

"Living room," he said at the top. There was a large, stiffly decorated area, and a dining room opposite. I explored both of them later, when I had a chance to spy them out. They were fusty, old-fashioned rooms with brocaded sofas and ponderous lamps. Swags of stiff draperies hung at the windows. There was a nearly concert-sized piano, and a formal array of family photographs, sailing prints, ornamental brasses. The dining room had a table that could have been used for board meetings, and a book of racing prints propped up on a stand, opened to a page showing *Man o' War*.

But Dacey walked straight past all this, as I guess he was accustomed to doing, back to the kitchen and den. This was one large room, with glass doors leading out to a deck. There was a recliner, television, an aquarium full of fish, a telephone desk with a pile of receipts and stray papers, like you'd find in anybody's house. He opened a cupboard to show me where the cat food was. Everything on the shelves was tidy and monastic, the kitchen of someone who never cooked: cereal, packets of instant soup, crackers, muffin mix, a box of neglected raisins, a tin of anchovies. I was so used to admiring things by now, I had to stop myself from exclaiming over his groceries.

"Now you probably won't even see Jake," he said. Jake was the cat. "He stays outside. I could leave all his food out before I left, but the raccoons would get it."

I repeated, idiotically, that I was happy to help him. I asked where he was going for the weekend.

Dacey blinked at me, as if I'd committed some trespass, and he'd found a reason to dislike me. But he said, "I've got a cabin up in the foothills. Going to do some fishing. Your husband like to fish?"

"No," I said.

Dacey raised his eyebrows, as if he couldn't imagine such a thing. Our conversation stalled, then went belly-up. We stared at each other for a moment more. I couldn't remember meeting anyone who damped down human speech as Dacey did. He showed me downstairs again, and we repeated our politenesses, and then I was outside, breathing in the cool morning air.

I hadn't lied, technically, about my husband, but I'd missed some chance to tell the truth. I wasn't sure if that had more to do with Dacey or myself, with his coldness—I put that name to it—or my own sulking. He didn't know or hadn't noticed that my husband no longer lived here, and I hadn't bothered to inform him. Maybe I didn't like the idea that the two of us might have anything in common. When I got back to my house, it had a welcoming look to it. Your own unhappiness is always preferable to someone else's, just as you sleep better in your own bed, even alone.

A little while later I saw Dacey's truck, a big Silverado that he used on weekends, rumble down the driveway. And later still, after the workmen had all gone home, and the sun had dropped behind that ridge crest, I took the ring of keys he'd given me and headed toward the iron gate. I thought how strange it was that he'd entrusted his house to me, whom he hardly knew. Maybe he didn't have anyone else, or maybe I was so insignificant as to be harmless.

That first visit I didn't stay long or poke around much. I left out food for the invisible cat, and strolled through the rooms I'd already seen, not touching anything. The fading sunset light and the huge emptiness of the place oppressed me. It was like wandering alone through a monument or a tomb. A corridor upstairs led to what I guessed was a wing of private rooms, and there were other doors that wouldn't give when I put a cautious hand to them. The ceilings in the hallways had panels of some thin reflecting glass, and it wasn't hard for me to imagine that Dacey, with his fondness for security, might have mounted cameras up there.

Still, he couldn't blame me for looking at the pictures. You were meant to do that. There was no photograph of his wife, but there was one of someone's elderly parents, looking timid and glassy-eyed. Dacey himself, posed in one of those elaborately casual shots where the photographer has attempted to do something expressive with the hands. And a large portrait, big as an oil painting, of Dacey's children: two teenaged girls—twins, it seemed—with glossy chestnut bobs, and two younger boys, grinning and freckled. I looked for family resemblances among them but there wasn't much, only the expression of glazed constraint common to overdressed children. From the hairstyles, I guessed the portrait was at least fifteen years old. They'd grown up in this house but they'd left it behind them. I looked at the portrait again, this time for clues, hints of their future flight. Were they happy here? I wasn't acquainted with any rich people. I didn't know if money made them unhappy in interesting ways, as it did on television. The faces in the photograph told me nothing. But their spirits were all around me, those shy childhoods, fluttering like trapped moths.

I was beginning to spook myself. I turned on the entrance lamps as Dacey had instructed me, locked and double-checked the doors, and walked up the driveway in the clear evening light. There was a little gold half-moon, like an earring, already high in the sky. The air was calm and smelled of wood smoke. I wished that my husband was waiting for me inside, that we could open a bottle of wine and I could tell him about Dacey's house, how it made me feel, how any place so fortified and empty was somehow wrong. I imagined scenes like that more and more, and remembered less and less of the things that had really happened between us. It was a different phase of loneliness, the one that came after the sharpest edges had worn off.

The next morning, Saturday, I was up early. I didn't really have to feed the cat—once every twenty-four hours was enough—but I wanted to turn the lights off, make sure nothing had burned down or gone amiss. I felt some anxious responsibility for the place. And I wasn't above nosing around more, although I wouldn't do anything crude like drink Dacey's liquor or make long-distance calls from his phone.

The morning light turned the rooms ordinary and unremarkable. The cat, or something, had cleaned out the food and I filled the dish again and changed the water bowl. I stood on the deck and looked out. I saw, a little ways up the valley, the line of the creek and the higher ground where deer and wild turkeys ranged. When I lowered my eyes I saw the ragged horse pasture and some pipe corral stalls. A boat trailer and a long-dry skiff had come to rest there, abandoned projects on abandoned land.

Then, closer in, there was the turquoise oblong of the swimming pool, and the chalk-lined tennis court, surrounded by strips of hyper-green sod. An L-shaped structure on one side of the pool deck, and a larger building with skylights in its roof. Everything below me was in deep blue shadow, with the sunlight just now touching the wood at my feet. Something moved in the shadow. A man looked up at me. "Morning," he said.

He was grinning. I don't know what my face was doing. I said, "I'm here to feed the cat." I don't know why I felt I had to explain myself. I could have just as easily demanded to know what he was doing there.

He came to stand at the border of the shadow, so he had to shade his eyes to look up at me. "Thought maybe you was his girlfriend."

"I live next door," I said, as if that ruled out my being anyone's girl-friend. He nodded, then seemed to lose interest in me. He walked across the deck, whistling, and unlocked the door to the pool house. I heard him rummaging inside, and noises of metal shifting against metal.

So he was a workman of some sort, and I didn't have to worry about him. But I was unsettled, as if I'd been caught actually rummaging the house, instead of just contemplating doing so. I locked the glass doors and went downstairs.

While I was securing the front door I heard him behind me, dragging something heavy. I turned around and he said, "Work's never done around here."

I said I could believe it. There was a hunk of metal housing on the deck, some part of a filtration system, I guessed. We both regarded it for a moment, as if it would explain us to each other.

"Does anybody ever swim in that pool?" I asked. I don't know why I was talking to him. It had something to do with the early-morning quiet, and the two of us there alone, and the blue unmoving water. Everything we said sounded like a secret.

"I do. When nobody else's here." He grinned at me again. He had a thin, mobile face with curious light, soft eyes, and a lot of feathery gray hair. There was nothing handsome about him but I kept sneaking glances at him. Scruffy, with that light-bodied, underfed look you see in some workingmen, as if they wear themselves down to smooth-running levers and pulleys. Blue jeans and a T-shirt whose fabrics had been sweated through and washed hot and fried in the dryer. He was maybe thirty, too young for the hair. These days I watched men the way you might an unknown species of bird, observing markings and calls, trying to determine their range and habits. Since my husband left, I didn't trust anything I thought I knew about them.

He said, "You ever see his playroom?"

"His what?"

"This here." He walked across the deck to the peak-roofed bungalow, the one with the skylights. It was made of blond wood and glass, and sat in its own sunken deck. He turned and waited for me at the door, like a host.

Inside there was a pool table, covered with a piece of crushed velvet, gold-colored and tasseled at the ends. The table itself was claw-footed, oversized, an antique of some sort. I said, "Does anybody ever use this?"

"When nobody else is here . . . ," he began.

I shook my head, pretending to disapprove of him. There was a Ping-

Pong table, and a model-train track that folded down from the wall, and a croquet set, and a poker table with stacks of chips. There was a wet bar in one corner. "I don't believe this," I said. It was too much. Nobody would ever be able to have this much organized fun. The room smelled of sawdust and plaster. Black wires dangled from the ceiling, and in one corner was a push broom and a small pile of construction trash.

"This is all new," I said, marveling. The sun was pouring in through the skylights and the room was turning hot.

"Remodeled."

"Why does he need all this? Why would anyone?"

"It gives him something to do, I guess." He patted down his pockets for cigarettes. "Gives me something to do. I'm Jesse."

I introduced myself and we shook hands. He said he thought he'd seen me from time to time, unloading groceries or at the mailbox. He hadn't really thought I was Dacey's girlfriend. That was just kidding. He worked for Dacey off and on, doing repairs and construction.

"I don't know him very well," I said. "Mr. Dacey." The sun was drilling straight into my scalp. It made me feel sleepy, like everything in me had slowed way down.

The man, Jesse, was squinting at his cigarette, angling it toward the small flame. He turned his head away to blow out a stream of smoke. Sometimes the simplest things men did seemed like magic tricks to me.

He turned back again. His eyes were gray. It had taken me that long to look at him straight on. "Isn't he a work of art, that guy."

I said I wouldn't know about that.

"He's got some house."

I said, "I wouldn't live here if you paid me."

"You seen it all?" I shook my head. "Well, come on."

Jesse had his own set of keys. I followed him inside without thinking twice about it.

Downstairs there were two guest bedrooms, neat and unused, and a locked door that Jesse said was an office, "Where he wheels and deals and steals." Beyond that was an exercise room, complete with weights and a stationary bicycle and those elaborate machines that make you think of scientifically engineered torture chambers. I didn't ask Jesse if Dacey ever came down here to work up a dutiful sweat. (The image of

him, pink and sagging, pedaling away in furious stasis, was something I
didn't care to dwell on.) By now I'd caught on that for Dacey buying
was the equivalent of, or the substitute for, doing. If Dacey had been
more personable, I might have felt sorry for him. I wouldn't have
wanted anyone in my house, doing this to me.

There was an overclean workroom with a tool bench off the garage,
and Dacey's big navy blue Lincoln, and a little green MG I'd never seen
him drive. Jesse held a hand over the curve of a headlight, the way another man might cup a woman's breast. "Now this is the only thing he's
got that I covet." *Covet*, a Bible word. It sounded strange in anybody's
mouth, and in all that echoing cement.

We climbed up to the second floor. He steered me toward the wing
I hadn't seen, and pointed to the deck outside. "The royal hot tub."

It was a big six-sided affair, with a tight-fitting lid like a stew pot.
Jesse said, "You should come up here sometime, check it out."

I did something—shook my head, I don't know—and moved away
from him. I didn't like him saying that. I was thinking I didn't know him
at all.

"Hey," he said. "It's a joke."

I muttered something like all right, never mind. It was the wrong
place for maidenly sensitivities, or maybe I'd acquired them too late. I
couldn't believe I was doing any of this.

Dacey's bedroom was a big unadorned chamber—like a hotel
room—with a separate dressing room littered with magazines and stray
coins and cardboard packs of batteries, with unpaired shoes, an elaborate silver-topped tankard of the kind no one ever uses for drinking, a
miniature TV, binoculars in a pebbled leather case, more. His bathroom was all onyx and dark green, like an underwater chamber, with a
sunken tub. The towels were oversized, the same funereal algae color.
Nothing was unclean, but the suite had a stale, burrow-like quality to it,
the one place where someone really lived.

His sons' rooms were across the hall, connected by a more utilitarian
bathroom done in earth tones. There was no furniture here, only open
cardboard boxes disgorging lamp bases, an electric space heater, ladies'
handbags, throw pillows, curtain rods, shoe trees, all manner of pawed-

over and unloved items. Jesse said, "His missus packed up all this when she left. Never came back for it."

"What was she like? Is she like, I mean."

"Nice lady. Nervous sort. She always looked like her belt was too tight, maybe."

I laughed at that. We were standing in front of a mirrored closet door and our reflections faced us. I looked into the mirror while I was still laughing, and I hardly knew myself, much less the man standing next to me. I closed my mouth and my familiar image returned: skittish, with my hair too ragged, legs too lumpy, all the things I wanted to reach out and brush away. The man beside the woman said, "Pretty." I saw his mouth move.

"Don't talk to me like that," I said, looking at him now, not the mirror.

"Sorry." He turned his palms upward and raised his eyebrows to indicate harmlessness. I was annoyed because I thought he was making fun of me. I didn't think I was pretty.

"I saved the best for last," he said, opening the door at the end of the hallway.

Twin canopy beds, decked in white ruffles, stood at opposite ends of the big L-shaped room. Each was freighted with stuffed animals. There were owlish-looking teddy bears, plush rabbits, happy tigers. Two white and gold desk sets shared a wall. One corner, the L end, was set up as a parlor, with a loveseat and a television.

Jesse said, "Which do you think he liked better, those girls, or his boys?"

On the walls were formal displays of medals (horsemanship, swimming), school pennants, heart-shaped picture frames, a program from a production of *Brigadoon*. All of it prim and fixed, like a museum of girlhood. "Unreal," I said. I walked to the center of the room. A single thread of spiderweb broke across my face.

Jesse said, "I mean, how far back would you want to go, if you was them?"

Each end of the room opened into a dressing room, with its own sink and vanity table, ruffled skirts and pretty little lamps. The rooms smelled like old powder.

"All his kids were adopted," Jesse told me. "If you're rich enough, I guess you can buy anything."

I said I'd seen enough. The house was stale and sad, arrogant and wrong-headed, even ugly. We trooped downstairs and I waited at the front door while Jesse set the burglar alarm.

"Can you imagine doing this," he said. "Every time you go in or out, you have to get permission from yourself."

"There's nothing here I'd want to steal," I said.

"Sure."

"I mean it." It irritated me that he might not believe me, but it wasn't the kind of thing you could prove.

"Well, back to work. Nice meeting you." I said it was nice to meet him too. He nodded and turned abruptly away. A minute later I heard him banging away at the hunk of metal again. I didn't know what to make of him. Odd duck, my husband would have called him. It was one of the things he said that I still heard from time to time.

I fed the cat again the next morning without seeing anyone. Dacey would be home that night and I wouldn't have to worry anymore about his grandiose bathrooms, his ignorance, his lonesome money.

My husband and I loved the valley. We'd moved there from our perfectly unremarkable suburbia, from traffic and hyperkinetic televisions and shopping malls and streets with fragrant, ultimately disappointing names: El Paseo Drive, Vista Del Sol. We moved because we had ideas about tranquility and solitude, nature and space, about a worthwhile life lived genuinely. It would be easy to make fun of those ideas now, or at least to treat them ironically, as untried romanticism, but I can't. I still believe they are good ideas; we just weren't good people to carry them out. But we didn't know that at first. We felt brave and lucky. The landscape's moods and weathers thrilled us. There were sharp-edged winter nights when the air was clear and the stars were as big as fists. One cold morning we stepped out on the front porch and saw an extraordinary thing: a bare tree with six turkey vultures perched in its branches, their wings spread out to warm in the sun, like black laundry. We loved the green rains and the yellow summer days when every dry wind could be the sound of fire.

I say *we* but I can't assume that anymore. I can't say for certain how he felt about anything. Maybe he never really loved those things, or maybe he changed his mind, like he did about me. He'd been mistaken in his first enthusiasms. Or he'd been deceived by me and by the life we'd chosen here. We'd misrepresented ourselves. We'd made false pretenses, raised his expectations and then failed to meet them. I think it scared him when he found himself feeling ordinary, bored or fretful or adrift. The new life was meant to change all that. And I was supposed to have been someone more interesting, but that seam in me played out quickly. I'd disguised my limitations and my unglamorous plodding nature behind intricate shimmering veils. I didn't recognize that version of myself, both cunning and dull. All I'd ever wanted was for someone to know me so thoroughly that I could love without apologies. Now it seemed that neither of us had known the other, or ourselves.

Monday morning the lanterns in the stone arches were on, as I'd left them, but I imagined Dacey had come home late and didn't think to turn them off. Before I left for work—I was still working in town, at my office job—I walked up the driveway, hoping to surrender the key. The upstairs windows were open and throw rugs were draped over the balcony railings. The doorbell chimed over the racket of a vacuum cleaner. The Mexican maid came to the door and shook her head when I asked for Dacey. I couldn't tell if she was denying knowledge or language or both. She kept shaking it when I tried to find out if he'd been there at all. When I stopped asking questions she shut the door again.

The maid's car was gone when I came home late that afternoon. The electric lights were beginning to reassert themselves when I thought about the cat, and whether he'd been fed. I set off up the driveway to Dacey's. It was becoming easier all the time to go there, like any habit. The house smelled of polish and atomized cleansers. I climbed the staircase, wondering what it was designed for, whether the twins had posed there with prom dates, wearing white net dresses and corsages.

In the kitchen I scooped up cat food, then walked out to the deck. I wasn't even looking for the cat—I'd pretty much given up on ever seeing him—when he came pattering around the corner of the deck, uttering little cries of reproach. He was a tiger cat, gray and rangy, and he let me stroke his back while he ate. "Jake," I said. I felt his ribs, and the greedy mechanics of his eating.

The phone rang. It was just inside the door, and the sound of it made me jump. After two rings an answering machine clicked, and Dacey's taped voice instructed callers to leave a message.

There was a silence, full of hesitation and listening. Then whoever it was hung up without speaking. Under my hand the cat thrummed and purred. I was glad he was there. The house was too full of ghosts, and each day I woke up to the ghost of my marriage, and there were times when it seemed I had only a remembered life. The cat at least was solid and real, even though after he finished eating he bolted away, escaping me.

Dacey didn't come home that night either. When I returned from work the next day the man Jesse appeared at my front door. That in itself seemed remarkable, as if I'd come to believe I might have invented him or conjured him up. But here he was, planted on the front porch, running a hand through his hair as he spoke. Dacey was missing, he said, or at least overdue. Dacey's office had called him, Jesse, to see what he knew.

"He was going fishing at his cabin," I said. "That's what he told me."

"Well he never got there. Least, nobody's seen him."

We watched each other thinking. The sun was tangled in the low trees across the road and the light from it was as level as a ruler. I said, "Two days. That's not a long time."

"It is for a money man not to be calling his office."

"Oh," I said. I was retrieving and dusting off the words used in such situations: misappropriation, embezzlement. "Do they think . . ."

"They don't know what to think. They didn't say anything to me. I could just tell."

I was turning over this new picture in my mind, Dacey the conniver, fiddling accounts, doing whatever it is you do to move a line of zeroes from one piece of paper to another, turning all that unreal money into something you could pocket and run off with. There was the way he'd looked at me when I'd asked him where he was going. It made sense, until I imagined him lying dead in some creek or canyon, and that made an equal amount of sense.

I said, "I guess I'll keep feeding that cat."

"I guess."

Jesse was looking behind me, through the half-open front door. "This is a nice place," he said.

"Thanks." I was trying to fill as much of the doorway as I could. I shaded my eyes with my hand. Everything was rimmed with red sunset light.

"Where you think he went?"

I don't know why I thought he meant my husband. I said, "I don't know. I'm sure that's the whole point, for me not to know."

Then he was confused, and I had to explain, and then I was confused and embarrassed in turn. We sidled around on the porch a bit. "Sorry," Jesse said.

"You didn't do anything."

"I mean, sorry for you."

I had to squint to see him. His hair was all sunset and his eyes were chips of light. He said, "What's he like, your husband? Tell me about him."

"I don't know him anymore. I don't know him any better than I do you."

When he moved closer I could smell the boiled cotton of his shirt, and the day's heat soaked into it, and his skin's salt. I stepped forward, closing the door behind me. "Not in here," I said.

Dacey didn't return the next day or the next. After a week had gone by the local papers carried stories about the search for him, identifying Dacey as a "prominent investor and businessman," indicating, in glum neutral journalese, that the investment firm's records were being examined. The Silverado was found in a highway rest area on I-5, a hundred and fifty miles north of Los Angeles. Just the truck, no helpful matchbooks or bloodstains or negotiable securities. Dacey himself had been magicked completely away.

After the first week the Mexican maid stopped coming, as well as the rest of the workers. The garden is left in unfinished half-splendor, although I water the rosebushes, and Jesse keeps the sod green. I bought a new bag of cat food when the old one ran out. We coaxed the cat inside and he prowls and sniffs the rooms and makes himself at home on the upholstery. I do my laundry in Dacey's big old-fashioned machines, even using his soap powder and bleach. For a time the phone still rang, then one day for some reason I picked it up, and the dial tone was gone. Jesse has other jobs now, but he comes by at the end of his day, and often spends the night. I assume he has a different life outside these gates, one he doesn't talk about, one I don't need to know. We float in the pool, me wearing the matronly bathing suit he teases me about. It's October now, but still blazing warm at times, with a sky of blue enamel. I still go to my job, and do errands, and fill up my day with ordinary things. It seems that part of my life will go on without changing while we float in the blue water under the perfect sky.

We talk about Dacey, Jesse and I, and what might happen to the property. Nothing, Jesse says. Nothing until Dacey turns up either dead or in Brazil, and even then nothing for a long time. Everything Dacey owns will be in legal paralysis. The house will be like Sleeping Beauty's castle, hidden behind a briar hedge of suits and injunctions. We will intercept the water and power bills somehow, keep things up and running. We can probably stay here for a long time, as long as we wish. Each night we sleep in a different bed; anything we wish for, towels or ice or firewood, the house provides.

Dacey is either living his new life on some palm-edged shore, or else the silver buckle of his belt tarnishes under a layer of leaf mold and dirt. Just as my husband is either a man who loved me or one who never loved me, just as I am either an ordinary woman or one who inhabits a secret. Stepping out of character, people call it, but that's not really the case. It's more about abandoning the house of our unhappiness, about the spirit moving on. Sometimes the house is really a house, and sometimes it's a body—our own or someone else's—that we leave behind. I'm convinced that Dacey wanted to leave, unbuild the life he had here, whether he knew it or planned it out, and that in the same fashion he chose me to inherit it.

Just yesterday morning I saw three wild peacocks, escapees from someone's misguided notion of an estate, dragging their tails across the old horse pasture. I clucked to them, wondering what you did to make them raise their fans, but they scurried uphill out of sight. When I went to bed that night, there was a long soft feather on my pillow, a single green-gold-blue eye. Jesse found it for me, a free treasure picked right up off the ground, then given away.

PART 4

Coming Up Short

Flannery O'Connor

GOOD COUNTRY PEOPLE

Flannery O'Connor *(1925–1964) was born in Savannah, Georgia, and spent most of her life in her hometown of Milledgeville, Georgia. She got to know her part of the world (and its people) pretty well, especially in view of the fact that she was afflicted with lupus, which killed her before she reached forty. Also in Milledgeville was the State Asylum for the Insane, an institution of which she was keenly aware, and her stories suggest it wasn't always all that easy to tell who belonged on which side of the asylum gates. "Good Country People" is, on the surface, comedy bordering on camp—Bible salesman meets professed atheist—but the disarming tactics of Manley Pointer point up the pretensions (religious, social, moral) of Hulga (née Joy) Hopewell and everyone else he encounters. Ultimately this insinuating salesman brings us all up short.*

Besides the neutral expression that she wore when she was alone, Mrs. Freeman had two others, forward and reverse, that she used for all her human dealings. Her forward expression was steady and driving like the advance of a heavy truck. Her eyes never swerved to left or right but turned as the story turned as if they followed a yellow line down the center of it. She seldom used the other expression because it was not often necessary for her to retract a statement, but when she did, her face came to a complete stop, there was an almost imperceptible movement of her black eyes, during which they seemed to be receding, and then the observer would see that Mrs. Freeman, though she might stand there as real as several grain sacks thrown on top of each other, was no longer there in spirit. As for getting anything across to her when this was the case, Mrs. Hopewell had given it up. She might talk her head off. Mrs. Freeman could never be brought to admit herself wrong on any point. She would stand there and if she could be brought to say anything, it was something like, "Well, I wouldn't of said it was and I wouldn't of said it wasn't," or letting her gaze range over the top kitchen shelf where there was an assortment of dusty bottles, she might remark, "I see you ain't ate many of them figs you put up last summer."

They carried on their most important business in the kitchen at breakfast. Every morning Mrs. Hopewell got up at seven o'clock and lit her gas heater and Joy's. Joy was her daughter, a large blonde girl who had an artificial leg. Mrs. Hopewell thought of her as a child though she was thirty-two years old and highly educated. Joy would get up while her mother was eating and lumber into the bathroom and slam the door, and before long, Mrs. Freeman would arrive at the back door. Joy would hear her mother call, "Come on in," and then they would talk for a while in low voices that were indistinguishable in the bathroom. By the time Joy came in, they had usually finished the weather report and were on one or the other of Mrs. Freeman's daughters, Glynese or Carramae, Joy called them Glycerin and Caramel. Glynese, a redhead, was eighteen and had many admirers; Carramae, a blonde, was only fifteen but already married and pregnant. She could not keep anything on her stomach. Every morning Mrs. Freeman told Mrs. Hopewell how many times she had vomited since the last report.

Mrs. Hopewell liked to tell people that Glynese and Carramae were two of the finest girls she knew and that Mrs. Freeman was a *lady* and that she was never ashamed to take her anywhere or introduce her to anybody they might meet. Then she would tell how she had happened to hire the Freemans in the first place and how they were a godsend to her and how she had had them four years. The reason for her keeping them so long was that they were not trash. They were good country people. She had telephoned the man whose name they had given as a reference and he had told her that Mr. Freeman was a good farmer but that his wife was the nosiest woman ever to walk the earth. "She's got to be into everything," the man said. "If she don't get there before the dust settles, you can bet she's dead, that's all. She'll want to know all your business. I can stand him real good," he had said, "but me nor my wife neither could have stood that woman one more minute on this place." That had put Mrs. Hopewell off for a few days.

She had hired them in the end because there were no other applicants but she had made up her mind beforehand exactly how she would handle the woman. Since she was the type who had to be into everything, then, Mrs. Hopewell had decided, she would not only let her be into everything, she would *see to it* that she was into everything—she would give her the responsibility of everything, she would put her in charge. Mrs. Hopewell had no bad qualities of her own but she was able to use other people's in such a constructive way that she never felt the lack. She had hired the Freemans and she had kept them four years.

Nothing is perfect. This was one of Mrs. Hopewell's favorite sayings. Another was: that is life! And still another, the most important, was: well, other people have their opinions too. She would make these statements, usually at the table, in a tone of gentle insistence as if no one held them but her, and the large hulking Joy, whose constant outrage had obliterated every expression from her face, would stare just a little to the side of her, her eyes icy blue, with the look of someone who has achieved blindness by an act of will and means to keep it.

When Mrs. Hopewell said to Mrs. Freeman that life was like that, Mrs. Freeman would say, "I always said so myself." Nothing had been arrived at by anyone that had not first been arrived at by her. She was quicker than Mr. Freeman. When Mrs. Hopewell said to her after they had been on the place a while, "You know, you're the wheel behind the wheel," and winked, Mrs. Freeman had said, "I know it. I've always been quick. It's some that are quicker than others."

"Everybody is different," Mrs. Hopewell said.

"Yes, most people is," Mrs. Freeman said.

"It takes all kinds to make the world."

"I always said it did myself."

The girl was used to this kind of dialogue for breakfast and more of it for dinner; sometimes they had it for supper too. When they had no guest they ate in the kitchen because that was easier. Mrs. Freeman always managed to arrive at some point during the meal and to watch them finish it. She would stand in the doorway if it were summer but in the winter she would stand with one elbow on top of the refrigerator and look down on them, or she would stand by the gas heater, lifting the back of her skirt slightly. Occasionally she would stand against the wall and roll her head from side to side. At no time was she in any hurry to leave. All this was very trying on Mrs. Hopewell but she was a woman of great patience. She realized that nothing is perfect and that in the Freemans she had good country people and that if, in this day and age, you get good country people, you had better hang onto them.

She had had plenty of experience with trash. Before the Freemans she had averaged one tenant family a year. The wives of these farmers were not the kind you would want to be around you for very long. Mrs. Hopewell, who had divorced her husband long ago, needed someone to walk over the fields with her; and when Joy had to be impressed for these services, her remarks were usually so ugly and her face so glum that Mrs. Hopewell would say, "If you can't come pleasantly, I don't want you at all," to which the girl, standing square and rigid-shouldered with her neck thrust slightly forward, would reply, "If you want me, here I am— LIKE I AM."

Mrs. Hopewell excused this attitude because of the leg (which had been shot off in a hunting accident when Joy was ten). It was hard for Mrs. Hopewell to realize that her child was thirty-two now and that for more than twenty years she had had only one leg. She thought of her still as a child because it tore her heart to think instead of the poor stout girl in her thirties who had never danced a step or had any *normal* good times. Her name was really Joy but as soon as she was twenty-one and away from home, she had had it legally changed. Mrs. Hopewell was certain that she had thought and thought until she had hit upon the ugliest name in any language. Then she had gone and had the beautiful name, Joy, changed without telling her mother until after she had done it. Her legal name was Hulga.

When Mrs. Hopewell thought the name, Hulga, she thought of the broad blank hull of a battleship. She would not use it. She continued to call her Joy to which the girl responded but in a purely mechanical way.

Hulga had learned to tolerate Mrs. Freeman who saved her from taking walks with her mother. Even Glynese and Carramae were useful when they occupied attention that might otherwise have been directed at her. At first she had thought she could not stand Mrs. Freeman for she had found that it was not possible to be rude to her. Mrs. Freeman would take on strange resentments and for days together she would be

sullen but the source of her displeasure was always obscure; a direct attack, a positive leer, blatant ugliness to her face—these never touched
her. And without warning one day, she began calling her Hulga.

She did not call her that in front of Mrs. Hopewell who would have
been incensed but when she and the girl happened to be out of the
house together, she would say something and add the name Hulga to
the end of it, and the big spectacled Joy-Hulga would scowl and redden
as if her privacy had been intruded upon. She considered the name her
personal affair. She had arrived at it first purely on the basis of its ugly
sound and then the full genius of its fitness had struck her. She had a vision of the name working like the ugly sweating Vulcan who stayed in
the furnace and to whom, presumably, the goddess had to come when
called. She saw it as the name of her highest creative act. One of her
major triumphs was that her mother had not been able to turn her dust
into Joy, but the greater one was that she had been able to turn it herself into Hulga. However, Mrs. Freeman's relish for using the name
only irritated her. It was as if Mrs. Freeman's beady steel-pointed eyes
had penetrated far enough behind her face to reach some secret fact.
Something about her seemed to fascinate Mrs. Freeman and then one
day Hulga realized that it was the artificial leg. Mrs. Freeman had a special fondness for the details of secret infections, hidden deformities,
assaults upon children. Of diseases, she preferred the lingering or in-
curable. Hulga had heard Mrs. Hopewell give her the details of the
hunting accident, how the leg had been literally blasted off, how she
had never lost consciousness. Mrs. Freeman could listen to it any time
as if it had happened an hour ago.

When Hulga stumped into the kitchen in the morning (she could
walk without making the awful noise but she made it—Mrs. Hopewell
was certain—because it was ugly-sounding), she glanced at them and
did not speak. Mrs. Hopewell would be in her red kimono with her hair
tied around her head in rags. She would be sitting at the table, finishing
her breakfast and Mrs. Freeman would be hanging by her elbow out-
ward from the refrigerator, looking down at the table. Hulga always put
her eggs on the stove to boil and then stood over them with her arms
folded, and Mrs. Hopewell would look at her—a kind of indirect gaze
divided between her and Mrs. Freeman—and would think that if she

would only keep herself up a little, she wouldn't be so bad looking. There was nothing wrong with her face that a pleasant expression wouldn't help. Mrs. Hopewell said that people who looked on the bright side of things would be beautiful even if they were not.

Whenever she looked at Joy this way, she could not help but feel that it would have been better if the child had not taken the Ph.D. It had certainly not brought her out any and now that she had it, there was no more excuse for her to go to school again. Mrs. Hopewell thought it was nice for girls to go to school to have a good time but Joy had "gone through." Anyhow, she would not have been strong enough to go again. The doctors had told Mrs. Hopewell that with the best of care, Joy might see forty-five. She had a weak heart. Joy had made it plain that if it had not been for this condition, she would be far from these red hills and good country people. She would be in a university lecturing to people who knew what she was talking about. And Mrs. Hopewell could very well picture her there, looking like a scarecrow and lecturing to more of the same. Here she went about all day in a six-year-old skirt and a yellow sweat shirt with a faded cowboy on a horse embossed on it. She thought this was funny; Mrs. Hopewell thought it was idiotic and showed simply that she was still a child. She was brilliant but she didn't have a grain of sense. It seemed to Mrs. Hopewell that every year she grew less like other people and more like herself—bloated, rude, and squint-eyed. And she said such strange things! To her own mother she had said—without warning, without excuse, standing up in the middle of a meal with her face purple and her mouth half full— "Woman! do you ever look inside? Do you ever look inside and see what you are *not*? God!" she had cried sinking down again and staring at her plate, "Malbranche was right: we are not our own light. We are not our own light!" Mrs. Hopewell had no idea to this day what brought that on. She had only made the remark, hoping Joy would take it in, that a smile never hurt anyone.

The girl had taken the Ph.D. in philosophy and this left Mrs. Hopewell at a complete loss. You could say, "My daughter is a nurse," or "My daughter is a schoolteacher," or even, "My daughter is a chemical engineer." You could not say, "My daughter is a philosopher." That was something that had ended with the Greeks and Romans. All day

Joy sat on her neck in a deep chair, reading. Sometimes she went for walks but she didn't like dogs or cats or birds or flowers or nature or nice young men. She looked at nice young men as if she could smell their stupidity.

One day Mrs. Hopewell had picked up one of the books the girl had just put down and opening it at random, she read, "Science, on the other hand, has to assert its soberness and seriousness afresh and declare that it is concerned solely with what-is. Nothing—how can it be for science anything but a horror and a phantasm? If science is right, then one thing stands firm: science wishes to know nothing of nothing. Such is after all the strictly scientific approach to Nothing. We know it by wishing to know nothing of Nothing." These words had been underlined with a blue pencil and they worked on Mrs. Hopewell like some evil incantation in gibberish. She shut the book quickly and went out of the room as if she were having a chill.

This morning when the girl came in, Mrs. Freeman was on Carramae. "She thrown up four times after supper," she said, "and was up twict in the night after three o'clock. Yesterday she didn't do nothing but ramble in the bureau drawer. All she did. Stand up there and see what she could run up on."

"She's got to eat," Mrs. Hopewell muttered, sipping her coffee, while she watched Joy's back at the stove. She was wondering what the child had said to the Bible salesman. She could not imagine what kind of a conversation she could possibly have had with him.

He was a tall gaunt hatless youth who had called yesterday to sell them a Bible. He had appeared at the door, carrying a large black suitcase that weighted him so heavily on one side that he had to brace himself against the door facing. He seemed on the point of collapse but he said in a cheerful voice. "Good morning, Mrs. Cedars!" and set the suitcase down on the mat. He was not a bad-looking young man though he had on a bright blue suit and yellow socks that were not pulled up far enough. He had prominent face bones and a streak of sticky-looking brown hair falling across his forehead.

"I'm Mrs. Hopewell," she said.

"Oh!" he said, pretending to look puzzled but with his eyes sparkling, "I saw it said 'The Cedars' on the mailbox so I thought you was Mrs. Cedars!" and he burst out in a pleasant laugh. He picked up the satchel and under cover of a pant, he fell forward into her hall. It was rather as if the suitcase had moved first, jerking him after it. "Mrs. Hopewell!" he said and grabbed her hand. "I hope you are well!" and he laughed again and then all at once his face sobered completely. He paused and gave her a straight earnest look and said, "Lady, I've come to speak of serious things."

"Well, come in," she muttered, none too pleased because her dinner was almost ready. He came into the parlor and sat down on the edge of a straight chair and put the suitcase between his feet and glanced around the room as if he were sizing her up by it. Her silver gleamed on the two sideboards; she decided he had never been in a room as elegant as this.

"Mrs. Hopewell," he began, using her name in a way that sounded almost intimate, "I know you believe in Chrustian service."

"Well yes," she murmured.

"I know," he said and paused, looking very wise with his head cocked on one side, "that you're a good woman. Friends have told me."

Mrs. Hopewell never liked to be taken for a fool. "What are you selling?" she asked.

"Bibles," the young man said and his eye raced around the room before he added, "I see you have no family Bible in your parlor, I see that is the one lack you got!"

Mrs. Hopewell could not say, "My daughter is an atheist and won't let me keep the Bible in the parlor." She said, stiffening slightly, "I keep my Bible by my bedside." This was not the truth. It was in the attic somewhere.

"Lady," he said, "the word of God ought to be in the parlor."

"Well, I think that's a matter of taste," she began. "I think . . ."

"Lady," he said, "for a Christian, the word of God ought to be in every room in the house besides in his heart. I know you're a Chrustian because I can see it in every line of your face."

She stood up and said, "Well, young man, I don't want to buy a Bible and I smell my dinner burning."

He didn't get up. He began to twist his hands and looking down at them, he said softly, "Well lady, I'll tell you the truth—not many people want to buy one nowadays and besides, I know I'm real simple. I don't know how to say a thing but to say it. I'm just a country boy." He glanced up into her unfriendly face. "People like you don't like to fool with country people like me!"

"Why!" she cried, "good country people are the salt of the earth! Besides, we all have different ways of doing, it takes all kinds to make the world go 'round. That's life!"

"You said a mouthful," he said.

"Why, I think there aren't enough good country people in the world!" she said, stirred. "I think that's what's wrong with it!"

His face had brightened. "I didn't inraduce myself," he said. "I'm Manley Pointer from out in the country around Willohobie, not even from a place, just from near a place."

"You wait a minute," she said. "I have to see about my dinner." She went out to the kitchen and found Joy standing near the door where she had been listening.

"Get rid of the salt of the earth," she said, "and let's eat."

Mrs. Hopewell gave her a pained look and turned the heat down under the vegetables. "*I* can't be rude to anybody," she murmured and went back into the parlor.

He had opened the suitcase and was sitting with a Bible on each knee.

"You might as well put those up," she told him. "I don't want one."

"I appreciate your honesty," he said. "You don't see any more real honest people unless you go way out in the country."

"I know," she said, "real genuine folks!" Through the crack in the door she heard a groan.

"I guess a lot of boys come telling you they're working their way through college," he said, "but I'm not going to tell you that. Somehow," he said, "I don't want to go to college. I want to devote my life to Chrustian service. See," he said, lowering his voice, "I got this heart condition. I may not live long. When you know it's something wrong with you and you may not live long, well then, lady . . ." He paused, with his mouth open, and stared at her.

He and Joy had the same condition! She knew that her eyes were filling with tears but she collected herself quickly and murmured, "Won't you stay for dinner? We'd love to have you!" and was sorry the instant she heard herself say it.

"Yes mam," he said in an abashed voice, "I would sher love to do that!"

Joy had given him one look on being introduced to him and then throughout the meal had not glanced at him again. He had addressed several remarks to her, which she had pretended not to hear. Mrs. Hopewell could not understand deliberate rudeness, although she lived with it, and she felt she had always to overflow with hospitality to make up for Joy's lack of courtesy. She urged him to talk about himself and he did. He said he was the seventh child of twelve and that his father had been crushed under a tree when he himself was eight year old. He had been crushed very badly, in fact, almost cut in two and was practically not recognizable. His mother had got along the best she could by hard working and she had always seen that her children went to Sunday School and that they read the Bible every evening. He was now nineteen year old and he had been selling Bibles for four months. In that time he had sold seventy-seven Bibles and had the promise of two more sales. He wanted to become a missionary because he thought that was the way you could do most for people. "He who losest his life shall find it," he said simply and he was so sincere, so genuine and earnest that Mrs. Hopewell would not for the world have smiled. He prevented his peas from sliding onto the table by blocking them with a piece of bread which he later cleaned his plate with. She could see Joy observing sidewise how he handled his knife and fork and she saw too that every few minutes, the boy would dart a keen appraising glance at the girl as if he were trying to attract her attention.

After dinner Joy cleared the dishes off the table and disappeared and Mrs. Hopewell was left to talk with him. He told her again about his childhood and his father's accident and about various things that had happened to him. Every five minutes or so she would stifle a yawn. He sat for two hours until finally she told him she must go because she had an appointment in town. He packed his Bibles and thanked her and prepared to leave, but in the doorway he stopped and wrung her hand and said that not on any of his trips had he met a lady as nice as her and he asked if he could come again. She had said she would always be happy to see him.

Joy had been standing in the road, apparently looking at something in the distance, when he came down the steps toward her, bent to the side with his heavy valise. He stopped where she was standing and confronted her directly. Mrs. Hopewell could not hear what he said but she trembled to think what Joy would say to him. She could see that after a minute Joy said something and that then the boy began to speak again, making an excited gesture with his free hand. After a minute Joy said something else at which the boy began to speak once more. Then to her amazement, Mrs. Hopewell saw the two of them walk off together, toward the gate. Joy had walked all the way to the gate with him and Mrs. Hopewell could not imagine what they had said to each other, and she had not yet dared to ask.

Mrs. Freeman was insisting upon her attention. She had moved from the refrigerator to the heater so that Mrs. Hopewell had to turn and face her in order to seem to be listening. "Glynese gone out with Harvey Hill again last night," she said. "She had this sty."

"Hill," Mrs. Hopewell said absently, "is that the one who works in the garage?"

"Nome, he's the one that goes to chiropracter school," Mrs. Freeman said. "She had this sty. Been had it two days. So she says when he brought her in the other night he says, 'Lemme get rid of that sty for you,' and she says, 'How?' and he says, 'You just lay yourself down acrost the seat of that car and I'll show you.' So she done it and he popped her neck. Kept on a-popping it several times until she made him quit. This morning," Mrs. Freeman said, "she ain't got no sty. She ain't got no traces of a sty."

"I never heard of that before," Mrs. Hopewell said.

"He ast her to marry him before the Ordinary," Mrs. Freeman went on, "and she told him she wasn't going to be married in no *office*."

"Well, Glynese is a fine girl," Mrs. Hopewell said. "Glynese and Carramae are both fine girls."

"Carramae said when her and Lyman was married Lyman said it sure felt sacred to him. She said he said he wouldn't take five hundred dollars for being married by a preacher."

"How much would he take?" the girl asked from the stove.

"He said he wouldn't take five hundred dollars," Mrs. Freeman repeated.

"Well we all have work to do," Mrs. Hopewell said.

"Lyman said it just felt more sacred to him," Mrs. Freeman said. "The doctor wants Carramae to eat prunes. Says instead of medicine. Says them cramps is coming from pressure. You know where I think it is?"

"She'll be better in a few weeks," Mrs. Hopewell said.

"In the tube," Mrs. Freeman said. "Else she wouldn't be as sick as she is."

Hulga had cracked her two eggs into a saucer and was bringing them to the table along with a cup of coffee that she had filled too full. She sat down carefully and began to eat, meaning to keep Mrs. Freeman there by questions if for any reason she showed an inclination to leave. She could perceive her mother's eye on her. The first round-about question would be about the Bible salesman and she did not wish to bring it on. "How did he pop her neck?" she asked.

Mrs. Freeman went into a description of how he had popped her neck. She said he owned a '55 Mercury but that Glynese said she would rather marry a man with only a '36 Plymouth who would be married by a preacher. The girl asked what if he had a '32 Plymouth and Mrs. Freeman said what Glynese had said was a '36 Plymouth.

Mrs. Hopewell said there were not many girls with Glynese's common sense. She said what she admired in those girls was their common sense. She said that reminded her that they had had a nice visitor yesterday, a young man selling Bibles. "Lord," she said, "he bored me to death but he was so sincere and genuine I couldn't be rude to him. He was just good country people, you know," she said, "just the salt of the earth."

"I seen him walk up," Mrs. Freeman said, "and then later—I seen him walk off," and Hulga could feel the slight shift in her voice, the slight insinuation, that he had not walked off alone, had he? Her face remained expressionless but the color rose into her neck and she seemed to swallow it down with the next spoonful of egg. Mrs. Freeman was looking at her as if they had a secret together.

"Well, it takes all kinds of people to make the world go 'round," Mrs. Hopewell said. "It's very good we aren't all alike."

"Some people are more alike than others," Mrs. Freeman said.

Hulga got up and stumped, with about twice the noise that was necessary, into her room and locked the door. She was to meet the Bible salesman at ten o'clock at the gate. She had thought about it half the night. She had started thinking of it as a great joke and then she had begun to see profound implications in it. She had lain in bed imagining dialogues for them that were insane on the surface but that reached below to depths that no Bible salesman would be aware of. Their conversation yesterday had been of this kind.

He had stopped in front of her and had simply stood there. His face was bony and sweaty and bright, with a little pointed nose in the center of it, and his look was different from what it had been at the dinner table. He was gazing at her with open curiosity, with fascination, like a child watching a new fantastic animal at the zoo, and he was breathing as if he had run a great distance to reach her. His gaze seemed somehow familiar but she could not think where she had been regarded with it before. For almost a minute he didn't say anything. Then on what seemed an insuck of breath, he whispered, "You ever ate a chicken that was two days old?"

The girl looked at him stonily. He might have just put this question up for consideration at the meeting of a philosophical association. "Yes," she presently replied as if she had considered it from all angles.

"It must have been mighty small!" he said triumphantly and shook all over with little nervous giggles, getting very red in the face, and subsiding finally into his gaze of complete admiration, while the girl's expression remained exactly the same.

"How old are you?" he asked softly.

She waited some time before she answered. Then in a flat voice she said, "Seventeen."

His smiles came in succession like waves breaking on the surface of a little lake. "I see you got a wooden leg," he said. "I think you're brave. I think you're real sweet."

The girl stood blank and solid and silent.

"Walk to the gate with me," he said. "You're a brave sweet little thing and I liked you the minute I seen you walk in the door."

Hulga began to move forward.

"What's your name?" he asked, smiling down on the top of her head.

"Hulga," she said.

"Hulga," he murmured, "Hulga. Hulga. I never heard of anybody name Hulga before. You're shy, aren't you, Hulga?" he asked.

She nodded, watching his large red hand on the handle of the giant valise.

"I like girls that wear glasses," he said. "I think a lot. I'm not like these people that a serious thought don't ever enter their heads. It's because I may die."

"I may die too," she said suddenly and looked up at him. His eyes were very small and brown, glittering feverishly.

"Listen," he said, "don't you think some people was meant to meet on account of what all they got in common and all? Like they both think serious thoughts and all?" He shifted the valise to his other hand so that the hand nearest her was free. He caught hold of her elbow and shook it a little. "I don't work on Saturday," he said. "I like to walk in the woods and see what Mother Nature is wearing. O'er the hills and far away. Pic-nics and things. Couldn't we go on a pic-nic tomorrow? Say yes, Hulga," he said and gave her a dying look as if he felt his insides about to drop out of him. He had even seemed to sway slightly toward her.

During the night she had imagined that she seduced him. She imagined that the two of them walked on the place until they came to the storage barn beyond the two back fields and there, she imagined, that things came to such a pass that she very easily seduced him and that then, of course, she had to reckon with his remorse. True genius can get an idea across even to an inferior mind. She imagined that she took his remorse in hand and changed it into a deeper understanding of life. She took all his shame away and turned it into something useful.

She set off for the gate at exactly ten o'clock, escaping without drawing Mrs. Hopewell's attention. She didn't take anything to eat, forgetting that food is usually taken on a picnic. She wore a pair of slacks and a dirty white shirt, and as an afterthought, she had put some Vapex on the collar of it since she did not own any perfume. When she reached the gate no one was there.

She looked up and down the empty highway and had the furious feeling that she had been tricked, that he had only meant to make her walk to the gate after the idea of him. Then suddenly he stood up, very tall, from behind a bush on the opposite embankment. Smiling, he lifted his hat which was new and wide-brimmed. He had not worn it yesterday and she wondered if he had bought it for the occasion. It was toast-colored with a red and white band around it and was slightly too large for him. He stepped from behind the bush still carrying the black valise. He had on the same suit and the same yellow socks sucked down in his shoes from walking. He crossed the highway and said, "I knew you'd come!"

The girl wondered acidly how he had known this. She pointed to the valise and asked, "Why did you bring your Bibles?"

He took her elbow, smiling down on her as if he could not stop. "You can never tell when you'll need the word of God, Hulga," he said. She had a moment in which she doubted that this was actually happening and then they began to climb the embankment. They went down into the pasture toward the woods. The boy walked lightly by her side, bouncing on his toes. The valise did not seem to be heavy today; he even swung it. They crossed half the pasture without saying anything and then, putting his hand easily on the small of her back, he asked softly, "Where does your wooden leg join on?"

She turned an ugly red and glared at him and for an instant the boy looked abashed. "I didn't mean you no harm," he said. "I only meant you're so brave and all. I guess God takes care of you."

"No," she said, looking forward and walking fast, "I don't even believe in God."

At this he stopped and whistled. "No!" he exclaimed as if he were too astonished to say anything else.

She walked on and in a second he was bouncing at her side, fanning with his hat. "That's very unusual for a girl," he remarked, watching her out of the corner of his eye. When they reached the edge of the wood, he put his hand on her back again and drew her against him without a word and kissed her heavily.

The kiss, which had more pressure than feeling behind it, produced that extra surge of adrenalin in the girl that enables one to carry a packed trunk out of a burning house, but in her, the power went at once to the brain. Even before he released her, her mind, clear and detached and ironic anyway, was regarding him from a great distance, with amusement but with pity. She had never been kissed before and she was pleased to discover that it was an unexceptional experience and all a matter of the mind's control. Some people might enjoy drain water if they were told it was vodka. When the boy, looking expectant but uncertain, pushed her gently away, she turned and walked on, saying nothing as if such business, for her, were common enough.

He came along panting at her side, trying to help her when he saw a root that she might trip over. He caught and held back the long swaying blades of thorn vine until she had passed beyond them. She led the way and he came breathing heavily behind her. Then they came out on a sunlit hillside, sloping softly into another one a little smaller. Beyond, they could see the rusted top of the old barn where the extra hay was stored.

The hill was sprinkled with small pink weeds. "Then you ain't saved?" he asked suddenly, stopping.

The girl smiled. It was the first time she had smiled at him at all. "In my economy," she said, "I'm saved and you are damned but I told you I didn't believe in God."

Nothing seemed to destroy the boy's look of admiration. He gazed at her now as if the fantastic animal at the zoo had put its paw through the bars and given him a loving poke. She thought he looked as if he wanted to kiss her again and she walked on before he had the chance.

"Ain't there somewheres we can sit down sometime?" he murmured, his voice softening toward the end of the sentence.

"In that barn," she said.

They made for it rapidly as if it might slide away like a train. It was a large two-story barn, cool and dark inside. The boy pointed up the ladder that led into the loft and said, "It's too bad we can't go up there."

"Why can't we?" she asked.

"Yer leg," he said reverently.

The girl gave him a contemptuous look and putting both hands on the ladder, she climbed it while he stood below, apparently awestruck. She pulled herself expertly through the opening and then looked down at him and said, "Well, come on if you're coming," and he began to climb the ladder, awkwardly bringing the suitcase with him.

"We won't need the Bible," she observed.

"You never can tell," he said, panting. After he had got into the loft, he was a few seconds catching his breath. She had sat down in a pile of straw. A wide sheath of sunlight, filled with dust particles, slanted over her. She lay back against a bale, her face turned away, looking out the front opening of the barn where hay was thrown from a wagon into the loft. The two pink-speckled hillsides lay back against a dark ridge of woods. The sky was cloudless and cold blue. The boy dropped down by her side and put one arm under her and the other over her and began methodically kissing her face, making little noises like a fish. He did not remove his hat but it was pushed far enough back not to interfere. When her glasses got in his way, he took them off of her and slipped them into his pocket.

The girl at first did not return any of the kisses but presently she began to and after she had put several on his cheek, she reached his lips and remained there, kissing him again and again as if she were trying to draw all the breath out of him. His breath was clear and sweet like a child's and the kisses were sticky like a child's. He mumbled about loving her and about knowing when he first seen her that he loved her, but the mumbling was like the sleepy fretting of a child being put to sleep by his mother. Her mind, throughout this, never stopped or lost itself for a second to her feelings. "You ain't said you loved me none," he whispered finally, pulling back from her. "You got to say that."

She looked away from him off into the hollow sky and then down at a black ridge and then down farther into what appeared to be two green swelling lakes. She didn't realize he had taken her glasses but this landscape could not seem exceptional to her for she seldom paid any close attention to her surroundings.

"You got to say it," he repeated. "You got to say you love me."

She was always careful how she committed herself. "In a sense," she began, "if you use the word loosely, you might say that. But it's not a word I use. I don't have illusions. I'm one of those people who see *through* to nothing."

The boy was frowning. "You got to say it. I said it and you got to say it," he said.

The girl looked at him almost tenderly. "You poor baby," she murmured. "It's just as well you don't understand," and she pulled him by the neck, face-down, against her. "We are all damned," she said, "but some of us have taken off our blindfolds and see that there's nothing to see. It's a kind of salvation."

The boy's astonished eyes looked blankly through the ends of her hair. "Okay," he almost whined, "but do you love me or don'tcher?"

"Yes," she said and added, "in a sense. But I must tell you something. There mustn't be anything dishonest between us." She lifted his head and looked him in the eye. "I am thirty years old," she said. "I have a number of degrees."

The boy's look was irritated but dogged. "I don't care," he said. "I don't care a thing about what all you done. I just want to know if you love me or don'tcher?" and he caught her to him and wildly planted her face with kisses until she said, "Yes, Yes."

"Okay then," he said, letting her go. "Prove it."

She smiled, looking dreamily out on the shifty landscape. She had seduced him without even making up her mind to try. "How?" she asked, feeling that he should be delayed a little.

He leaned over and put his lips to her ear. "Show me where your wooden leg joins on," he whispered.

The girl uttered a sharp little cry and her face instantly drained of color. The obscenity of the suggestion was not what shocked her. As a child she had sometimes been subject to feelings of shame but education had removed the last traces of that as a good surgeon scrapes for cancer; she would no more have felt it over what he was asking than she would have believed in his Bible. But she was as sensitive about the artificial leg as a peacock about his tail. No one ever touched it but her. She took care of it as someone else would his soul, in private and almost with her own eyes turned away, "No," she said.

"I known it," he muttered, sitting up. "You're just playing me for a sucker."

"Oh no no!" she cried. "It joins on at the knee. Only at the knee. Why do you want to see it?"

The boy gave her a long penetrating look. "Because," he said, "it's what makes you different. You ain't like anybody else."

She sat staring at him. There was nothing about her face or her round freezing-blue eyes to indicate that this had moved her; but she felt as if her heart had stopped and left her mind to pump her blood. She decided that for the first time in her life she was face to face with real innocence. This boy, with an instinct that came from beyond wisdom, had touched the truth about her. When after a minute, she said in a hoarse high voice, "All right," it was like surrendering to him completely. It was like losing her own life and finding it again, miraculously, in his.

Very gently he began to roll the slack leg up. The artificial limb, in a white sock and brown flat shoe, was bound in a heavy material like canvas and ended in an ugly jointure where it was attached to the stump. The boy's face and his voice were entirely reverent as he uncovered it and said, "Now show me how to take it off and on."

She took it off for him and put it back on again and then he took it off himself, handling it as tenderly as if it were a real one. "See!" he said with a delighted child's face. "Now I can do it myself!"

"Put it back on," she said. She was thinking that she would run away with him and that every night he would take the leg off and every morning put it back on again. "Put it back on," she said.

"Not yet," he murmured, setting it on its foot out of her reach. "Leave it off for a while. You got me instead."

She gave a little cry of alarm but he pushed her down and began to kiss her again. Without the leg she felt entirely dependent on him. Her brain seemed to have stopped thinking altogether and to be about some other function that it was not very good at. Different expressions raced back and forth over her face. Every now and then the boy, his eyes like two steel spikes, would glance behind him where the leg stood. Finally she pushed him off and said, "Put it back on me now."

"Wait," he said. He leaned the other way and pulled the valise toward him and opened it. It had a pale blue spotted lining and there were only two Bibles in it. He took one of these out and opened the cover of it. It was hollow and contained a pocket flask of whiskey, a pack of cards, and a small blue box with printing on it. He laid these out in front of her one at a time in an evenly-spaced row, like one presenting offerings at the shrine of a goddess. He put the blue box in her hand. THIS PRODUCT TO BE USED ONLY FOR THE PREVENTION OF DISEASE, she read, and dropped it. The boy was unscrewing the top of the flask. He stopped and pointed, with a smile, to the deck of cards. It was not an ordinary deck but one with an obscene picture on the back of each card. "Take a swig," he said, offering her the bottle first. He held it in front of her, but like one mesmerized, she did not move.

Her voice when she spoke had an almost pleading sound. "Aren't you," she murmured, "aren't you just good country people?"

The boy cocked his head. He looked as if he were just beginning to understand that she might be trying to insult him. "Yeah," he said, curling his lip slightly, "but it ain't held me back none. I'm as good as you any day in the week."

"Give me my leg," she said.

He pushed it farther away with his foot. "Come on now, let's begin to have us a good time," he said coaxingly. "We ain't got to know one another good yet."

"Give me my leg!" she screamed and tried to lunge for it but he pushed her down easily.

"What's the matter with you all of a sudden?" he asked, frowning as he screwed the top on the flask and put it quickly back inside the Bible. "You just a while ago said you didn't believe in nothing. I thought you was some girl!"

Her face was almost purple. "You're a Christian!" she hissed. "You're a fine Christian! You're just like them all—say one thing and do another. You're a perfect Christian, you're . . ."

The boy's mouth was set angrily. "I hope you don't think," he said in a lofty indignant tone, "that I believe in that crap! I may sell Bibles but I know which end is up and I wasn't born yesterday and I know where I'm going!"

"Give me my leg!" she screeched. He jumped up so quickly that she barely saw him sweep the cards and the blue box into the Bible and throw the Bible into the valise. She saw him grab the leg and then she saw it for an instant slanted forlornly across the inside of the suitcase with a Bible at either side of its opposite ends. He slammed the lid shut and snatched up the valise and swung it down the hole and then stepped through himself.

When all of him had passed but his head, he turned and regarded her with a look that no longer had any admiration in it. "I've gotten a lot of interesting things," he said. "One time I got a woman's glass eye this way. And you needn't to think you'll catch me because Pointer ain't really my name. I use a different name at every house I call at and don't stay nowhere long. And I'll tell you another thing, Hulga," he said, using the name as if he didn't think much of it, "you ain't so smart. I been believing in nothing ever since I was born!" and then the toast-colored hat disappeared down the hole and the girl was left, sitting on the straw in the dusty sunlight. When she turned her churning face toward the opening, she saw his blue figure struggling successfully over the green speckled lake.

Mrs. Hopewell and Mrs. Freeman, who were in the back pasture, digging up onions, saw him emerge a little later from the woods and head across the meadow toward the highway. "Why, that looks like that nice dull young man that tried to sell me a Bible yesterday," Mrs. Hopewell said, squinting. "He must have been selling them to the Negroes back in there. He was so simple," he said, "but I guess the world would be better off if we were all that simple."

Mrs. Freeman's gaze drove forward and just touched him before he disappeared under the hill. Then she returned her attention to the evil-smelling onion shoot she was lifting from the ground. "Some can't be that simple," she said. "I know I never could."

Michael Thomas

THE LOSER

Michael Thomas *(1972–) peers into the interior of a man at the cusp of either success or failure. The protagonist of Thomas's first novel,* Man Gone Down *(2007), has come up short lately, and the past is coming back at him. Early slights, discords and disadvantages, and squandered opportunities now seem more pivotal. Early triumphs, once interpreted as assurances of an upward arc, now seem more contingent. The way he listens to his fretting self carries both the exoticism of unknowable past circumstances and the banality of financial and moral perils in midlife—a poised agony akin, in its brave intimacy, to Cheever's Johnny Hake (see page 105), not to mention Ralph Ellison's invisible man and, farther afield, Dostoevsky's man from underground. Michael Thomas was raised in Boston and has spent time working as a cab driver, carpenter, and filmmaker, among other things. He teaches creative writing at Hunter College, where he earned his bachelor's degree; he received his MFA from Warren Wilson College. He lives in Brooklyn with his wife and three children.*

I know I'm not doing well. I have an emotional relationship with a fish—Thomas Strawberry. My oldest son, C, named him, and that name was given weight because a six-year-old voiced it as though he'd had an epiphany: *"He looks like a strawberry."* The three adults in the room had nodded in agreement.

"I only gave you one," his godfather, Jack, the marine biologist, told him. "If you have more than one, they kill each other." Jack laughed. He doesn't have kids. He doesn't know that one's not supposed to speak of death in front of them and cackle. One speaks of death in hushed, sober tones—the way one speaks of alcoholism, race, or secret bubble gum a younger sibling can't have. Jack figured it out on some level from

the way both C and X looked at him blankly and then stared into the small aquarium, perhaps envisioning a battle royal between a bowlful of savage little fish, or the empty space left behind. We left the boys in their bedroom and took the baby with us. *"They don't live very long,"* he whispered to us. *"About six weeks."* That was C's birthday in February. It's August, and he's not dead.

He's with me on the desk, next to my stack of books and legal pads. I left my laptop at my mother-in-law's for C to use. She'd raised an eyebrow as I started to the door. Allegedly, my magnum opus was on that hard drive—the book that would launch my career and provide me with the financial independence she desired. *"I write better if the first draft is longhand."* She hadn't believed me. It had been a Christmas gift from Claire. I remember opening it and being genuinely surprised. All three children had stopped to see what was in the box.

"Merry Christmas, honey," she'd cooed in my ear. She then took me by the chin and gently turned my face to meet hers. *"This is your year."* She kissed me—too long—and the children, in unison, looked away. The computer was sleek and gray and brimming with the potential to organize my thoughts, my work, my time. It would help extract that last portion of whatever it was that I was working on and buff it with the requisite polish to make it salable. *"This is our year."* Her eyes looked glazed, as though she had been intoxicated by the machine's power, the early hour, and the spirit of the season. It had been bought, I was sure, with her mother's money. And I knew Edith had never believed me to have any literary talent, but she'd wanted to make her daughter feel supported and loved—although she probably had expected it to end like this. C had seemed happy when I left, though, sitting on the floor with his legs stretched under the coffee table, the glow from the screen washing out his copper skin.

"Bye, C."

"By-ye." He'd made it two syllables. He hadn't looked up.

Marco walks up the stairs and stops outside his kid's study, where I'm working. He knocks on the door. I don't know whether to be thankful or annoyed, but the door's open and it's his house. I try to be as friendly as I can.

"Yo!"

"Yo! What's up?" He walks in. I turn halfway and throw him a wave. He comes to the desk and looks down at the stack of legal pads.

"Damn, you're cranking it out, man."

"I'm writing for my life." He laughs. I don't. I wonder if he notices.

"Is it a novel?"

I can't explain to him that three pads are one novel and seven are another, but what I'm working on is a short story. I can't tell him that each hour I have what I believe to be an epiphany, and I must begin again—thinking about my life.

"Want to eat something?"

"No thanks, man, I have to finish this part."

I turn around on the stool. I'm being rude. He's moved back to the doorway, leaning. His tie's loose. He holds his leather bag in one hand and a fresh beer in the other. He's dark haired, olive skinned, and long nosed. He's five-ten and in weekend racquetball shape. He stands there, framed by a clear, solid maple jamb. Next to him is more millwork—a solid maple bookcase, wonderfully spare, with books and photos and his son's trophies. There's a picture of his boy with C. They were on the same peewee soccer team. They're grinning, holding trophies in front of what I believe to be my leg. Marco clinks his wedding band on the bottle. I stare at him. I've forgotten what we were talking about. I hope he'll pick me up.

"Want me to bring you something back?"

"No, man. Thanks, I'm good."

I'm broke, but I can't tell him this because while his family's away on Long Island for the summer, I'm sleeping in his kid's bed and he earns daily what I, at my best, earn in a month, because he has a beautiful home, because in spite of all this, I like him. I believe he's a decent man.

"All right, man." He goes to take a sip, then stops. He's probably learned of my drinking problem through the neighborhood gossip channels, but he's never confirmed any of it with me.

"Call me on the cell if you change your mind."

He leaves. In the margins, I tally our monthly costs. *We need to make $140,000 a year,*" Claire told me last week. I compute that I'll have to teach twenty-two freshman comp sections a semester as well as pick up full-time work as a carpenter. Thomas Strawberry swims across his bowl to face me.

"I fed you," I say to him as though he's my dog. He floats, puckering his fish lips. Thomas, at one time, had the whole family copying his pucker face, but the boys got tired of it. The little one, my girl, kept doing it—the fish, the only animal she'd recognize. *What does the cow say?* I'd ask *What does the cat say?* She'd stare at me, blankly, giving me the deadeye that only children can give—a glimpse of her indecipherable consciousness. *What does the fish say?* She'd pucker, the same way as when I'd ask her for a kiss—the fish face and a forehead to the cheekbone.

I packed my wife and kids into my mother-in-law's enormous Mercedes Benz at 7:45 p.m. on Friday, June 26. It was essential for both Claire and her mother to leave Brooklyn by eight with the kids fed and washed and ready for sleep for the three-and-a-half-hour drive to Massachusetts. Claire, I suppose, had learned the trick of planning long drives around sleeping schedules from her mother. Road trips required careful planning and the exact execution of those plans. I'd have to park in the bus stop on Atlantic Avenue in front of our building then run the bags, toys, books, and snacks down the stairs, trying to beat the thieves and meter maids. Then I'd signal for Claire to bring the kids down, and we'd strap them into their seats, equipping them with juice and crackers and their special toys. Then, in her mind, she'd make one last sweep of the house, while I'd calculate the cost of purchasing whatever toiletries I knew I'd left behind.

After the last bathroom check and the last seatbelt check, we'd be off. We'd sing. We'd tell stories. We'd play I Spy. Then one kid would drop off and we'd shush the other two until Jersey or Connecticut and continue to shush until the last one dropped. There's something about children sleeping in cars, perhaps something felt by parents, and perhaps only by the parents of multiple children—their heads tilted, their mouths open, eyes closed. The stillness and the quiet that had vanished from your life returns, but you must be quiet—respect their stillness, their silence. You must also make the most of it. It's when you speak about important things that you don't want them to hear: money, time, death—we'd almost whisper. We'd honor their breath, their silence, knowing that their faces would be changed each time they awoke, one nap older, that less easily lulled to sleep. Before we had children, we joked, we played music loud, we talked about a future with children. *"What do you think they'll be like?"* she'd ask. But I knew I could never voice the image in my head and make it real for her—our child; my broad head, her sharp nose, blond afro, and freckles—the cacophony phenotype alone caused. I would shake my head. She'd smile and whine, *"What?"* playfully, as though I was flirting with or teasing her, but in actuality, I was reeling from the picture of the imagined face, the noise inside her dichotomized mind, and the ache of his broken mongrel heart.

X was already beginning to fade when Edith turned on the engine. The sun was setting over the East River. The corrugated metal warehouses, the giant dinosaur-like cranes, and the silver chassis of the car were swept with a mix of rosy light and shadow. I used to drink on a hill in a park outside of Boston with my best friend, Gavin. He'd gotten too drunk at too many high school parties and he wasn't welcome at them anymore, so we drank by ourselves outside. We'd say nothing and watch the sun set. And when the light was gone from the sky, one of us would try to articulate whatever was troubling us that day.

"Okay, honey." Claire was buckling up. "We're all in." Edith tried to smile at me and mouthed, *"Bye."* She took a hand off the wheel and gave a short wave. I closed C's door and looked in at him to wave good-bye, but he was watching the dome light slowly fade from halogen white through orange to umber—soft and warm enough through its transitions to temporarily calm the brassiness of Edith's hair. I saw him say, *"Cool"* as it dulled, suspended on the ceiling, emberlike. Perhaps it reminded him of a fire he'd once seen in its dying stages, or a sunset. I watched him until it went off, and there was more light outside the car than in and he was partially obscured by my reflection.

C said something to his grandmother and his window lowered. He unbuckled himself and got up on his knees. Edith put the car in gear.

"Sit down and buckle up, hon." C didn't acknowledge her and stuck his hand out the window.

"Say good-bye to your dad."

"Bye, Daddy."

There was something about *daddy* versus *dad*. Something that made it seem as though it was the last good-bye he'd say to me as a little boy: X's eyes were closed. My girl yawned, shook her head, searched for and then found her bottle in her lap. C was still waving. Edith rolled up all the windows. Claire turned to tell him to sit, and they pulled away.

Thomas Strawberry's bowl looks cloudy. There's bright green algae growing on the sides, leftover food and what I imagine to be fish poop on the bottom—charcoal-green balls that list back and forth, betraying an underwater current. Cleaning his bowl is always difficult for me because the risk of killing him seems so high. I don't know how much trauma a little fish can handle. So I hold off cleaning until his habitat resembles something like a bayou backwater—more suitable for a catfish than for Thomas. He has bright orange markings and elaborate fins. He looks flimsy—effete. I can't imagine him fighting anything, especially one of his own.

I tap the glass and remember aquarium visits and classroom fish tanks. There was always a sign or a person in charge warning not to touch the glass. Thomas swims over to me, and while he examines my fingertip, I sneak the net in behind him. I scoop him out of the water. He wriggles and then goes limp. He does this every time, and every time I think I've killed him. I let him out into his temporary lodgings. He darts out of the net, back to life, and swims around the much smaller confines of the cereal bowl. I clean his bowl in the bathroom sink and refill it with the tepid water I believe he likes. I go back to the desk. He's stopped circling. I slowly pour him back in. I wonder if his stillness, in the net is because of shock or if he's playing possum. The latter of the two ideas suggests the possibility of a fishy consciousness. Since school begins for the boys in two weeks and I haven't found an apartment, a job, or paid tuition, I let it go.

I wonder if I'm too damaged. Baldwin somewhere once wrote about someone who had *"a wound that he would never recover from,"* but I don't remember where. He also wrote about a missing member that was lost but still aching. Maybe something inside of me was no longer intact. Perhaps something had been cut off or broken down—collateral damage of the diaspora. Marco seems to be intact. Perhaps he was damaged, too. Perhaps whatever he'd had was completely lost, or never there. I wonder if I'm too damaged. Thomas Strawberry puckers at me. I tap the glass. He swims away.

I had a girlfriend in high school named Sally, and one day I told her everything. How at the age of six I'd been treed by an angry mob of adults who hadn't liked the idea of Boston busing. They threw rocks up at me, yelling, *"Nigger go home!"* And how the policeman who rescued me called me *"Sammy."* How I'd been sodomized in the bathroom of the Brighton Boys Club when I was seven, and how later that year, my mother, divorced and broke, began telling me that she should've flushed me down the toilet when she'd had the chance. I told Sally that from the day we met, I'd been writing poems about it all, for her, which I then gave to her. She held the book of words like it was a cold brick, with a glassy film, not tears, forming in front of her eyes. I fear, perhaps, that I'm too damaged. In the margins of the yellow pad I write down titles for the story—unholy trinities: *Drunk, Black, and Stupid. Black, Broke, and Stupid. Drunk, Black, and Blue.* The last seems the best the most melodic, the least concrete. Whether or not it was a mystery remained to be seen.

The phone rings. It's Claire.

"Happy almost birthday."

"Thanks."

It's been three weeks since I've seen my family. Three weeks of over-the-phone progress reports. We've used up all the platitudes we know. Neither of us can stand it.

"Are you coming?"

"Yeah."

"How?"

It's a setup. She knows I can't afford the fare.

"Do you have something lined up for tomorrow?"

"Yeah," I answer. As of now it's a lie, but it's nine. I have till Labor Day to come up with several thousand dollars for a new apartment and long overdue bills, plus an extra fifty for the bus. It's unlikely, but not unreasonable.

"Did you get the security check from Marta?" she asks, excited for a moment that someone owes us money.

"No."

"Fuck." She breathes. Claire's never been convincing when she curses. She sighs purposefully into the receiver. "Do you have a plan?"

"I'll make a plan."

"Will you let me know?"

"I'll let you know."

"I dropped my mother at the airport this morning."

"It's her house. I like your mother." It's a lie, but I've never, in the twelve years we've been together, shown any evidence of my contempt.

"I think C wants a Ronaldo shirt." She stops. "Not the club team. He wants a Brazil one." Silence again. "Is that possible?"

"I'll try." More silence. "How's your nose?"

"It's fine." She sighs. She waits. I can tell she's crunching numbers in her head. She turns her voice up to sound excited. "We'd all love to see you," then turns it back down—soft, caring, to pad the directive. "Make a plan."

James Agee

MONEY

James Agee *(1909–1955) was born in Tennessee and educated at Phillips Ex-
eter Academy and Harvard College, from which he graduated in 1932, amid the
throes of the Great Depression. He soon joined the staff of* Fortune *magazine,
Henry Luce's inspired monthly tribute to ascendant capitalism, whose first issue
was published in February 1930. In 1936, Agee was sent on assignment with a
fellow staffer, the photographer Walker Evans, to report on conditions among the
rural tenant farms in Hale County, Alabama.* Fortune *declined to publish the
report Agee and Evans sent back, but their book* Let Us Now Praise Famous
Men—*a classic double take of documentary observation (without recourse to "fiction") asking what a certain kind of grinding economic frustration does not only
of the person suffering it, but also to two observers diligently reporting, though not
without opinions, or even a healthy dose of righteous rancor—made it into print
in 1941. The excerpts below are from that book. Agee distinguished himself as a
novelist, poet, and screenwriter before his cruelly early death, at age forty-five, of
a heart attack he suffered while riding in a New York taxicab on the way to a doctor's appointment.*

Woods and Ricketts work for Michael and T. Hudson Margraves, two
brothers, in partnership, who live in Cookstown. Gudger worked for
the Margraves for three years; he now (1936) works for Chester Boles,
who lives two miles south of Cookstown.

On their business arrangements, and working histories, and on their
money, I wrote a chapter too long for inclusion in this volume without
sacrifice of too much else. I will put in its place here as extreme a précis
as I can manage.

Gudger has no home, no land, no mule; none of the more important
farming implements. He must get all these of his landlord. Boles, for

his share of the corn and cotton, also advances him rations money during four months of the year, March through June, and his fertilizer.

Gudger pays him back with his labor and with the labor of his family.

At the end of the season he pays him back further: with half his corn; with half his cotton; with half his cottonseed. Out of his own half of these crops he also pays him back the rations money, plus interest, and his share of the fertilizer, plus interest, and such other debts, plus interest, as he may have incurred.

What is left, once doctors' bills and other debts have been deducted, is his year's earnings.

Gudger is a straight half-crop or sharecropper.

Woods and Ricketts own no home and no land, but Woods owns one mule and Ricketts owns two, and they own their farming implements. Since they do not have to rent these tools and animals, they work under a slightly different arrangement. They give over to the landlord only a third of their cotton and a fourth of their corn. Out of their own parts of the crop, however, they owe him the price of two thirds of their cotton fertilizer and three fourths of their corn fertilizer, plus interest; and, plus interest, the same debts on rations money.

Woods and Ricketts are tenants: they work on third and fourth.

A very few tenants pay cash rent: but these two types of arrangement, with local variants (company stores; food instead of rations money; slightly different divisions of the crops) are basic to cotton tenantry all over the South.

From March through June, while the cotton is being cultivated, they live on the rations money.

From July through to late August, while the cotton is making, they live however they can.

From late August through October or into November, during the picking and ginning season, they live on the money from their share of the cottonseed.

From then on until March, they live on whatever they have earned in the year; or however they can.

During six to seven months of each year, then—that is, during exactly such time as their labor with the cotton is of absolute necessity to the landlord—they can be sure of whatever living is possible in rations advances and in cottonseed money.

During five to six months of the year, of which three are the hardest months of any year, with the worst of weather, the least adequacy of shelter, the worst and least of food, the worst of health, quite normal and inevitable, they can count on nothing except that they may hope least of all for any help from their landlords.

Gudger—a family of six—lives on ten dollars a month rations money during four months of the year. He has lived on eight, and on six. Woods—a family of six—until this year was unable to get better than eight a month during the same period; this year he managed to get it up to ten. Ricketts—a family of nine—lives on ten dollars a month during this spring and early summer period.

This debt is paid back in the fall at eight per cent interest. Eight per cent is charged also on the fertilizer and on all other debts which tenants incur in this vicinity.

At the normal price, a half-sharing tenant gets about six dollars a bale from his share of the cottonseed. A one-mule, half-sharing tenant makes on the average three bales. This half-cropper, then, Gudger, can count on eighteen dollars, more or less, to live on during the picking and ginning: though he gets nothing until his first bale is ginned.

Working on third and fourth, a tenant gets the money from two thirds of the cottonseed of each bale: nine dollars to the bale. Woods, with one mule, makes three bales, and gets twenty-seven dollars. Ricketts, with two mules, makes and gets twice that, to live on during the late summer and fall.

What is earned at the end of a given year is never to be depended on and, even late in a season, is never predictable. It can be enough to tide through the dead months of the winter, sometimes even better: it can be enough, spread very thin, to take through two months, and a sickness, or six weeks, or a month: it can be little enough to be completely meaningless: it can be nothing: it can be enough less than nothing to insure a tenant only of an equally hopeless lack of money at the end of his next year's work: and whatever one year may bring in the way of good luck, there is never any reason to hope that that luck will be repeated in the next year or the year after that.

The best that Woods has ever cleared was $1300 during a war year. During the teens and twenties he fairly often cleared as much as $300; he fairly often cleared $50 and less; two or three times he ended the year in debt. During the depression years he has more often cleared $50 and less; last year he cleared $150, but serious illness during the winter ate it up rapidly.

The best that Gudger has ever cleared is $125. That was in the plow-under year. He felt exceedingly hopeful and bought a mule: but when his landlord warned him of how he was coming out the next year, he sold it. Most years he has not made more than $25 to $30; and about one year in three he has ended in debt. Year before last he wound up $80 in debt; last year, $12; of Boles, his new landlord, the first thing he had to do was borrow $15 to get through the winter until rations advances should begin.

Years ago the Ricketts were, relatively speaking, almost prosperous. Besides their cotton farming they had ten cows and sold the milk, and they lived near a good stream and had all the fish they wanted. Ricketts went $400 into debt on a fine young pair of mules. One of the mules died before it had made its first crop; the other died the year after; against his fear, amounting to full horror, of sinking to the half-crop level where nothing is owned, Ricketts went into debt for other, inferior mules; his cows went one by one into debts and desperate exchanges and by sickness; he got congestive chills; his wife got pellagra; a number of his children died; he got appendicitis and lay for days on end under the ice cap; his wife's pellagra got into her brain; for ten consecutive years now, though they have lived on so little rations money, and have turned nearly all their cottonseed money toward their debts, they have not cleared or had any hope of clearing a cent at the end of the year.

* * *

It is not often, then, at the end of the season, that a tenant clears
enough money to tide him through the winter, or even an appreciable
part of it. More generally he can count on it that, during most of the
four months between settlement time in the fall and the beginning of
work and resumption of rations advances in the early spring, he will
have no money and can expect none, nor any help, from his landlord:
and of having no money during the six midsummer weeks of laying by,
he can be still more sure. Four to six months of each year, in other
words, he is much more likely than not to have nothing whatever, and
during these months he must take care for himself: he is no responsibility of the landlord's. All he can hope to do is find work. This is hard, because there are a good many chronically unemployed in the towns, and
they are more convenient to most openings for work and can at all
times be counted on if they are needed; also there is no increase, during
these two dead farming seasons, of other kinds of work to do. And so,
with no more jobs open than at any other time of year, and with plenty
of men already convenient to take them, the whole tenant population,
hundreds and thousands in any locality, are desperately in need of work.

A landlord saves up certain odd jobs for these times of year: they go,
at less than he would have to pay others, to those of his tenants who
happen to live nearest or to those he thinks best of; and even at best
they don't amount to much.

When there is wooded land on the farm, a landlord ordinarily per-
mits a tenant to cut and sell firewood for what he can get. About the
best a tenant gets of this is a dollar a load, but more often (for the market is glutted, so many are trying to sell wood) he can get no better than
half that and less, and often enough, at the end of a hard day's peddling,
miles from home, he will let it go for a quarter or fifteen cents rather
than haul it all the way home again: so it doesn't amount to much.
Then, too, by no means everyone has wood to cut and sell: in the whole
southern half of the county we were working mainly in, there was so little wood that the negroes, during the hard winter of 1935–36, were
burning parts of their fences, outbuildings, furniture and houses, and
were dying off in great and not seriously counted numbers, of pneumo-
nia and other afflictions of the lungs.

WPA work is available to very few tenants: they are, technically, employed, and thus have no right to it: and if by chance they manage to get it, landlords are more likely than not to intervene. They feel it spoils a tenant to be paid wages, even for a little while. A tenant who so much as tries to get such work is under disapproval.

There is not enough direct relief even for the widows and the old of the county.

Gudger and Ricketts, during this year, were exceedingly lucky. After they, and Woods, had been turned away from government work, they found work in a sawmill. They were given the work on condition that they stay with it until the mill was moved, and subject strictly to their landlords' permission: and their employer wouldn't so much as hint how long the work might last. Their landlords quite grudgingly gave them permission, on condition that they pay for whatever help was needed in their absence during the picking season. Gudger hired a hand, at eight dollars a month and board. Ricketts did not need to: his family is large enough. They got a dollar and a quarter a day five days a week and seventy-five cents on Saturday, seven dollars a week, ten hours' work a day. Woods did not even try for this work: he was too old and too sick.

The family exists for work. It exists to keep itself alive. It is a cooperative economic unit. The father does one set of tasks; the mother another; the children still a third, with the sons and daughters serving apprenticeship to their father and mother respectively. A family is called a force, without irony; and children come into the world chiefly that they may help with the work and that through their help the family may increase itself. Their early years are leisurely, a child's life work begins as play. Among his first imitative gestures are gestures of work; and the whole initiative course of his maturing and biologic envy is a stepladder of the learning of physical tasks and skills.

This work solidifies, and becomes steadily more and more, in greater and greater quantity and variety, an integral part of his life.

Besides imitation, he works if he is a man under three compulsions, in three stages. First for his parents. Next for himself, single and wandering in the independence of his early manhood: "for himself," in the sense that he wants to stay alive, or better, and has no one dependent on him. Third, for himself and his wife and his family, under an employer. A woman works just for her parents; next, without a transition phase, for her husband and family.

Work for your parents is one thing: work "for yourself" is another. They are both hard enough, yet light, relative to what is to come. On the day you are married, at about sixteen if you are a girl, at about twenty if you are a man, a key is turned, with a sound not easily audible, and you are locked between the stale earth and the sky; the key turns in the lock behind you, and your full life's work begins, and there is nothing conceivable for which it can afford to stop short of your death, which is a long way off. It is perhaps at its best during the first two years or so, when you are young and perhaps are still enjoying one another or have not yet lost all hope, and when there are not yet so many children as to weigh on you. It is perhaps at its worst during the next ten to twelve years, when there are more and more children, but none of them old enough, yet, to be much help. One could hardly describe it as slackening off after that, for in proportion with the size of the family, it has been necessary to take on more land and more work, and, too, a son or daughter gets just old enough to be any full good to you, and marries or strikes out for himself: yet it is true, anyhow, that from then on there are a number of strong and fairly responsible people in the household besides the man and his wife. In really old age, with one of the two dead, and the children all married, and the widowed one making his home among them in the slow rotations of a floated twig, waiting to die, it does ease off some, depending more then on the individual: one may choose to try to work hard and seem still capable, out of duty and the wish to help, or out of "egoism," or out of the dread of dropping out of life; or one may relax, and live unnoticed, never spoken to, dead already; or again, life may have acted on you in such a way that you have no choice in it: or still again, with a wife dead, and children gone, and a long hard lifetime behind you, you may choose to marry again and begin the whole cycle over, lifting onto your back the great weight a young man carries, as Woods has done.

Studs Terkel

I WAS DROPPED

Studs Terkel *(1912–) has devoted much of his eventful life to recording the stories of ordinary Americans. He has also turned his microphone on himself, in memoirs including* Talking to Myself: A Memoir of My Times *(1977) and most recently* Touch and Go *(2007), published when he was ninety-five. Terkel was awarded a Pulitzer Prize for* "The Good War": An Oral History of World War II *(1984). Among his many other books are* Hard Times *(1980),* American Dreams: Lost and Found *(1983), and his classic oral history* Working: People Talk About What They Do All Day and How They Feel About What They Do *(1974), from which the selection below is reprinted.*

PETER KEELEY

"I sell draperies. I've done that for many years. In the past I've manufactured them. It was my business. It's no longer my business. I sell the product I used to make. It was a come down when I went broke. I don't believe it is today. I believe it is an adjustment to age. I think it's a victory. There's many men in the same condition, have given up and first rotted. Quite a few of my old friends. Not me."

He is sixty-five years old.

"Originally, I started selling in New England. Broad silks. Small stores, hardheaded New England Yankees. It was quite an education. If you can sell them, you can sell anybody. In 1941 they moved me to Pittsburgh for forty dollars a week, I became branch manager. I was quite successful—until the present day."

* * *

The company I was running the business for sold out to a corporation on the West Coast—a merger. I was dropped. It was company policy: no man older than forty-five. Everybody was merging. A lot of people got dropped by the wayside. I didn't bounce. That hurt my ego. It hurt me in twenty directions. I got cold feet, scared. It was a year ago, November. I was sixty-four. Many friends drop you, many people don't know you. You have to fight your own way—which I've done all my life. I'm damn well adjusted now.

I brought this branch from about a hundred thousand dollars a year to a million and a half. There was no great shakes over that. I was frantically, insanely mad. (Laughs.) I spent four months going insane. Another month, I probably would burn the building down and kill myself. I blamed everything on everybody.

These days I'm drawing $128 a week for a company I'm handling inventory for. And purchasing. He has a seventy-thousand-dollar inventory, about a hundred thousand yards. No fabric can come in, be cut, go out without me knowing it. I work very hard until about noon.

I run a little business of my own and make about three hundred dollars a month—a decorating business, a tiny company. A few jobs here and there. I work on this a couple of hours in the afternoon. I very seldom go out to lunch.

I call my customers cold turkey. I look in the book and call ten people: "Do you want draperies or don't you?" You'd be surprised. (Laughs.) It's like the guy that said to twenty girls, "Would you go to bed with me?" Nineteen said no, but one said yes. (Laughs.)

I use a telephone directory, I read the paper. Here's a new office building. I'll call the builder, the architect, or the company that's gonna manage it. I get a lead off that. Usually I get nowhere. All of a sudden you get that one guy and you have him. General Electric, a nationwide corporation, right? They got my name out of the Yellow Pages: Kee of Pittsburgh. The head porter—they now call him superintendent of maintenance—this janitor called me up and said, "This is General Electric. We want to have our offices decorated." They didn't know me from Adam. It was a lead out of a phonebook. That's one way.

I say, "This is Kee of Pittsburgh. My name's Pete Keeley. May I speak with the doctor?" You never talk to him, he's busier than a dog with fleas. So you talk to the nurse. "How about your draperies? I want to make some money off you. I can make about forty bucks on it. But you'll be satisfied." That's a good pitch. Either she'll think you're crazy or she'll say, "Okay, come on up." I never say I'm the cheapest. He can go to Penney's, you can go to Sears and get it cheaper, but you won't get me. I just cannot sell a cheap fabric. It always had to be the best. We're talking now about very small stuff, very small business. (*Laughs.*) I can get the job, maybe one out of ten, one out of twenty. That's enough. If I got 'em all, I wouldn't be talking to you. I'd own the building. I pick up about five a month. I've never used the stereotype approach. "My name is Pete Keeley. I'm Kee of Pittsburgh. I want to make some dough off you."

I try to pick carefully. I just feel it. I won't take a dentist who's been there forty-five years and cleans his drapes every five years. That's not the guy to approach. When I hear of new buildings, I may drive by and get the list off the front.

All my life, everytime I make a cold call, I've had cold feet. Whether I call the president of General Motors—as I have in the past—or on a little mama-and-papa store, the same butterfly, always. If you make enough calls and make the butterfly fly away, you're gonna hit. One out of ten, twenty. Like the old guy that sells doughnuts. If he makes enough calls, he's gonna sell a doughnut.

They hang up on me many times. A baseball player doesn't bat more than .300. When he hangs up on me, I say, "Look, Kee, what did you do wrong with this guy? Theoretically you're a genius in selling." Then I'll say to myself, "I did nothing wrong. I'm a genius. This guy's a dumb son of a bitch."

I've never felt humiliated. I got into a fistfight once with the head buyer of a store in Boston. He was a very nasty son of a bitch. He told me I was overpriced and no damn good. He and I resented back and forth, right there on the fifth floor. It ended in the elevator. The merchandise man separated us. The only time I got mad at a buyer. A lousy buyer is a buyer who won't buy from you, but there's no physical combat. We both got arrested. (*Pause.*) Maybe he did humiliate me. (*A longer pause.*) The more I think about it . . . It's the only time of my life I ever resorted to violence—in selling.

It's been a very bad year emotionally. I worried a lot, I sweat a lot of blood, and spent a lot of sleepless nights. Because of this let-out, this comedown. I felt it. I knew it was comin'. I knew the policy of this coast company. I didn't do anything about it. I should have. It's a shock to an egotist. All of a sudden you find you're not the smartest guy in the world. (*Laughs.*)

It's much easier to say, "Mr. Keeley resigned from X Company," than it is to say, "Mr. Keeley was dropped by X Company." (*Pause.*) Just like that, they dropped me. They handed me a couple of checks. "We regret this, Mr. Keeley, and thank you, good-bye." That was it.

I should have made the change myself when I had the opportunity. When a man has a responsible position, there are many offerings open to him. When he's out of it, these offerings disappear. They're gone. To look for another job when you have a job is not too difficult. But when you haven't got one, to look for a job—that was my mistake. I felt I failed bitterly. It came close to destroying me.

I have no regrets. I never met a man yet that didn't make mistakes. I feel I'm a tremendous success—to a point. Monetarily I'm no success. But mentally I'm a tremendous success. At sixty-five I'm still selling. I can't help it. You can't give up something you love. I'm doing it to keep my mind awake and clear. I'm doing it to keep myself alive.

"The word sell *is the key to my life. I was a scared boy. I couldn't even talk on the phone. I'd sweat blood, I'd perspire, I'd fall down, I'd have to go to the bathroom. I'd walk around the building twenty times and smoke two packs of cigarettes. I never had the nerve to go in. I was a complete introvert. But the minute I found out people liked me and I liked them, I started selling. It's the best thing that ever happened to me. You have to like every slob that ever was. There's something in every guy."*

I ran up against an unbeatable fact with corporation—age. Competence didn't enter into it. Nothing entered into it. No, uh-uh. I don't look forward to retirement. It would kill me. There is no such thing as re-tirement. It's a slow death.

Maybe I'm still trying to prove something. I've had a very bad stock in life. I went to grammar school four years late. I finished high school at night eleven years late. I went two years to college, twelve years late. I was trying to catch up. I've had to prove a lot of things later than other people did. Every man has to have a victory in something. To me, my life's a victory. Now at this moment I can sell you whatever I want to sell you. But I still have something to prove . . . and I'm not sure what it is.

LOIS KEELEY NOVAK

Peter Keeley's daughter. She is a schoolteacher. She has been seated nearby, listening to her father's reflections.

My dad lost his business the year I was married. (*To him*) I remember you coming home and sitting on the bed. You had to fire all those people. He had to post a notice: their employment was terminated. It was the end of Kee of Pittsburgh. I'd never seen a man cry. That really frightened me. Nineteen fifty-six. I thought my father was the wisest man that ever lived. He was always telling me how I could do all these things. He used to help me with math. I used to dread those sessions at the kitchen table when my father would help me. Actually I resented it. I wondered, Could I ever be as intelligent, as successful as he was?

I was a sophomore in college when everything went down the drain. I never thought it would happen. It was like the end of the world. We had those great plush years. I remember the house. The kids say, "Is that *your* house?" The schools we went to, Palm Springs, inviting your friends down for the weekends, swimming pools, fancy dresses. It was all tied up with my father. Finally I had to face my father being a real person.

And when it happened a year ago, his discharge, I knew it. My mother told me on the phone, "Please come home. Something's wrong." I knew it, but it was a strange feeling. My father's work was the key, my father's success was the key to how we lived.

O. Henry

THE MAN HIGHER UP

O. Henry *(pseudonym of William Sydney Porter, 1862–1910) was born in Greensboro, North Carolina. He was accused of embezzling funds while working as a bank teller, and in 1898 he was sentenced to five years in the federal penitentiary in Columbus, Ohio. During his time in prison he submitted short stories to the popular magazines of the day, and more than a dozen were published, mostly under the pen name O. Henry (whose letters can be found, in order, within "Ohio Penitentiary"). He was released in 1901, moved to New York the next year, and was soon writing one story a week for the* New York World; *these stories were generally very short and tended to have surprise endings. "The Man Higher Up" was originally collected in* The Gentle Grafters *(1908) and is about drifters, including a huckster who preys on the foolish pretensions of others. In this regard at least, it can be read alongside the story by Flannery O'Connor on page 159. Like O'Connor, O. Henry had an ear for the dissonant music of American regional vernacular.*

Across our two dishes of spaghetti, in a corner of Provenzano's restaurant, Jeff Peters was explaining to me the three kinds of graft.

Every winter Jeff comes to New York to eat spaghetti, to watch the shipping in East River from the depths of his chinchilla overcoat, and to lay in a supply of Chicago-made clothing at one of the Fulton Street stores. During the other three seasons he may be found further west—his range is from Spokane to Tampa. In his profession he takes a pride which he supports and defends with a serious and unique philosophy of ethics. His profession is no new one. He is an incorporated, uncapitalized, unlimited asylum for the reception of the restless and unwise dollars of his fellowmen.

In the wilderness of stone in which Jeff seeks his annual lonely holiday he is glad to palaver of his many adventures, as a boy will whistle after sundown in a wood. Wherefore, I mark on my calendar the time of his coming, and open a question of privilege at Provenzano's concerning the little wine-stained table in the corner between the rakish rubber plant and the framed palazzo della something on the wall.

"There are two kinds of graft," said Jeff, "that ought to be wiped out by law. I mean Wall Street speculation and burglary."

"Nearly everybody will agree with you as to one of them," said I, with a laugh.

"Well, burglary ought to be wiped out, too," said Jeff; and I wondered if the laugh had been redundant.

"About three months ago," said Jeff, "it was my privilege to become familiar with a sample of each of the aforesaid branches of illegitimate art. I was *sine qua grata* with a member of the housebreakers' union and one of the John D. Napoleons of finance at the same time."

"Interesting combination," said I, with a yawn. "Did I tell you I bagged a duck and a ground-squirrel at one shot last week over in the Ramapos?" I knew well how to draw Jeff's stories.

"Let me tell you first about these barnacles that clog the wheels of society by poisoning the springs of rectitude with their upas-like eye," said Jeff, with the pure gleam of the muckraker in his own.

"As I said, three months ago I got into bad company. There are two times in a man's life when he does this—when he's dead broke, and when he's rich.

"Now and then the most legitimate business runs out of luck. It was out in Arkansas I made the wrong turn at a crossroad, and drives into this town of Peavine by mistake. It seems I had already assaulted and disfigured Peavine the spring of the year before. I had sold $600 worth of young fruit trees there—plums, cherries, peaches and pears. The Peaviners were keeping an eye on the country road and hoping I might pass that way again. I drove down Main Street as far as the Crystal Palace drugstore before I realized I had committed ambush upon myself and my white horse Bill.

"The Peaviners took me by surprise and Bill by the bridle and began a conversation that wasn't entirely disassociated with the subject of fruit trees. A committee of 'em ran some trace-chains through the armholes of my vest, and escorted me through their gardens and orchards.

"Their fruit trees hadn't lived up to their labels. Most of 'em had turned out to be persimmons and dogwoods, with a grove or two of blackjacks and poplars. The only one that showed any signs of bearing anything was a fine young cottonwood that had put forth a hornet's nest and half of an old corset-cover.

"The Peaviners protracted our fruitless stroll to the edge of town. They took my watch and money on account; and they kept Bill and the wagon as hostages. They said the first time one of them dogwood trees put forth an Amsden's June peach I might come back and get my things. Then they took off the trace-chains and jerked their thumbs in the direction of the Rocky Mountains; and I struck a Lewis and Clark lope for the swollen rivers and impenetrable forests.

"When I regained intellectualness I found myself walking into an unidentified town on the A., T. & S. F. railroad. The Peaviners hadn't left anything in my pockets except a plug of chewing—they wasn't after my life—and that saved it. I bit off a chunk and sits down on a pile of ties by the track to recogitate my sensations of thought and perspicacity.

"And then along comes a fast freight which slows up a little at the town; and off of it drops a black bundle that rolls for twenty yards in a cloud of dust and then gets up and begins to spit soft coal and interjections. I see it is a young man broad across the face, dressed more for Pullmans than freights, and with a cheerful kind of smile in spite of it all that made Phoebe Snow's job look like a chimney-sweep's.

"'Fall off?' says I.

"'Nunk,' says he. 'Got off. Arrived at my destination. What town is this?'

"'Haven't looked it up on the map yet,' says I. 'I got in about five minutes before you did. How does it strike you?'

"'Hard,' says he, twisting one of his arms around. 'I believe that shoulder—no, it's all right.'

"He stoops over to brush the dust off his clothes, when out of his pocket drops a fine, nine-inch burglar's steel jimmy. He picks it up and looks at me sharp, and then grins and holds out his hand.

"'Brother,' says he, 'greetings. Didn't I see you in Southern Missouri last summer selling colored sand at half-a-dollar a teaspoonful to put into lamps to keep the oil from exploding?'

"'Oil,' says I, 'never explodes. It's the gas that forms that explodes.' But I shakes hands with him, anyway.

"'My name's Bill Bassett,' says he to me, 'and if you'll call it professional pride instead of conceit, I'll inform you that you have the pleasure of meeting the best burglar that ever set a gum-shoe on ground drained by the Mississippi River.'

"Well, me and this Bill Bassett sits on the ties and exchanges brags as artists in kindred lines will do. It seems he didn't have a cent, either, and we went into close caucus. He explained why an able burglar sometimes had to travel on freights by telling me that a servant girl had played him false in Little Rock, and he was making a quick get away.

"'It's part of my business,' says Bill Bassett, 'to play up to the ruffles when I want to make a riffle as Raffles. 'Tis loves that make the bit go 'round. Show me a house with the swag in it and a pretty parlor-maid and you might as well call the silver melted down and sold, and me spilling truffles and that Château stuff on the napkin under my chin, while the police are calling it an inside job because the old lady's nephew teaches a Bible class. I first make an impression on the girl,' says Bill, 'and when she lets me inside I make an impression on the locks. But this one in Little Rock done me,' says he. 'She saw me taking a trolley ride with another girl, and when I came 'round on the night she was to leave the door open for me it was fast. And I had keys made for the doors upstairs. But, no sir. She had sure cut off my locks. She was a Delilah,' says Bill Bassett.

"It seems that Bill tried to break in anyhow with his jimmy, but the girl emitted a succession of bravura noises like the top-riders of a tally-ho, and Bill had to take all hurdles between there and the depot. As he had no baggage they tried hard to check his departure, but he made a train that was just pulling out.

"'Well,' says Bassett, when we had exchanged memoirs of our dead lives, 'I could eat. This town don't look like it was kept under a Yale lock. Suppose we commit some mild atrocity that will bring in temporary expense money. I don't suppose you've brought along any hair tonic or rolled gold watch-chains, or similar law-defying swindles that you could sell on the plaza to the pilers of the paretic populace, have you?'

"'No,' says I, 'I left an elegant line of Patagonian diamond earrings and rainy-day sunbursts in my valise at Peavine. But they're to stay there till some of them black-gum trees begin to glut the market with yellow clings and Japanese plums. I reckon we can't count on them unless we take Luther Burbank in for a partner.'

"'Very well,' says Bassett, 'we'll do the best we can. Maybe after dark I'll borrow a hairpin from some lady, and open the Farmers and Drovers Marine Bank with it.'

"While we were talking, up pulls a passenger train to the depot near by. A person in a high hat gets off on the wrong side of the train and comes tripping down the track towards us. He was a little, fat man with a big nose and rat's eyes, but dressed expensive, and carrying a hand-satchel careful, as if it had eggs or railroad bonds in it. He passes by us and keeps on down the track, not appearing to notice the town.

"'Come on,' says Bill Bassett to me, starting after him.

"'Where?' I asks.

"'Lordy!' says Bill, "had you forgot you was in the desert? Didn't you see Colonel Manna drop down right before your eyes? Don't you hear the rustling of General Raven's wings? I'm surprised at you, Elijah.'

"We overtook the stranger in the edge of some woods, and, as it was after sun-down and in a quiet place, nobody saw us stop him. Bill takes the silk hat off the man's head and brushes it with his sleeve and puts it back.

"'What does this mean, sir?' says the man.

"'When I wore one of these,' says Bill, 'and felt embarrassed, I always done that. Not having one now I had to use yours. I hardly know how to begin, sir, in explaining our business with you, but I guess we'll try your pockets first.'

"Bill Bassett felt in all of them, and looked disgusted.

"'Not even a watch,' he says. 'Ain't you ashamed of yourself, you whited sculpture? Going about dressed like a headwaiter, and financed like a Count! You haven't even got carfare. What did you do with your transfer?'

"The man speaks up and says he has no assets or valuables of any sort. But Bassett takes his hand-satchel and opens it. Out comes some collars and socks and a half a page of a newspaper clipped out. Bill reads the clipping careful, and holds out his hand to the help-up party.

"'Brother,' says he, 'greetings! Accept the apologies of friends. I am Bill Bassett, the burglar. Mr. Peters, you must make the acquaintance of Mr. Alfred E. Ricks. Shake hands. Mr. Peters,' says Bill, 'stands about halfway between me and you, Mr. Ricks, in the line of havoc and corruption. He always gives something for the money he gets. I'm glad to meet you, Mr. Ricks—you and Mr. Peters. This is the first time I ever attended a full gathering of the National Synod of Sharks—housebreaking, swindling, and financiering all represented. Please examine Mr. Rick's credentials, Mr. Peters.'

"The piece of newspaper that Bill Bassett handed me had a good picture of this Ricks on it. It was a Chicago paper, and it had obloquies of Ricks in every paragraph. By reading it over I harvested the intelligence that said alleged Ricks had laid off all that portion of the State of Florida that lies under water into town lots and sold 'em to alleged innocent investors from his magnificently furnished offices in Chicago. After he had taken in a hundred thousand or so dollars one of these fussy purchasers that are always making trouble (I've had 'em actually try gold watches I've sold 'em with acid) took a cheap excursion down to the land where it is always just before supper to look at his lot and see if it didn't need a new paling or two on the fence, and market a few lemons in time for the Christmas present trade. He hires a surveyor to find his lot for him. They run the line out and find the flourishing town of Paradise Hollow, so advertised, to be about 40 rods and 16 poles S., 27° E. of the middle of Lake Okeechobee. This man's lot was under thirty-six feet of water, and, besides, had been preempted so long by the alligators and gars that his title looked fishy.

"Naturally, the man goes back to Chicago and makes it as hot for Alfred E. Ricks as the morning after a prediction of snow by the weather bureau. Ricks defied the allegation, but he couldn't deny the alligators. One morning the papers came out with a column about it, and Ricks come out by the fire escape. It seems the alleged authorities had beat him to the safe-deposit box where he kept his winnings, and Ricks has to westward ho! with only feetwear and a dozen 15½ English pokes in his shopping bag. He happened to have some mileage left in his book, and that took him as far as the town in the wilderness where he was spilled out on me and Bill Bassett as Elijah III with not a raven in sight for any of us.

"Then this Alfred E. Ricks lets out a squeak that he is hungry, too, and denies the hypothesis that he is good for the value, let alone the price of a meal. And so, there was the three of us, representing, if we had a mind to draw syllogisms and parabolas, labor and trade and capital. Now, when trade has no capital there isn't a dicker to be made. And when capital has no money there's a stagnation in steak and onions. That put it up to the man with the jimmy.

"'Brother bushrangers,' says Bill Bassett, 'never yet, in trouble, did I desert a pal. Hard-by, in yon wood, I seem to see unfurnished lodgings. Let us go there and wait till dark.'

"There was an old, deserted cabin in the grove, and we three took possession of it. After dark Bill Bassett tells us to wait, and goes out for half an hour. He comes back with an armful of bread and spareribs and pies.

"'Panhandled 'em at a farmhouse on Washita Avenue,' says he. 'Eat, drink and be leary.'

"The full moon was coming up bright, so we sat on the floor of the cabin and ate in the light of it. And this Bill Bassett begins to brag.

"'Sometimes,' says he, with his mouth full of country produce, 'I lose all patience with you people that think you are higher up in the profession than I am. Now, what could either of you have done in the present emergency to set us on our feet again? Could you do it, Ricksy?'

"'I must confess, Mr. Bassett,' says Ricks, speaking nearly inaudible out of a slice of pie, 'that at this immediate juncture I could not, perhaps, promote an enterprise to relieve the situation. Large operations, such as I direct, naturally require careful preparation in advance. I—'

"'I know, Ricksy,' breaks in Bill Bassett. 'You needn't finish. You need $500 to make the first payment on a blond typewriter, and four roomsful of quartered oak furniture. And you need $500 more for advertising contracts. And you need two weeks' time for the fish to begin to bite. Your line of relief would be about as useful in an emergency as advocating municipal ownership to cure a man suffocated by eighty-cent gas. And your graft ain't much swifter, Brother Peters,' he winds up.

"'Oh,' says I, 'I haven't seen you turn anything into gold with your wand yet, Mr. Good Fairy. 'Most anybody could rub the magic ring for a little leftover vituals.'

"'That was only getting the pumpkin ready,' says Bassett, braggy and cheerful. 'The coach and six'll drive up to the door before you know it, Miss Cinderella. Maybe you've got some scheme under your sleeve-holders that will give us a start.'

"'Son,' says I, 'I'm fifteen years older than you are, and young enough yet to take out an endowment policy. I've been broke before. We can see the lights of that town not half a mile away. I learned under Montague Silver, the greatest street man that ever spoke from a wagon. There are hundreds of men walking the streets this moment with grease spots on their clothes. Give me a gasoline lamp, a dry-goods box, and a two-dollar bar of white castile soap, cut into little—'

"'Where's your two dollars?' snickered Bill Bassett into my discourse. There was no use arguing with that burglar.

"'No,' he goes on; 'you're both babes-in-the-wood. Finance has closed the mahogany desk, and trade has put the shutters up. Both of you look to labor to start the wheels going. All right. You admit it. To-night I'll show you what Bill Bassett can do.'

"Bassett tells me and Ricks not to leave the cabin till he comes back, even if it's daylight, and then he struts off toward town, whistling gay.

"This Alfred E. Ricks pulls off his shoes and his coat, lays a silk handkerchief over his hat, and lays down on the floor.

"'I think I will endeavour to secure a little slumber,' he squeaks. 'The day has been fatiguing. Goodnight, my dear Mr. Peters.'

"'My regards to Morpheus,' says I. 'I think I'll sit up a while.'

"About two o'clock, as near as I could guess by my watch in Peavine, home comes our laboring man and kicks up Ricks, and calls us to the streak of bright moonlight shining in the cabin door. Then he spreads out five packages of one thousand dollars each on the floor, and begins to cackle over the nestegg like a hen.

"'I'll tell you a few things about that town,' says he. 'It's named Rocky Springs, and they're building a Masonic Temple, and it looks like the Democratic candidate for mayor is going to get soaked by a Pop, and Judge Tucker's wife, who has been down with pleurisy, is some better. I had a talk with these liliputian thesises before I got a siphon in the fountain of knowledge that I was after. And there's a bank there called the Lumberman's Fidelity and Plowman's Savings Institution. It closed for business yesterday with $23,000 cash on hand. It will open this morning with $18,000—all silver—that's the reason I didn't bring more. There you are, trade and capital. Now, will you be bad?'

"'My young friend,' says Alfred E. Ricks, holding up his hands, 'have you robbed this bank? Dear me, dear me!'

"'You couldn't call it that,' says Bassett. '"Robbing" sounds harsh. All I had to do was to find out what street it was on. That town is so quiet that I could stand on the corner and hear the tumblers clicking in that safe lock—"right to 45; left twice to 80; right to 60; left to 15"—as plain as the Yale captain giving orders in the football dialect. Now, boys,' says Bassett, 'this is an early rising town. They tell me the citizens are all up and stirring before daylight. I asked what for, and they said because breakfast was ready at that time. And what of merry Robin Hood? It must be Yoicks! and away with the tinkers' chorus. I'll stake you. How much do you want? Speak up. Capital.'

"'My dear young friend,' says this ground squirrel of a Ricks, standing on his hind legs and juggling nuts in his paws, 'I have friends in Denver who would assist me. If I had a hundred dollars I—'

"Bassett unpins a package of the currency and throws five twenties to Ricks.

"'Trade, how much?' he says to me.

"'Put your money up, Labor,' says I. 'I never yet drew upon honest toil for its hard-earned pittance. The dollars I get are surplus ones that are burning the pockets of damfools and greenhorns. When I stand on a street corner and sell a solid gold diamond ring to a yap for $3.00, I make just $2.60. And I know he's going to give it to a girl in return for all the benefits accruing from a $125.00 ring. His profits are $122.00. Which of us is the biggest fakir?'

"'And when you sell a poor woman a pinch of sand for fifteen cents to keep her lamp from exploding,' says Bassett, 'what do you figure her gross earnings to be, with sand at forty cents a ton?'

"'Listen,' says I, 'I instruct her to keep her lamp clean and well filled. If she does that it can't burst. And with the sand in it she knows it can't, and she don't worry. It's a kind of Industrial Christian Science. She pays fifty cents, and gets both Rockefeller and Mrs. Eddy on the job. It ain't everybody that can let the gold-dust twins do their work.'

"Alfred E. Ricks all but licks the dust off of Bill Bassett's shoes.

"'My dear young friend,' says he, 'I will never forget your generosity. Heaven will reward you. But let me implore you to turn from your ways of violence and crime.'

"'Mousie,' says Bill, 'the hole in the wainscoting for yours. Your dogmas and inculcations sound to me like the last words of a bicycle pump. What has your high moral, elevator-service system of pillage brought you to? Penuriousness and want. Even Brother Peters, who insists upon contaminating the art of robbery with theories of commerce and trade, admitted he was on the lift. Both of you live by the gilded rule. Brother Peters,' says Bill, 'you'd better choose a slice of his embalmed currency. You're welcome.'

"I told Bill Bassett once more to put his money in his pocket. I never had the respect for burglary that some people have. I always gave something for the money I took, even if it's only some little trifle for a souvenir to remind 'em not to get caught again.

"And then Alfred E. Ricks grovels at Bill's feet again, and bids us adieu. He says he will have a team at a farmhouse, and drive to the station below, and take the train for Denver. It salubrified the atmosphere when that lamentable boll-worm took his departure. He was a disgrace to every non-industrial profession in the country. With all his big schemes and fine offices he had wound up unable even to get an honest meal except by the kindness of a strange and maybe unscrupulous burglar. I was glad to see him go, though I felt a little sorry for him, now that he was ruined forever. What could such a man do without a big capital to work with? Why, Alfred E. Ricks, as we left him, was as helpless as a turtle on its back. He couldn't have worked a scheme to beat a little girl out of a penny slate-pencil.

"When me and Bill Bassett was left alone I did a little sleight-of-mind turn in my head with a trade secret at the end of it. Thinks I, I'll show this Mr. Burglar Man the difference between business and labor. He had hurt some of my professional self-adulation by casting his Persians upon commerce and trade.

"'I won't take any of your money as a gift, Mr. Bassett,' says I to him, 'but if you'll pay my expenses as a traveling companion until we get out of the danger zone of the immoral deficit you have caused in this town's finances tonight, I'll be obliged.'

"Bill Bassett agreed to that, and we hiked westward as soon as we could catch a safe train.

"When we got to a town in Arizona called Los Perros I suggested that we once more try our luck on terra-cotta. That was the home of Montague Silver, my old instructor, now retired from business. I knew Monty would stake me to web money if I could show him a fly buzzing 'round in the locality. Bill Bassett said all towns looked alike to him as he worked mainly in the dark. So we got off the train in Los Perros, a fine little town in the silver region.

"I had an elegant little sure thing in the way of a commercial slung-shot that I intended to hit Bassett behind the ear with. I wasn't going to take his money while he was asleep, but I was going to leave him with a lottery ticket that would represent in experience to him $4,755—I think that was the amount he had when he got off the train. But the first time I hinted to him about an investment, he turns on me and disencumbers himself of the following terms and expressions.

"'Brother Peters,' says he, 'it ain't a bad idea to go into an enterprise of some kind, as you suggest. I think I will. But if I do it will be such a cold proposition that nobody but Robert E. Peary and Charlie Fairbanks will be able to sit on the board of directors.'

"'I thought you might want to turn your money over,' says I.

"'I do,' says he, 'frequently. I can't sleep on one side all night. I'll tell you, Brother Peters,' says he, 'I'm going to start a poker room. I don't seem to care for the humdrum in swindling, such as peddling egg-beaters and working off breakfast food on Barnum and Bailey for sawdust to strew in their circus rings. But the gambling business,' says he, 'from the profitable side of the table is a good compromise between swiping silver spoons and selling penwipers at a Waldorf-Astoria charity bazaar.'

"'Then,' says I, 'Mr. Bassett, you don't care to talk over my business proposition?'

"'Why,' says he, 'do you know, you can't get a Pasteur Institute to start up within fifty miles of where I live. I bite so seldom.'

"So, Bassett rents a room over a saloon and looks around for some furniture and chromos. The same night I went to Monty Silver's house, and he let me have $200 on my prospects. Then I went to the only store in Los Perros that sold playing cards and bought every deck in the house. The next morning when the store opened I was there bringing all the cards back with me. I said that my partner that was going to back me in the game had changed his mind; and I wanted to sell the cards back again. The storekeeper took 'em at half price.

"Yes, I was seventy-five dollars loser up to that time. But while I had the cards that night I marked every one in every deck. That was labor. And then trade and commerce had their innings, and the bread I had cast upon the waters began to come back in the form of cottage pudding with wine sauce.

"Of course I was among the first to buy chips at Bill Bassett's game. He had bought the only cards there was to be had in town; and I knew the back of every one of them better than I know the back of my head when the barber shows me my haircut in the two mirrors.

"When the game closed I had the five thousand and a few odd dollars, and all Bill Bassett had was the wanderlust and a black cat he had bought for a mascot. Bill shook hands with me when I left.

"'Brother Peters,' says he, 'I have no business being in business. I was preordained to labor. When a No. 1 burglar tries to make a James out of his jimmy he perpetrates an improfundity. You have a well-oiled and efficacious system of luck at cards,' says he. 'Peace go with you.' And I never afterward sees Bill Bassett again."

"Well, Jeff," said I, when the Autolycan adventure seemed to have divulged the gist of his life, "I hope you took care of the money. That would be a respecta—that is a considerable working capital if you should choose some day to settle down to some sort of regular business."

"Me?" said Jeff, virtuously. "You can bet I've taken care of that five thousand."

He tapped his coat over the region of his chest exultantly.

"Gold mining stock," he explained "every cent of it. Shares par value one dollar. Bound to go up 500 percent within a year. Non-assessable. The Blue Gopher Mine. Just discovered a month ago. Better get in yourself if you've any spare dollars on hand."

"Sometimes," said I, "these mines are not—"

"Oh, this one's solid as an old goose," said Jeff. "Fifty thousand dollars worth of ore in sight, and 10 percent monthly earnings guaranteed."

He drew a long envelope from his pocket and cast it on the table.

"Always carry it with me," said he. "So the burglar can't corrupt or the capitalist break in and water it."

I looked at the beautifully engraved certificate of stock.

"In Colorado, I see," said I. "And, by the way, Jeff, what was the name of the little man who went to Denver—the one you and Bill met at the station?"

"Alfred E. Ricks," said Jeff, "was the toad's designation."

"I see," said I, "the president of this mining company signs himself A.L. Fredericks. I was wondering—"

"Let me see that stock," said Jeff quickly, almost snatching it from me.

To mitigate, even though slightly, the embarrassment I summoned the waiter and ordered another bottle of the Barbera. I thought it was the least I could do.

PART 5

You Can't Take
It With You

Arthur Miller

from *DEATH OF A SALESMAN*

Arthur Miller *(1915–2005) nearly gave up playwriting after the dismal reception of* The Man Who Had All the Luck *(1940). But he kept at it, and in 1948 came* Death of a Salesman, *which won a Tony Award, a Pulitzer Prize, and a New York City Drama Critic's Circle Award. The character of Willy Loman stands alongside George Babbitt (see page 132) and Johnny Hake (see page 105) as a lasting emblem of the cruel radiance of American capitalism in the twentieth century. The pathos of Loman's final confrontation with his much younger boss—his last stab at salesmanship— encapsulates the mood of the play.*

WILLY. (*Sits on chair, puts hat under it.*) Well . . . tell you the truth, Howard . . . I've come to the decision that I'd rather not travel any more.

HOWARD. Not travel! Well, what'll you do?

WILLY. (*Definite.*) Remember, Christmas time—when you had the party here? You said you'd try to think of some spot for me here in town.

HOWARD. (*Incredulous.*) With us?

WILLY. Well, sure.

HOWARD. (*Businesslike—drops head.*) Oh, yeah, yeah . . . I remember. Well . . . I couldn't think of anything for you, Willy.

WILLY. I tell ya, Howard . . . the kids are all grown up, y'know. . . . I don't need much any more. If I could take home . . . well, sixty-five dollars a week, I could swing it.

HOWARD. (*Crosses R. few steps.*) Yeah, but, Willy, see I . . .

WILLY. I tell ya why, Howard . . . speaking frankly and between the two of us, y'know?—I'm just a little tired. (*Starting to resent having to grovel.*)

HOWARD. (*Crosses to R. of table.*) Oh, I could understand that, Willy. (*Businesslike.*) But you're a road man, Willy, and we do a road business. (*WILLY rises.*) We've only got a half dozen salesmen on the floor here.

WILLY. (*Crosses to above table.*) God knows, Howard, I never asked a favor of any man. But I was with the firm when your father used to carry you in here on his arms. . . .

HOWARD. (*Embarrassed and irritated.*) I know that, Willy, but . . .

WILLY. Your father came to me the day you were born and asked me what I thought of the name of Howard, may he rest in peace! (*Crosses to L. end of table.*)

HOWARD. I appreciate that, Willy, if I had a spot I'd slam you right in, but I just don't have a single solitary spot. (*Turns, crosses few steps R. Pause.*)

WILLY. (*With increasing anger. Swallowing his pride.*) Howard, all I need to set my table is fifty dollars a week.

HOWARD. But where am I going to put you, kid?

WILLY. Look, it isn't a question of whether I can sell merchandise, is it?

HOWARD. No, but it's a business, kid, and everybody's gotta pull his own weight.

WILLY. (*Desperately.*) Just let me tell you a story, Howard. . . .

HOWARD. (*Crosses to table.*) 'Cause you gotta admit, business is business.

WILLY. (*Sits chair L. of table.*) Business is definitely business, but just listen for a minute. You don't understand this. When I was a boy . . . eighteen, nineteen, I was already on the road. And there was a question in my mind as to whether selling had a future for me. Because in those days I had a yearning to go to Alaska. See, there were three gold strikes in one month in Alaska, and I felt like going out; just for the ride, you might say.

HOWARD. (*Barely interested.*) Is that so? (*Sits on table R. of recorder.*)

WILLY. (*The effect of this speech is to put HOWARD in his place.*) Oh, yeah, my father lived many years in Alaska . . . he was an *adventurous* man. . . . We've got quite a little streak of self-reliance in our family. I thought I'd go out with my older brother and try to locate him, and maybe settle in the North with the old man. And I was almost decided to go, when I met a *salesman* in the Parker House. His name was Dave Singleman.

And he was eighty-four years old, and he'd drummed merchandise in thirty-one states. And old Dave . . . he'd go up to his room, y' understand, put on his green velvet slippers—I'll never forget—and pick up his phone and call the buyers and without ever leaving his room, at the age of eighty-four, he made his living. And when I saw that, I realized that selling was the greatest career a man could want. 'Cause what could be more satisfying than to be able to go, at the age of eighty-four, into twenty or thirty different cities, and pick up a phone, and be remembered and loved and helped, by so many different people? Do you know; when he died—and by the way he died the *death of a salesman*, in his green velvet slippers in the smoker of the New York, New Haven and Hartford, going into Boston—but when he died, hundreds of salesmen and buyers were at his funeral. Things were sad on a lotta trains for months after that. (*Rises.*) See what I mean? In those days there was personality in it, Howard; there was respect, and comradeship, and gratitude in it. Today, it's all cut and dried, and there's no chance for bringing friendship to bear . . . or personality. They don't know me any more.

HOWARD. (*Angry. Rises, moves away R.*) That's just the thing, Willy. . . .

WILLY. (*Pleading. Crosses R. to above R. of table.*) If I had *forty* dollars a week . . . that's all I'd need. Forty dollars, Howard.

HOWARD. (*Definite.*) Kid, I can't take blood from a stone, I . . .

WILLY. (*Cuts in. Desperation is on him now.*) Howard, the year Al Smith was nominated your father came to me and . . .

HOWARD. (*Starts off L.—to WILLY, impatiently.*) I've got to see some people, kid. . . . (*WILLY stops him.*)

WILLY. I'm talking about your *father*! There were promises made in this office! You mustn't tell me you've got people to see—(*Shouting.*) I put thirty-four years into this firm, Howard, and now I can't pay my insurance! You can't eat the orange and throw the peel away—a man is not a piece of fruit! (*Pause.*) Now pay attention. Your father—in 1928—I had a big year. I averaged a hundred and seventy dollars a week in commissions.

HOWARD. (*Snorts. Turns away.*) Now, Willy, you never averaged . . .

WILLY. (*Bangs his hand on desk.*) I averaged a hundred and seventy dollars a week in the year of 1928! And your father came to me . . . or rather I was in the office here . . . it was right over this desk . . . and he put his hand on my shoulder . . .

HOWARD. Willy, I gotta see some people. Pull yourself together. . . . *(Goes off L.)*

WILLY. *(Facing R.)* Pull myself together! What the hell did I say to him! My God, I was yelling at him! How could I! . . . ?

Joseph Conrad

AN OUTPOST OF PROGRESS

Joseph Conrad *(pseudonym of Teodor Józef Konrad Nalecz-Korzeniowski, 1857–1924) was born in Poland and spent the better part of his young adulthood working in the French and British merchant marine. His travels to the Belgian Congo in Africa informed his most famous work, the novella* Heart of Darkness *(1899), as well as "An Outpost of Progress," published two years earlier. As in many of his works, Conrad here mocks an all-too-common one-time European conceit: the supposed civilizing effect of imperial commerce on the so-called savages in the colonies.*

I

There were two white men in charge of the trading station. Kayerts, the chief, was short and fat; Carlier, the assistant, was tall, with a large head and a very broad trunk perched upon a long pair of thin legs. The third man on the staff was a Sierra Leone nigger, who maintained that his name was Henry Price. However, for some reason or other, the natives down the river had given him the name of Makola, and it stuck to him through all his wanderings about the country. He spoke English and French with a warbling accent, wrote a beautiful hand, understood bookkeeping, and cherished in his innermost heart the worship of evil spirits. His wife was a negress from Loanda, very large and very noisy. Three children rolled about in sunshine before the door of his low, shed-like dwelling. Makola, taciturn and impenetrable, despised the two white men. He had charge of a small clay storehouse with a dried-grass roof, and pretended to keep a correct account of beads, cotton cloth, red kerchiefs, brass wire, and other trade goods it contained. Besides the storehouse and Makola's hut, there was only one large building in the cleared ground of the station. It was built neatly of reeds, with a verandah on all the four sides. There were three rooms in it. The one in the middle was the living-room, and had two rough tables and a few stools in it. The other two were the bedrooms for the white men. Each had a bedstead and a mosquito net for all furniture. The plank floor was littered with the belongings of the white men: open half-empty boxes, torn wearing apparel, old boots; all the things dirty, and all the things broken, that accumulate mysteriously round untidy men. There was also another dwelling-place some distance away from the buildings. In it, under a tall cross much out of the perpendicular, slept the man who had seen the beginning of all this; who had planned and had watched the construction of this outpost of progress. He had been, at home, an unsuccessful painter who, weary of pursuing fame on an empty stomach, had gone out there through high protections. He had been the first chief of that station. Makola had watched the energetic artist die of fever in the just finished house with his usual kind of "I told you so" indifference. Then, for a time, he dwelt alone with his family, his account books, and the Evil Spirit that rules the lands under the equator. He got on very well with his god. Perhaps he had propitiated him by a promise of more white men to play with, by and by. At any rate the director of the Great Trading Company, coming up in a steamer that resembled an enormous sardine box with a flat-roofed shed erected on it, found the station in good order, and Makola as usual quietly diligent. The director had the cross put up over the first agent's grave, and appointed Kayerts to the post. Carlier was told off as second in charge. The director was a man ruthless and efficient, who at times, but very imperceptibly, indulged in grim humor. He made a speech to Kayerts and Carlier, pointing out to them the promising aspect of their station. The nearest trading-post was about three hundred miles away. It was an exceptional opportunity for them to distinguish themselves and to earn percentages on the trade. This appointment was a favor done to beginners. Kayerts was moved almost to tears by his director's kindness. He would, he said, by doing his best, try to justify the flattering confidence, etc., etc. Kayerts had been in the Administration of the Telegraphs, and knew how to express himself correctly. Carlier, an ex-noncommissioned officer of cavalry in an army guaranteed from harm by several European Powers, was less impressed. If there were commissions to get, so much the better; and, trailing a sulky glance over the river, the forests, the impenetrable bush that seemed to cut off the station from the rest of the world, he muttered between his teeth, "We shall see, very soon."

Next day, some bales of cotton goods and a few cases of provisions having been thrown on shore, the sardine-box steamer went off, not to return for another six months. On the deck the director touched his cap to the two agents, who stood on the bank waving their hats, and turning to an old servant of the company on his passage to headquarters, said, "Look at those two imbeciles. They must be mad at home to send me such specimens. I told those fellows to plant a vegetable garden, build new storehouses and fences, and construct a landing-stage. I bet nothing will be done! They won't know how to begin. I always thought the station on this river useless, and they just fit the station!"

"They will form themselves there," said the old stager with a quiet smile.

"At any rate, I am rid of them for six months," retorted the director.

The two men watched the steamer round the bend, then, ascending arm in arm the slope of the bank, returned to the station. They had been in this vast and dark country only a very short time, and as yet always in the midst of other white men, under the eye and guidance of their superiors. And now, dull as they were to the subtle influences of surroundings, they felt themselves very much alone when suddenly left unassisted to face the wilderness: a wilderness rendered more strange, more incomprehensible by the mysterious glimpses of the vigorous life it contained. They were two perfectly insignificant and incapable individuals, whose existence is only rendered possible through the high organization of civilized crowds. Few men realize that their life, the very essence of their character, their capabilities and their audacities, are only the expression of their belief in the safety of their surroundings. The courage, the composure, the confidence; the emotions and principles; every great and every insignificant thought belongs not to the individual but to the crowd: to the crowd that believes blindly in the irresistible force of its institutions and of its morals, in the power of its police and of its opinion. But the contact with pure unmitigated savagery, with primitive nature and primitive man, brings sudden and profound trouble into the heart. To the sentiment of being alone of one's kind, to the clear perception of the loneliness of one's thoughts, of one's sensations—to the negation of the habitual, which is safe, there is added the affirmation of the unusual, which is dangerous; a suggestion of things vague, uncontrollable, and repulsive, whose discomposing intrusion excites the imagination and tries the civilized nerves of the foolish and the wise alike.

Kayerts and Carlier walked arm in arm drawing close to one another as children do in the dark; and they had the same, not altogether unpleasant, sense of danger which one half suspects to be imaginary. They chatted persistently in familiar tones. "Our station is prettily situated," said one. The other assented with enthusiasm, enlarging volubly on the beauties of the situation. Then they passed near the grave. "Poor devil!" said Kayerts. "He died of fever, didn't he?" muttered Carlier, stopping short. "Why," retorted Kayerts, with indignation, "I've been told that the fellow exposed himself recklessly to the sun. The climate here, everybody says, is not at all worse than at home, as long as you keep out of the sun. Do you hear that, Carlier? I am chief here, and my orders are that you should not expose yourself to the sun!" He assumed his superiority jocularly, but his meaning was serious. The idea that he would, perhaps, have to bury Carlier and remain alone, gave him an inward shiver. He felt suddenly that this Carlier was more precious to him here, in the center of Africa, than a brother could be anywhere else. Carlier, entering into the spirit of the thing, made a military salute and answered in a brisk tone, "Your orders shall be attended to, chief!" Then he burst out laughing, slapped Kayerts on the back, and shouted, "We shall let life run easily here! Just sit still and gather in the ivory those savages will bring. This country has its good points, after all!" They both laughed loudly while Carlier thought: That poor Kayerts; he is so fat and unhealthy. It would be awful if I had to bury him here. He is a man I respect . . . Before they reached the verandah of their house they called one another "my dear fellow."

The first day they were very active, pottering about with hammers and nails and red calico, to put up curtains, make their house habitable and pretty; resolved to settle down comfortably to their new life. For them an impossible task. To grapple effectually with even purely material problems requires more serenity of mind and more lofty courage than people generally imagine. No two beings could have been more unfitted for such a struggle. Society, not from any tenderness, but because of its strange needs, had taken care of those two men, forbidding them all independent thought, all initiative, all departure from routine; and forbidding it under pain of death. They could only live on condition of being machines. And now, released from the fostering care of men with pens behind the ears, or of men with gold lace on the sleeves, they were like those lifelong prisoners who, liberated after many years, do not know what use to make of their freedom. They did not know what use to make of their faculties, being both, through want of practice, incapable of independent thought.

At the end of two months Kayerts often would say, "If it was not for my Melie, you wouldn't catch me here." Melie was his daughter. He had thrown up his post in the Administration of the Telegraphs, though he had been for seventeen years perfectly happy there, to earn a dowry for his girl. His wife was dead, and the child was being brought up by his sisters. He regretted the streets, the pavements, the cafés, his friends of many years; all the things he used to see, day after day; all the thoughts suggested by familiar things—the thoughts effortless, monotonous, and soothing of a government clerk; he regretted all the gossip, the small enmities, the mild venom, and the little jokes of government offices. "If I had had a decent brother-in-law," Carlier would remark, "a fellow with a heart, I would not be here." He had left the army and had made himself so obnoxious to his family by his laziness and impudence, that an exasperated brother-in-law had made superhuman efforts to procure him an appointment in the Company as a second-class agent. Having not a penny in the world, he was compelled to accept this means of livelihood as soon as it became quite clear to him that there was nothing more to squeeze out of his relations. He, like Kayerts, regretted his old life. He regretted the clink of saber and spurs on a fine afternoon, the barrack-room witticisms, the girls of garrison towns; but, besides, he had also a sense of grievance. He was evidently a much ill-used man. This made him moody, at times. But the two men got on well together in the fellowship of their stupidity and laziness. Together they did nothing, absolutely nothing, and enjoyed the sense of the idleness for which they were paid. And in time they came to feel something resembling affection for one another.

They lived like blind men in a large room, aware only of what came in contact with them (and of that only imperfectly), but unable to see the general aspect of things. The river, the forest, all the great land throbbing with life, were like a great emptiness. Even the brilliant sunshine disclosed nothing intelligible. Things appeared and disappeared before their eyes in an unconnected and aimless kind of way. The river seemed to come from nowhere and flow nowhither. It flowed through a void. Out of that void, at times, came canoes, and men with spears in their hands would suddenly crowd the yard of the station. They were naked, glossy black, ornamented with snowy shells and glistening brass wire, perfect of limb. They made an uncouth babbling noise when they spoke, moved in a stately manner, and sent quick, wild glances out of their startled, never-resting eyes. Those warriors would squat in long rows, four or more deep, before the verandah, while their chiefs bargained for hours with Makola over an elephant tusk. Kayerts sat on his chair and looked down on the proceedings, understanding nothing. He stared at them with his round blue eyes, called out to Carlier, "Here, look! look at that fellow there—and that other one, to the left. Did you ever see such a face? Oh, the funny brute."

Carlier, smoking native tobacco in a short wooden pipe, would swagger up twirling his moustaches, and, surveying the warriors with haughty indulgence, would say—

"Fine animals. Brought any bone? Yes? It's not any too soon. Look at the muscles of that fellow—third from the end. I wouldn't care to get a punch on the nose from him. Fine arms, but legs no good below the knee. Couldn't make cavalry men of them." And after glancing down complacently at his own shanks, he always concluded. "Pah! Don't they stink! You, Makola! Take that herd over to the fetish" (the storehouse was in every station called the fetish, perhaps because of the spirit of civilization it contained) "and give them up some of the rubbish you keep there. I'd rather see it full of bone than full of rags."

Kayerts approved.

"Yes, yes! Go and finish that palaver over there, Mr. Makola. I will come round when you are ready, to weigh the tusk. We must be careful." Then, turning to his companion: "This is the tribe that lives down the river; they are rather aromatic. I remember, they have been once before here. D'ye hear that row? What a fellow has got to put up with in this dog of a country! My head is split."

Such profitable visits were rare. For days the two pioneers of trade and progress would look on their empty courtyard in the vibrating brilliance of vertical sunshine. Below the high bank, the silent river flowed on, glittering and steady. On the sands in the middle of the stream, hippos and alligators sunned themselves side by side. And stretching away in all directions, surrounding the insignificant cleared spot of the trading post, immense forests, hiding fateful complications of fantastic life, lay in the eloquent silence of mute greatness. The two men understood nothing, cared for nothing but for the passage of days that separated them from the streamer's return. Their predecessor had left some torn books. They took up these wrecks of novels, and, as they had never read anything of the kind before, they were surprised and amused. Then during long days there were interminable and silly discussions about plots and personages. In the centre of Africa they made the acquaintance of Richelieu and of d'Artagnan, of Hawk's Eye and of Father Goriot, and of many other people. All these imaginary personages became subjects for gossip as if they had been living friends. They discounted their virtues, suspected their motives, decried their successes; were scandalized at their duplicity or were doubtful about their courage. The accounts of crimes filled them with indignation, while tender or pathetic passages moved them deeply. Carlier cleared his throat and said in a soldierly voice, "What nonsense!" Kayerts, his round eyes suffused with tears, his fat cheeks quivering, rubbed his bald head, and declared, "This is a splendid book. I had no idea there were such clever fellows in the world." They also found some old copies of a home paper. That print discussed what it was pleased to call "Our Colonial Expansion" in high-flown language. It spoke much of the rights and duties of civilization, of the sacredness of the civilizing work, and extolled the merits of those who went about bringing light, and faith, and commerce to the dark places of the earth. Carlier and Kayerts read, wondered, and began to think better of themselves. Carlier said one evening, waving his hand about, "In a hundred years, there will be perhaps a town here. Quays, and warehouses, and barracks, and—and—billiard-rooms. Civilization, my boy, and virtue—and all. And then, chaps will read that two good fellows, Kayerts and Carlier, were the first civilized men to live in this very spot!" Kayerts nodded, "Yes, it is a consolation to think of that." They seemed to forget their dead predecessor; but, early one day, Carlier went out and replanted the cross firmly. "It used to make me squint whenever I walked that way," he explained to Kayerts over the morning coffee. "It made me squint, leaning over so much. So I just planted it upright. And solid, I promise you! I suspended myself with both hands to the cross-piece. Not a move. Oh, I did that properly."

At times Gobila came to see them. Gobila was the chief of the neighboring villages. He was a gray-headed savage, thin and black, with a white cloth round his loins and a mangy panther skin hanging over his back. He came up with long strides of his skeleton legs, swinging a staff as tall as himself, and, entering the common room of the station, would squat on his heels to the left of the door. There he sat, watching Kayerts, and now and then making a speech which the other did not understand. Kayerts, without interrupting his occupation, would from time to time say in a friendly manner: "How goes it, you old image?" and they would smile at one another. The two whites had a liking for that old and incomprehensible creature, and called him Father Gobila. Gobila's manner was paternal, and he seemed really to love all white men. They all appeared to him very young, indistinguishably alike (except for stature), and he knew that they were all brothers, and also immortal. The death of the artist, who was the first white man whom he knew intimately, did not disturb this belief, because he was firmly convinced that the white stranger had pretended to die and got himself buried for some mysterious purpose of his own, into which it was useless to enquire. Perhaps it was his way of going home to his own country? At any rate, these were his brothers, and he transferred his absurd affection to them. They returned it in a way. Carlier slapped him on the back, and recklessly struck off matches for his amusement. Kayerts was always ready to let him have a sniff at the ammonia bottle. In short, they behaved just like that other white creature that had hidden itself in a hole in the ground. Gobila considered them attentively. Perhaps they were the same being with the other—or one of them was. He couldn't decide—clear up that mystery; but he remained always very friendly. In consequence of that friendship the women of Gobila's village walked in single file through the reedy grass, bringing every morning to the station, fowls, and sweet potatoes, and palm wine, and sometimes a goat. The Company never provisioned the stations fully, and the agents required those local supplies to live. They had them through the goodwill of Gobila, and lived well. Now and then one of them had a bout of fever, and the other nursed him with gentle devotion. They did not think much of it. It left them weaker, and their appearance changed for the worse. Carlier was hollow-eyed and irritable, Kayerts showed a drawn, flabby face above the rotundity of his stomach, which gave him a weird aspect. But being constantly together, they did not notice the change that took place gradually in their appearance, and also in their dispositions.

Five months passed in that way.

Then, one morning, as Kayerts and Carlier, lounging in their chairs under the verandah, talked about the approaching visit of the steamer, a knot of armed men came out of the forest and advanced towards the station. They were strangers to that part of the country. They were tall, slight, draped classically from neck to heel in blue fringed cloths, and carried percussion muskets over their bare right shoulders. Makola showed signs of excitement, and ran out of the storehouse (where he spent all his days) to meet these visitors. They came into the courtyard and looked about them with steady, scornful glances. Their leader, a powerful and determined-looking negro with bloodshot eyes, stood in front of the verandah and made a long speech. He gesticulated much, and ceased very suddenly.

There was something in his intonation, in the sounds of the long sentences he used, that startled the two whites. It was like a reminiscence of something not exactly familiar, and yet resembling the speech of civilized men. It sounded like one of those impossible languages which sometimes we hear in our dreams.

"What lingo is that?" said the amazed Carlier. "In the first moment

I fancied the fellow was going to speak French. Anyway, it is a different kind of gibberish to what we ever heard."

"Yes," replied Kayerts. "Hey, Makola, what does he say? Where do they come from? Who are they?"

But Makola, who seemed to be standing on hot bricks, answered hurriedly, "I don't know. They come from very far. Perhaps Mrs. Price will understand. They are perhaps bad men."

The leader, after waiting for a while, said something sharply to Makola, who shook his head. Then the man, after looking round, noticed Makola's hut and walked over there. The next moment Mrs. Makola was heard speaking with great volubility. The other strangers—they were six in all—strolled about with an air of ease, put their heads through the door of the storeroom, congregated round the grave, pointed understandingly at the cross, and generally made themselves at home.

"I don't like those chaps—and, I say, Kayerts, they must be from the coast; they've got firearms," observed the sagacious Carlier.

Kayerts also did not like those chaps. They both, for the first time, became aware that they lived in conditions where the unusual may be dangerous, and that there was no power on earth outside of themselves to stand between them and the unusual. They became uneasy, went in and loaded their revolvers. Kayerts said, "We must order Makola to tell them to go away before dark."

The strangers left in the afternoon, after eating a meal prepared for them by Mrs. Makola. The immense woman was excited, and talked much with the visitors. She rattled away shrilly, pointing here and pointing there at the forests and at the river. Makola sat apart and watched. At times he got up and whispered to his wife. He accompanied the strangers across the ravine at the back of the station-ground, and returned slowly looking very thoughtful. When questioned by the white men he was very strange, seemed not to understand, seemed to have forgotten French—seemed to have forgotten how to speak altogether. Kayerts and Carlier agreed that the nigger had had too much palm wine.

There was some talk about keeping a watch in turn, but in the evening everything seemed so quiet and peaceful that they retired as usual. All night they were disturbed by a lot of drumming in the villages. A deep, rapid roll near by would be followed by another far off—then all ceased. Soon short appeals would rattle out here and there, then all mingle together, increase, become vigorous and sustained, would spread out over the forest, roll through the night, unbroken and ceaseless, near and far, as if the whole land had been one immense drum booming out steadily an appeal to heaven. And through the deep and tremendous noise sudden yells that resembled snatches of songs from a madhouse darted shrill and high in discordant jets of sound which seemed to rush far above the earth and drive all peace from under the stars.

Carlier and Kayerts slept badly. They both thought they had heard shots fired during the night—but they could not agree as to the direction. In the morning Makola was gone somewhere. He returned about noon with one of yesterday's strangers, and eluded all Kayerts's attempts to close with him: had become deaf apparently. Kayerts wondered. Carlier, who had been fishing off the bank, came back and remarked while he showed his catch, "The niggers seem to be in a deuce of a stir; I wonder what's up. I saw about fifteen canoes cross the river during the two hours I was there fishing." Kayerts, worried, said, "Isn't this Makola very queer today?" Carlier advised, "Keep all our men together in case of some trouble."

II

There were ten station men who had been left by the director. Those fellows, having engaged themselves to the Company for six months (without having any idea of a month in particular and only a very faint notion of time in general), had been serving the cause of progress for upwards of two years. Belonging to a tribe from a very distant part of this land of darkness and sorrow, they did not run away, naturally supposing that as wandering strangers they would be killed by the inhabitants of the country; in which they were right. They lived in straw huts on the slope of a ravine overgrown with reedy grass, just behind the station buildings. They were not happy, regretting the festive incantations, the sorceries, the human sacrifices of their own land; where they also had parents, brothers, sisters, admired chiefs, respected magicians, loved friends, and other ties supposed generally to be human. Besides, the rice rations served out by the Company did not agree with them, being a food unknown to their land, and to which they could not get used. Consequently they were unhealthy and miserable. Had they been of any other tribe they would have made up their minds to die—for nothing is easier to certain savages than suicide—and so have escaped from the puzzling difficulties of existence. But belonging, as they did, to a warlike tribe with filed teeth, they had more grit, and went on stupidly living through disease and sorrow. They did very little work, and had lost their splendid physique. Carlier and Kayerts doctored them assiduously without being able to bring them back into condition again. They were mustered every morning and told off to different tasks— grass-cutting, fence-building, tree-felling, etc., etc., which no power on earth could induce them to execute efficiently. The two whites had practically very little control over them.

In the afternoon Makola came over to the big house and found Kayerts watching three heavy columns of smoke rising above the forests. "What is that?" asked Kayerts. "Some villages burn," answered Makola, who seemed to have regained his wits. Then he said abruptly: "We have got very little ivory; bad six months' trading. Do you like get a little more ivory?"

"Yes," said Kayerts eagerly. He thought of percentages which were low.

"Those men who came yesterday are traders from Loanda who have got more ivory than they can carry home. Shall I buy? I know their camp."

"Certainly," said Kayerts, "What are those traders?"

"Bad fellows," said Makola indifferently. "They fight with people, and catch women and children. They are bad men, and got guns. There is a great disturbance in the country. Do you want ivory?"

"Yes," said Kayerts. Makola said nothing for a while. Then: "Those workmen of ours are no good at all," he muttered, looking round. "Station in very bad order, sir. Director will growl. Better get a fine lot of ivory, then he say nothing."

"I can't help it; the men won't work," said Kayerts. "When will you get that ivory?"

"Very soon," said Makola. "Perhaps tonight. You leave it to me, and keep indoors, sir. I think you had better give some palm wine to our men to make a dance this evening. Enjoy themselves. Work better tomorrow. There's plenty palm wine—gone a little sour."

Kayerts said yes, and Makola, with his own hands, carried the big calabashes to the door of his hut. They stood there till the evening, and Mrs. Makola looked into every one. The men got them at sunset. When Kayerts and Carlier retired, a big bonfire was flaring before the men's huts. They could hear their shouts and drumming. Some men from Gobila's village had joined the station hands, and the entertainment was a great success.

In the middle of the night, Carlier, waking suddenly, heard a man shout loudly; then a shot was fired. Only one. Carlier ran out and met Kayerts on the verandah. They were both startled. As they went across the yard to call Makola, they saw shadows moving in the night. One of them cried, "Don't shoot! It's me, Price." Then Makola appeared close to them. "Go back, go back, please," he urged, "you spoil all." "There are strange men about," said Carlier. "Never mind; I know," said Makola. Then he whispered, "All right. Bring ivory. Say nothing! I know my business." The two white men reluctantly went back to the house, but did not sleep. They heard footsteps, whispers, some groans. It seemed as if a lot of men came in, dumped heavy things on the ground, squabbled a long time, then went away. They lay on their hard beds and thought: "This Makola is invaluable." In the morning Carlier came out, very sleepy, and pulled at the cord of the big bell. The station hands mustered every morning to the sound of the bell. That morning nobody came. Kayerts turned out also, yawning. Across the yard they saw Makola come out of his hut, a tin basin of soapy water in his hand. Makola, a civilized nigger, was very neat in his person. He threw the soapsuds skilfully over a wretched little yellow cur he had, then turning his face to the agent's house, he shouted from the distance, "All the men gone last night!"

They heard him plainly, but in their surprise they both yelled out together: "What!" Then they stared at one another. "We are in a proper fix now," growled Carlier. "It's incredible!" muttered Kayerts. "I will go to the huts and see," said Carlier, striding off. Makola coming up found Kayerts standing alone.

"I can hardly believe it," said Kayerts tearfully. "We took care of them as if they had been our children."

"They went with the coast people," said Makola after a moment of hesitation.

"What do I care with whom they went—the ungrateful brutes!" exclaimed the other. Then with sudden suspicion, and looking hard at Makola, he added: "What do you know about it?"

Makola moved his shoulders, looking down on the ground. "What do I know? I think only. Will you come and look at the ivory I've got there? It is a fine lot. You never saw such."

He moved towards the store. Kayerts followed him mechanically, thinking about the incredible desertion of the men. On the ground before the door of the fetish lay six splendid tusks.

"What did you give for it?" asked Kayerts, after surveying the lot with satisfaction.

"No regular trade," said Makola. "They brought the ivory and gave it to me. I told them to take what they most wanted in the station. It is a beautiful lot. No station can show such tusks. Those traders wanted carriers badly, and our men were no good here. No trade, no entry in books; all correct."

Kayerts nearly burst with indignation. "Why!" he shouted, "I believe you have sold our men for these tusks!" Makola stood impassive and silent. "I—I—will—I," stuttered Kayerts. "You fiend!" he yelled out.

"I did the best for you and the Company," said Makola imperturbably. "Why you shout so much? Look at this tusk."

"I dismiss you! I will report you—I won't look at the tusk. I forbid you to touch them. I order you to throw them into the river. You—you!"

"You very red, Mr. Kayerts. If you are so irritable in the sun, you will get fever and die—like the first chief!" pronounced Makola impressively.

They stood still, contemplating one another with intense eyes, as if they had been looking with effort across immense distances. Kayerts shivered. Makola had meant no more than he said, but his words seemed to Kayerts full of ominous menace! He turned sharply and went away to the house. Makola retired into the bosom of his family; and the tusks, left lying before the store, looked very large and valuable in the sunshine.

Carlier came back on the verandah. "They're all gone, hey?" asked Kayerts from the far end of the common room in a muffled voice. "You did not find anybody?"

"Oh, yes," said Carlier, "I found one of Gobila's people lying dead before the huts—shot through the body. We heard that shot last night."

Kayerts came out quickly. He found his companion staring grimly over the yard at the tusks, away by the store. They both sat in silence for a while. Then Kayerts related his conversation with Makola. Carlier said nothing. At the midday meal they ate very little. They hardly exchanged a word that day. A great silence seemed to lie heavily over the station and press on their lips. Makola did not open the store; he spent the day playing with his children. He lay full-length on a mat outside his door, and the youngsters sat on his chest and clambered all over him. It was a touching picture. Mrs. Makola was busy cooking all day as usual. The white men made a somewhat better meal in the evening. Afterwards, Carlier smoking his pipe strolled over to the store; he stood for a long time over the tusks, touched one or two with his foot, even tried to lift the largest one by its small end. He came back to his chief, who had not stirred from the verandah, threw himself in the chair and said—

"I can see it! They were pounced upon while they slept heavily after drinking all that palm wine you'd allowed Makola to give them. A put-up job! See? The worst is, some of Gobila's people were there, and got carried off too, no doubt. The least drunk woke up, and got shot for his sobriety. This is a funny country. What will you do now?"

"We can't touch it, of course," said Kayerts.

"Of course not," assented Carlier.

"Slavery is an awful thing," stammered out Kayerts in an unsteady voice.

"Frightful—the sufferings," grunted Carlier, with conviction.

They believed their words. Everybody shows a respectful deference to certain sounds that he and his fellows can make. But about feelings people really know nothing. We talk with indignation or enthusiasm;

we talk about oppression, cruelty, crime, devotion, self-sacrifice, virtue, and we know nothing real beyond the words. Nobody knows what suffering or sacrifice mean—except, perhaps, the victims of the mysterious purpose of these illusions.

Next morning they saw Makola very busy setting up in the yard the big scales used for weighing ivory. By and by Carlier said: "What's that filthy scoundrel up to?" and lounged out into the yard. Kayerts followed. They stood by watching. Makola took no notice. When the balance was swung true, he tried to lift a tusk into the scale. It was too heavy. He looked up helplessly without a word, and for a minute they stood round that balance as mute and still as three statues. Suddenly Carlier said: "Catch hold of the other end, Makola—you beast!" and together they swung the tusk up. Kayerts trembled in every limb. He muttered, "I say! Oh! I say!" and putting his hand in his pocket found there a dirty bit of paper and the stump of a pencil. He turned his back on the others, as if about to do something tricky, and noted stealthily the weights which Carlier shouted out to him with unnecessary loudness. When all was over, Makola whispered to himself: "The sun's very strong here for the tusks." Carlier said to Kayerts in a careless tone: "I say, chief, I might just as well give him a lift with this lot into the store."

As they were going back to the house Kayerts observed with a sigh: "It had to be done." And Carlier said: "It's deplorable, but, the men being Company's men, the ivory is Company's ivory. We must look after it."

"I will report to the director, of course," said Kayerts. "Of course; let him decide," approved Carlier.

At midday they made a hearty meal. Kayerts sighed from time to time. Whenever they mentioned Makola's name they always added to it an opprobrious epithet. It eased their conscience. Makola gave himself a half-holiday, and bathed his children in the river. No one from Gobila's villages came near the station that day. No one came the next day, and the next, nor for a whole week. Gobila's people might have all been dead and buried for any sign of life they gave. But they were only mourning for those they had lost by the witchcraft of white men, who had brought wicked people into their country. The wicked people were gone, but fear remained. Fear always remains. A man may destroy everything within himself, love and hate and belief, and even doubt; but as long as he clings to life he cannot destroy fear: the fear, subtle, indestructible, and terrible, that pervades his being; that tinges his thoughts; that lurks in his heart; that watches on his lips the struggle of his last breath. In his fear, the mild old Gobila offered extra human sacrifices to all the evil spirits that had taken possession of his white friends. His heart was heavy. Some warriors spoke about burning and killing, but the cautious old savage dissuaded them. Who could foresee the woe those mysterious creatures, if irritated, might bring? They should be left alone. Perhaps in time they would disappear into the earth as the first one had disappeared. His people must keep away from them, and hope for the best.

Kayerts and Carlier did not disappear, but remained above on this earth, that, somehow, they fancied had become bigger and very empty. It was not the absolute and dumb solitude of the post that impressed them so much as an inarticulate feeling that something from within them was gone, something that worked for their safety, and had kept the wilderness from interfering with their hearts. The images of home; the memory of people like them, of men that thought and felt as they used to think and feel, receded into distances made indistinct by the glare of unclouded sunshine. And out of the great silence of the surrounding wilderness, its very hopelessness and savagery seemed to approach them nearer, to draw them gently, to look upon them, to envelop them with a solicitude irresistible, familiar, and disgusting.

Days lengthened into weeks, then into months. Gobila's people drummed and yelled to every new moon, as of yore, but kept away from the station. Makola and Carlier tried once in a canoe to open communications, but were received with a shower of arrows, and had to fly back to the station for dear life. That attempt set the country up and down the river into an uproar that could be very distinctly heard for days. The steamer was late. At first they spoke of delay jauntily, then anxiously, then gloomily. The matter was becoming serious. Stores were running short. Carlier cast his lines off the bank, but the river was low, and the fish kept out in the stream. They dared not stroll far away from the station to shoot. Moreover, there was no game in the impenetrable forest. Once Carlier shot a hippo in the river. They had no boat to secure it, and it sank. When it floated up it drifted away, and Gobila's people secured the carcass. It was the occasion for a national holiday, but Carlier had a fit of rage over it, and talked about the necessity of exterminating all the niggers before the country could be made habitable. Kayerts mooned about silently; spent hours looking at the portrait of his Melie. It represented a little girl with long bleached tresses and a rather sour face. His legs were much swollen, and he could hardly walk. Carlier, undermined by fever, could not swagger anymore, but kept tottering about, still with a devil-may-care air, as became a man who remembered his crack regiment. He had become hoarse, sarcastic, and inclined to say unpleasant things. He called it "being frank with you." They had long ago reckoned their percentages on trade, including in them that last deal of "this infamous Makola." They had also concluded not to say anything about it. Kayerts hesitated at first—was afraid of the director.

"He has seen worse things done on the quiet," maintained Carlier, with a hoarse laugh. "Trust him! He won't thank you if you blab. He is no better than you or me. Who will talk if we hold our tongues? There is nobody here."

That was the root of the trouble! There was nobody there; and being left there alone with their weakness, they became daily more like a pair of accomplices than like a couple of devoted friends. They had heard nothing from home for eight months. Every evening they said, "Tomorrow we shall see the steamer." But one of the Company's steamers had been wrecked, and the director was busy with the other, relieving very distant and important stations on the main river. He thought that the useless station, and the useless men, could wait. Meantime Kayerts and Carlier lived on rice boiled without salt, and cursed the Company, all Africa, and the day they were born. One must have lived on such diet to discover what ghastly trouble the necessity of swallowing one's food may become. There was literally nothing else in the station but rice and coffee; they drank the coffee without sugar. The last fifteen lumps Kayerts had solemnly locked away in his box, together with a half-bottle of Cognac, "in case of sickness," he explained. Carlier approved. "When one is sick," he said, "any little extra like that is cheering."

They waited. Rank grass began to sprout over the courtyard. The bell never rang now. Days passed, silent, exasperating, and slow. When the two men spoke, they snarled; and their silences were bitter, as if tinged by the bitterness of their thoughts.

One day after a lunch of boiled rice, Carlier put down his cup untasted, and said: "Hang it all! Let's have a decent cup of coffee for once. Bring out that sugar, Kayerts."

"For the sick," muttered Kayerts, without looking up.

"For the sick," mocked Carlier. "Bosh! . . . Well! I am sick."

"You are no more sick than I am, and I go without," said Kayerts in a peaceful tone.

"Come! out with that sugar, you stingy old slave-dealer."

Kayerts looked up quickly. Carlier was smiling with marked insolence. And suddenly it seemed to Kayerts that he had never seen that man before. Who was he? He knew nothing about him. What was he capable of? There was a surprising flash of violent emotion within him, as if in the presence of something undreamt of, dangerous, and final. But he managed to pronounce with composure—

"That joke is in very bad taste. Don't repeat it."

"Joke!" said Carlier, hitching himself forward on his seat. "I am hungry—I am sick—I don't joke! I hate hypocrites. You are a hypocrite. You are a slave-dealer. I am a slave-dealer. There's nothing but slave-dealers in this cursed country. I mean to have sugar in my coffee today, anyhow!"

"I forbid you to speak to me in that way," said Kayerts with a fair show of resolution.

"You!—What?" shouted Carlier, jumping up.

Kayerts stood up also. "I am your chief," he began, trying to master the shakiness of his voice.

"What?" yelled the other. "Who's chief? There's no chief here. There's nothing here: there's nothing but you and I. Fetch the sugar—you potbellied ass."

"Hold your tongue. Go out of this room," screamed Kayerts. "I dismiss you—you scoundrel!"

Carlier swung a stool. All at once he looked dangerously in earnest. "You flabby, good-for-nothing civilian—take that!" he howled.

Kayerts dropped under the table, and the stool struck the grass inner wall of the room. Then, as Carlier was trying to upset the table, Kayerts in desperation made a blind rush, head low, like a cornered pig would do, and overturning his friend, bolted along the verandah and into his room. He locked the door, snatched his revolver, and stood panting. In less than a minute Carlier was kicking at the door furiously, howling, "If you don't bring out that sugar, I will shoot you at sight, like a dog. Now then—one—two—three. You won't? I will show you who's the master."

Kayerts thought the door would fall in, and scrambled through the square hole that served for a window in his room. There was then the whole breadth of the house between them. But the other was apparently not strong enough to break in the door, and Kayerts heard him running round. Then he also began to run laboriously on his swollen legs. He ran as quickly as he could, grasping the revolver, and unable yet to understand what was happening to him. He saw in succession Makola's house, the store, the river, the ravine, and the low bushes; and he saw all those things again as he ran for the second time round the house. Then again they flashed past him. That morning he could not have walked a yard without a groan.

And now he ran. He ran fast enough to keep out of sight of the other man.

Then as, weak and desperate, he thought "Before I finish the next round I shall die," he heard the other man stumble heavily, then stop. He stopped also. He had the back and Carlier the front of the house, as before. He heard him drop into a chair cursing, and suddenly his own legs gave way, and he slid down into a sitting posture with his back to the wall. His mouth was as dry as a cinder, and his face was wet with perspiration—and tears. What was it all about? He thought it must be a horrible illusion; he thought he was dreaming; he thought he was going mad! After a while he collected his senses. What did they quarrel about? That sugar! How absurd! He would give it to him—didn't want it himself. And he began scrambling to his feet with a sudden feeling of security. But before he had fairly stood upright, a commonsense reflection occurred to him and drove him back into despair. He thought: If I give way now to that brute of a soldier, he will begin this horror again tomorrow—and the day after—every day—raise other pretensions, trample on me, torture me, make me his slave—and I will be lost! Lost! The steamer may not come for days—may never come. He shook so that he had to sit down on the floor again. He shivered forlornly. He felt he could not, would not move any more. He was completely distracted by the sudden perception that the position was without issue—that death and life had in a moment become equally difficult and terrible.

All at once he heard the other push his chair back; and he leaped to his feet with extreme facility. He listened and got confused. Must run again! Right or left? He heard footsteps. He darted to the left, grasping his revolver, and at the very same instant, as it seemed to him, they came into violent collision. Both shouted with surprise. A loud explosion took place between them; a roar of red fire, thick smoke; and Kayerts, deafened and blinded, rushed back thinking: I am hit—it's all over. He expected the other to come round—to gloat over his agony. He caught hold of an upright of the roof—"all over!" Then he heard a crashing fall on the other side of the house, as if somebody had tumbled headlong over a chair—then silence. Nothing more happened. He did not die. Only his shoulder felt as if it had been badly wrenched, and he had lost his revolver. He was disarmed and helpless! He waited for his fate. The other man made no sound. It was stratagem. He was stalking him now! Along what side? Perhaps he was taking aim this very minute!

After a few moments of an agony frightful and absurd, he decided to go and meet his doom. He was prepared for every surrender. He turned the corner, steadying himself with one hand on the wall, made a few paces, and nearly swooned. He had seen on the floor, protruding past the other corner, a pair of turned-up feet. A pair of white naked feet in red slippers. He felt deadly sick, and stood for a time in profound darkness. Then Makola appeared before him, saying quietly: "Come along, Mr. Kayerts. He is dead." He burst into tears of gratitude; a loud, sobbing fit of crying. After a time he found himself sitting in a chair and looking at Carlier, who lay stretched on his back. Makola was kneeling over the body.

"Is this your revolver?" asked Makola, getting up.

"Yes," said Kayerts; then he added very quickly, "He ran after me to shoot me—you saw!"

"Yes, I saw," said Makola. "There is only one revolver; where's his?"

"Don't know," whispered Kayerts in a voice that had become suddenly very faint.

"I will go and look for it," said the other gently. He made the round along the verandah, while Kayerts sat still and looked at the corpse. Makola came back empty-handed, stood in deep thought, then stepped quietly into the dead man's room, and came out directly with a revolver, which he held up before Kayerts. Kayerts shut his eyes. Everything was going round. He found life more terrible and difficult than death. He had shot an unarmed man.

After meditating for a while, Makola said softly, pointing at the dead man who lay there with his right eye blown out—

"He died of fever." Kayerts looked at him with a stony stare. "Yes," repeated Makola thoughtfully, stepping over the corpse, "I think he died of fever. Bury him tomorrow."

And he went away slowly to his expectant wife, leaving the two white men alone on the verandah.

Night came, and Kayerts sat unmoving on his chair. He sat quiet as if he had taken a dose of opium. The violence of the emotions he had passed through produced a feeling of exhausted serenity. He had plumbed in one short afternoon the depths of horror and despair, and now found repose in the conviction that life had no more secrets for him: neither had death! He sat by the corpse thinking; thinking very actively, thinking very new thoughts. He seemed to have broken loose from himself altogether. His old thoughts, convictions, likes and dislikes, things he respected and things he abhorred, appeared in their true light at last! Appeared contemptible and childish, false and ridiculous. He reveled in his new wisdom while he sat by the man he had killed. He argued with himself about all things under heaven with that kind of wrong-headed lucidity which may be observed in some lunatics. Incidentally he reflected that the fellow dead there had been a noxious beast anyway; that men died every day in thousands; perhaps in hundreds of thousands—who could tell?—and that, in the number, that one death could not possibly make any difference; couldn't have any importance, at least to a thinking creature. He, Kayerts, was a thinking creature. He had been all his life, till that moment, a believer in a lot of nonsense like the rest of mankind—who are fools; but now he thought! He knew! He was at peace; he was familiar with the highest wisdom! Then he tried to imagine himself dead, and Carlier sitting in his chair watching him; and his attempt met with such unexpected success, that in a very few moments he became not at all sure who was dead and who was alive. This extraordinary achievement of his fancy startled him, however, and by a clever and timely effort of mind he saved himself just in time from becoming Carlier. His heart thumped, and he felt hot all over at the thought of that danger. Carlier! What a beastly thing! To compose his now disturbed nerves—and no wonder!—he tried to whistle a little. Then, suddenly, he fell asleep, or thought he had slept; but at any rate there was a fog, and somebody had whistled in the fog.

He stood up. The day had come, and a heavy mist had descended upon the land: the mist penetrating, enveloping, and silent; the morning mist of tropical lands; the mist that clings and kills; the mist white and deadly, immaculate and poisonous. He stood up, saw the body, and threw his arms above his head with a cry like that of a man who, waking from a trance, finds himself immured for ever in a tomb. *"Help! . . . My God!"*

A shriek, inhuman, vibrating and sudden, pierced like a sharp dart the white shroud of that land of sorrow. Three short, impatient screeches followed, and then, for a time, the fog-wreaths rolled on, undisturbed, through a formidable silence. Then many more shrieks, rapid and piercing, like the yells of some exasperated and ruthless creature, rent the air. Progress was calling to Kayerts from the river. Progress and civilization and all the virtues. Society was calling to its accomplished child to come, to be taken care of, to be instructed, to be judged, to be condemned; it called him to return to that rubbish heap from which he had wandered away, so that justice could be done.

Kayerts heard and understood. He stumbled out of the verandah, leaving the other man quite alone for the first time since they had been thrown there together. He groped his way through the fog, calling in his ignorance upon the invisible heaven to undo its work. Makola flitted by in the mist, shouting as he ran—

"Steamer! Steamer! They can't see. They whistle for the station. I go ring the bell. Go down to the landing, sir. I ring."

He disappeared. Kayerts stood still. He looked upwards; the fog rolled low over his head. He looked round like a man who has lost his way; and he saw a dark smudge, a cross-shaped stain, upon the shifting purity of the mist. As he began to stumble towards it, the station bell rang in a tumultuous peal its answer to the impatient clamor of the steamer.

The managing director of the Great Civilizing Company (since we know that civilization follows trade) landed first, and incontinently lost sight of the steamer. The fog down by the river was exceedingly dense; above, at the station, the bell rang unceasing and brazen.

The director shouted loudly to the steamer: "There is nobody down to meet us; there may be something wrong, though they are ringing. You had better come, too!"

And he began to toil up the steep bank. The captain and the engine-driver of the boat followed behind. As they scrambled up the fog thinned, and they could see their director a good way ahead. Suddenly they saw him start forward, calling to them over his shoulder: "Run! Run to the house! I've found one of them. Run, look for the other!"

He had found one of them! And even he, the man of varied and startling experience, was somewhat discomposed by the manner of this finding. He stood and fumbled in his pockets (for a knife) while he faced Kayerts, who was hanging by a leather strap from the cross. He had evidently climbed the grave, which was high and narrow, and after tying the end of the strap to the arm, had swung himself off. His toes were only a couple of inches above the ground; his arms hung stiffly down; he seemed to be standing rigidly at attention, but with one purple cheek playfully posed on the shoulder. And, irreverently, he was putting out a swollen tongue at his managing director.

John Updike

MY UNCLE'S DEATH

John Updike *(1932–) was born in Shillington, Pennsylvania, and graduated from Harvard College in 1954. He is among our most honored and prolific writers, and he continues, well into his seventies, to produce a wonderful
torrent of novels, short fiction, literary criticism, and poetry. "My Uncle's
Death," which first appeared in the* Saturday Evening Post *in 1963, is a
reminder that children absorb a lot from the grown-ups around them, even
people they don't see often. The uncle in this story "played to win" and had notable success in business; in death, he left behind a not-inconsiderable legacy of
memories and words of advice taken on board by the narrator, now an adult.*

He died while shaving; when I was told of this, I pictured him stagger-
ing back heavily, stricken, his own amazed face in the mirror the last
thing he ever saw. His face flashed there for him, hung there, slipped
backward; and then the mirror was full of the blank bathroom wall. I
pictured this so sharply I seemed to have been there.

At his funeral I felt, for the first time, my adult height. The Manatees
are not a family of breeders, and the number of relatives was small; walking up the aisle to the front pew with my parents, my aunt and my two
cousins, I felt tall and prominent. Walking back down the aisle after the
service, I caught, from the faces of those still seated, an odd, motionless,
intent look, almost an odor, of sympathy and curiosity and reverence for
grief. The look, no doubt, was primarily directed at my aunt, the widow,
who, on the arm of my father, led our ragged, rustling procession. But
we all—all the relatives—shared in it and were for the moment heroes of
bereavement: a surviving band, a clan. I carried my role proudly, though
doubting that I had felt enough sorrow to earn it. I was just sixteen, still

an inch or two short of my eventual height, but walking down that aisle I entered, through that strange odor of respect, pity, and wonder, the company of adulthood. I became a Manatee. Unfairly enough, my two cousins, my uncle's daughters, were a little younger than I and emerged from the church, with all their bewildering weight of loss, still children, though fatherless.

Yet I had loved my uncle, as much as the distance between us permitted. He was famous and rich. Not so famous and rich, I have since discovered, as our branch of the family imagined, but enough for a head shot and a half column on the obituary page of *The New York Times*. Trained as an architect—though he never got his degree—he speculated in real estate, and there are several blocks of Manhattan that would not look quite the same if he had never lived. The phantom presence of his importance hovered about our family table long before I first saw him seated there as a guest, and when I try to remember him as he was, his fame and wealth, which I so obtrusively wanted for myself, inflate and blur his face, making it unreally large and distant—a clown-faced moon hung in the skimpy branches of my family tree.

I cannot reach him. I can remember nothing about him that is quite real except his death; he is like a celestial body which only eclipse renders measurable. He was six feet, four inches tall, but his immensity was narrow-shouldered, small-boned and unmuscular. He was vain of having, for so outsized a man, rather small feet. He usually wore neat black loafers, virtually slippers, of English leather, and, sprawling soddenly in a chair, he generally contrived to thrust his feet forward on the floor, or up on a stool, so they were noticed. I remember my mother—I must have been ten or eleven—teasing him about his dainty feet. I cannot recapture her words, but she was still slim then, and her pose as she spoke—head tilted back, hands half lifted—stuck in my mind; she so seldom struck an unmotherly attitude that it was as if a strange spirit had come and for a moment possessed her body. My uncle, presumably, responded with a dry flutter of the sheepish gallantry that he seemed to reserve for my mother and for waitresses in restaurants. My mother seemed exempt from the rather lazy distaste with which my uncle viewed the rest of the world, and perhaps, as her son, I was included in the exemption, for he was kind to me.

He taught me gin rummy. The very name of the game excited me with visions of parlor cars and high hotel rooms full of heavy, expensive men—world-wielders—smoking cigars and playing for a dollar a point. We would play gin rummy for hours on the side porch of our homely little green-shingled house in our once-rural suburb of Providence. My uncle and his wife and daughters would visit us here once a year, always in the summer, and for exactly three days—never more. He would cite the adage about fish and guests stinking after three days, adding, "And we're both." The manatee is, of course, an aquatic mammal, with a flat snout and rounded tail—but my uncle was willing to twist the truth to cinch a joke.

"Leonard, how's your friend Christ?" would be, with each visit, the first and virtually the only question that he would direct at my father. It was a joke, but my father would answer the question seriously; his involvement with church and community affairs was so consuming that he was rarely at home in the evenings. He was older than my uncle by two years but had long ago ceased to be a challenge to him. As my father talked about church feuds and Lions' Club politics, my uncle would sink silently deeper into his chair, a kind of fine powder of resignation would whiten his large face, and the thrust-out, exquisitely shod feet would conspicuously fidget.

Humiliated that my uncle, who manipulated city blocks like a giant, should be bored by the petty details of our timid lives, I scolded my father privately. He said, "No, he's interested. He's my brother. You're an only child, Freddy, so that probably doesn't make any sense to you."

I was an only child, and there was little in my life beyond my uncle's annual visits to broaden my definition of "family." *He's my brother*: this simple assertion plunged me backward into depths I could never understand. By the time I reached my mid-teens, my mind, like a soft surface lightly but repeatedly tapped, had received from these visits some confusing impressions. My father, dismissed by his brother, had turned in his heart toward Thelma, my uncle's wife, a stoic, chain-smoking woman whose face seemed to have suffered so many jolts that certain corners of it would never relax again. She must have found much in her pious, modest brother-in-law that was soothing; she was an amateur gardener in much the same obsessed way that he was a deacon, and the two of them would go for long walks together, she looking at the vegetation, he performing altruistic errands. Sitting side by side on the couch looking at old family photographs, *they* seemed the siblings; there was even a physical resemblance. The skin of both had grown darker with age; their faces were wrinkled as if with the cracks of a tough varnish. Meanwhile my uncle, so fragilely pale and pink, hovering humorously on his pampered feet while my mother, more gracefully than usual, performed the motions of housework, showered upon her a kind of antic indulgence which I supposed was fraternal. These impressions, bafflingly contradicted at the end of each visit when my uncle and aunt got into their gray Cadillac with their girls and, waving, disappeared down the driveway together, suggested to me that in the depths of the mystery called "family" there lay, necessarily, an irrevocable mistake.

"Freddy, who ate the cards?" With this absurd question my uncle would invite me to play rummy. My father would be off at work. My aunt and my mother would be somewhere in the house tugging, with the elaborate and pained tact that lay between them, the housekeeping duties back and forth. My cousins, who lived in a small chaste bivalve world in which they always faced each other, would be engaged underfoot in some conspiratorial girlish game. I would find the cards. My uncle would sit down and deal. We would play for hours on the porch, the side screens sieving the songs of insects, the sounds of traffic swelling from a whisper at noon to a waterfall roar by suppertime. Timidly I would ask if I weren't wasting his time.

He would laugh and shuffle the cards once more. He had a loud, easy way of riffling them together that I could never quite master. "Most of my time, Freddy, is wasted time. I've sat in railroad stations all day long."

"But isn't there something important you should be doing?"

"Because I'm important? You don't understand, Freddy—importance is entirely a matter of belief. The more important you are, the less important what you do is. When you reach my stage, nothing you do matters at all. The most important thing in my life right now is to whump you at this witless game. Your draw."

He played to win, and I loved him for that. So many adults refuse to give a child the compliment of a contest. Now and then, as he deliberated over the upturned pile, and then plunged and took them all into his hand, I felt for an instant the decisive thrust that had carried him so far into the world of money.

I was still groping, trying to discover in him what it was like to be rich and famous. I searched his face; it was an ugly face, a clown's and giant's both. His cheekbones seemed broadened by the extreme closeness of his old-fashioned, centrally parted haircut. His small slanting eyes twitched alertly in their puffy mountings of sleeplessness. His nose, battered by college football, was rose pink, and his teeth were yellowed by tobacco.

"Someday *you'll* be important," he said suddenly.

Startled, I lied, "Oh, I don't think so."

"I think so. You'll do it to please your mother."

"Really? You think she cares?"

He didn't answer, but instead lay down three triplets and went out. As he totted up the points caught in my hand, he said, "Don't do everything to please your mother. It's a mistake."

It was the only advice my uncle ever gave me, and I am not sure I understand it still. I have, in an unimportant way, become important; if I died tomorrow, I might receive three or four inches in the *Times*—about as much, say, as the mother superior of an upstate nunnery. I have taken a slower, more scholarly route than my uncle, and the other day, in reading a treatise on fools, I encountered a certain King Suibhne, of ancient Ireland, who abruptly became a fool in the tumult of battle: "Unsteadiness, restlessness, and unquiet filled him, likewise disgust with every place in which he used to be and desire for every place which he had not reached." I recognized the sensations. They are ours, the Manatees'. I feel now how my father roved the streets, seeking good to do, because he was possessed by "disgust with every place in which he used to be and desire for every place which he had not reached." And my uncle, too, though he sought to escape the curse by remaining in a chair, was an unquiet traveler; the family discontent vibrated in him until he collapsed. Because shuffling cards and striking matches were the most strenuous things I ever saw him do, when I heard of his first heart attack it seemed a mistake. How could a man overwork his heart when he was always sitting with his feet preeningly stretched out before him?

The summer after the winter of his first attack I was invited, alone, to visit his home in Rye, New York. They lived in a big white house on what seemed to my semirural eyes a rather small lawn. My aunt's flower-and-vegetable garden took up most of the land. I was disappointed that the difference between their house and ours was one of degree rather than kind. A maid came in on Mondays and Fridays, and in the living room there was a paneled closet full of liquor bottles, with a faucet for water and a small pine counter like a bar; otherwise it was a house like ours, with rooms (only more) and rugs (only deeper) and chairs and windows and books. Their bookcases smelled like my parents' college yearbooks and held dark brown Modern Library editions from the twenties, with jiggly type and stingy margins, and an English edition of *Ulysses* bearing a longbow on the spine. I opened *Ulysses* and was appalled, in the middle of a blank August afternoon, by the keen scent of death the packed words gave off; my uncle had long ago marked a few passages in the margins, and his pencilings were like the tracks of someone who had preceded me through Hell.

I was fifteen that summer and stayed two weeks, reading books and mowing the lawn and playing badminton with my cousins. Several times my aunt drove me into Manhattan. She became confiding; as an only child I was susceptible to adult confidences. She told me about my uncle's heart. It had been weakened by his work, his weight, his total lack of exercise, his drinking, his smoking, and—her eyes suddenly glittered with tears, making my stomach clench—his lack of will to live. "He doesn't care enough, Freddy, if he lives or dies; he just doesn't see that great a difference." But my attention had snagged on the first thing she had said. His work? But many days he came home from New York on the shoppers' train, and some says he did not go in at all, just loafed around the house in his bathrobe all morning and had lunch by himself at a restaurant in downtown Rye. Though he and Aunt Thelma never quarreled in my presence, I soon learned to detect, from the atmosphere in the house, when he had returned with liquor on his breath. His doctors had ordered him to stop smoking and drinking.

In the evenings, often, my cousins and my aunt would go to bed while my uncle and I sat up playing gin rummy. As soon as his wife's footsteps hit the stair, he would take a rumpled pack of Camels out of his pocket and begin to smoke. His big, crimped, clownish mouth did not so much smoke the cigarettes as swallow them; one after another they vanished in front of his face, and the light of the bridge lamp over his shoulder turned blue. When it was my turn to shuffle, he would go to the paneled closet; there would be a soft tinkling noise, and he would bring back a glass of ice cubes and amber liquid. I would drink ginger ale to keep him company; many nights I drank a whole quart. We often stayed up past one o'clock, and, though little was said that did not relate to the cards, I felt trusted. My parents kept regular hours, so the region of time beyond midnight still held a romance for me. As the sounds of traffic outside dwindled to an occasional speeder spurting from one horizon of silence to another, my uncle and I seemed to be traveling together like two card players on a perfectly greased train riding absolutely level tracks into a hushed beyond where his harrowed, puffy face was no longer ugly but utterly appropriate, like an angel's in ether. His presence, in the beginning a mere inflated projection on the flat facts of his fame and wealth, was given a shadowy third dimension by what I knew now of his life. His attack had caused my parents to reminisce about him. He had been the precocious, favored baby of my grandmother's house; he had had a double aptitude, for drawing and mathematics, and had resolved it into the ambition to be an architect. He had finished half his training, when his father, in a swift street accident, died, leaving nothing but debts. He had faced the choice of completing his training and beginning his years of apprenticeship, or of quitting and immediately helping my father support their mother; with his slightly brusque decisiveness, he had chosen the latter. Henceforth he lived, as my father put it, "by his wits," and apparently thrived. Their mother lived for twenty more years.

Invariably he kept the score of our games, in precise penciled numerals, the fours closed at the top, the ones fashioned like small sevens. After several glasses of amber liquid, his architect's printing would become mechanically small and even, and all his motions took on the deliberately slowed efficiency of someone determined to complete a distasteful job. When he finished a pack of Camels, he would crumple it in his hand and stuff the paper ball back into his coat pocket. Once he paused and showed the crumpled pack to me. It lay in his wide white palm like a garish pill, or like a tinfoil-headed beetle with a camel's brown sneer buckled into its back. "You needn't tell Thelma about this," he said mildly, stuffing it into his pocket and drawing out a fresh pack. He took care to return the red cellophane strip to his pocket.

"Should you be doing it?" I asked.

"Oh, sure," he said, huffing through his pink nose with an asthmatic effort I had not noticed before. "I'm an old expert, Freddy, at taking care of myself. In forty-nine years I've never had an accident."

And, anxious to win, I obligingly shuffled another hand, and he heaved to his feet through the blue veil and went to hover, tinkling, at the bar. I suppose I felt that beating him at cards would somehow give me access—if not now, later—to the millions I imagined he had won from the world. In fact, his fortune, inscrutably submerged in loans and options and fractional titles to property, was not so large as my family had thought; his sole bequest to me was a beautiful suitcase of English leather, which I still use.

I never told my aunt how my uncle drank and smoked, though several times an opportunity for telling seemed to have been created. I was fifteen and assumed that adults were their own responsibility. I was flattered by his trust and do not believe now that my betraying it would have significantly added to her knowledge, or helped anyone. Nevertheless, when my mother, one noon in the following autumn, came back from the telephone with a shocked face and told us, "Ed died this morning," I had this sharp sense, for all the intervening distance, of witnessing my uncle's death.

Leo Tolstoy

MASTER AND MAN

Initially, "Master and Man" is about a busy merchant who encounters a major obstacle to an important business transaction. But this timeless tale by **Leo Tolstoy** *(1828–1910) is also a meditation on power, ego, subservience, and ultimately, humility before God. Vasily Andreevich Brekhunov's conversion of faith requires a crisis: only then does the master become fully a man. Perhaps, hints Tolstoy with measured optimism, we'll all have such an opportunity to discover our true relationship to our fellow-travelers, and to God. The text provided here is a newly revised version of an earlier translation from the Russian by Louise and Aylmer Maude.*

I

It happened in the seventies, in winter, the day after St. Nicholas's Day. There was a festival in the parish, and the innkeeper, Vasily Andreevich Brekhunov, a second guild merchant, being a church elder, had to go to church and also had to entertain his relatives and friends at home.

But as soon as the last of his guests had left, he prepared to drive over to see a neighboring landowner about a grove he had been bargaining over for a long time. He was in a hurry to set off, lest buyers from the town should interfere with his making a profitable purchase.

The young landowner was asking ten thousand rubles for the grove simply because Vasily Andreevich was offering seven thousand. Seven thousand was, however, only a third of its real value. Vasily Andreevich might have been able to get the price down further, for the woods were in his district and he had a longstanding agreement with the other village dealers that no one should run up the price in another's district, but he had recently learned that some timber dealers from town were planning to bid on the Goryachkin grove, and he resolved to go at once and get the matter settled. So as soon as the feast was over, he took seven hundred rubles from his strongbox and added twenty-three hundred rubles of church money he had in his keeping, for a total of three thousand; he carefully counted the notes, put them into his pocket-book, and set off in haste.

Nikita, the only one of Vasily Andreevich's laborers who wasn't drunk that day, ran to harness the horse. Nikita, though a habitual drunkard, wasn't drunk that day because he had sworn off drinking since the eve of the fast, when he had drunk away his coat and leather boots; he kept his vow for two months and was still keeping it despite the temptation of the vodka that had been drunk everywhere during the first two days of the feast.

Nikita was a peasant of about fifty from a neighboring village, "not a manager," as the peasants said of him, meaning that he was not the thrifty head of a household but lived most of his time away from home as a laborer. He was valued everywhere for his industry, dexterity, and strength at work, and still more for his kindly and pleasant demeanor. But he never settled down anywhere for long, because about twice a year, or even oftener, he would have a drinking bout and then, besides spending all his clothes on drink, he would grow agitated and quarrel-some. Vasily Andreevich himself had turned Nikita away several times, but had afterward taken him back, valuing his honesty, his kindness to animals, and especially his low wages. Vasily Andreevich did not pay Nikita the eighty rubles a year such a man was worth, but only about forty, which he paid him in haphazard way, in small sums, and mostly not in cash but in goods from his own shop and at high prices.

Nikita's wife, Martha, who had once been a handsome, vigorous woman, managed the homestead with the help of her son and two daughters, and did not urge Nikita to live at home, first because she had been living for some twenty years already with a cooper, a peasant from another village who lodged in their house, and second because, although she managed her husband as she pleased when he was sober, she feared him like fire when he was drunk. Once he got drunk at home and, probably out of a need to make up for his submissiveness when sober, he broke open her box, took out her best clothes, snatched up an ax, and chopped all her undergarments and dresses to bits. All the wages Nikita earned went to his wife, and he raised no objection to that. So now, two days before the holiday, Martha had been twice to see Vasily Andreevich and had got from him wheat flour, tea, sugar, and a quart of vodka, at a total cost of three rubles, and he advanced her an additional five rubles in cash, for which she thanked him as if it were a special favor, even though he owed Nikita at least twenty rubles in back pay.

"What agreement did we ever draw up with you?" said Vasily Andreevich to Nikita. "If you need anything, take it; you'll work it off. I'm not like others, who would keep you waiting, and make up accounts and impose fines. We deal straightforwardly. You serve me and I don't neglect you."

And when saying this, Vasily Andreevich was honestly convinced that he was Nikita's benefactor, and he knew how to say it so plausibly that all those who depended on him for their money, beginning with Nikita, was convinced he was their benefactor and did not exploit them.

"Yes, I understand, Vasily Andreevich," Nikita would reply. "You know I take pains to serve you just as I would my own father. I understand very well!" He was well aware that Vasily Andreevich was cheating him, but at the same time it seemed useless to try to clear up his accounts with him or explain his side of the matter, and that as long as he had nowhere else to go he had to take what he could get.

Now, having heard his master's order to harness the horse, he went as usual cheerfully and willingly to the shed, stepping briskly and easily on his rather pigeon-toed feet. He took the heavy tasseled leather bridle down off a nail on the wall and, jingling the rings of the bit, went to the covered stable where the horse he was to harness was standing by himself.

"What, feeling lonely, feeling lonely, little silly?" said Nikita in answer to the low whinny with which he was greeted by the good-tempered, medium-sized bay stallion, with a rather slanting rump. "Now then, now then, there's time enough, let me water you first," he went on, speaking to the horse just as if he were addressing someone who under-stood the words he was using. He whisked the dusty, grooved back of the well-fed young stallion with the skirt of his coat, put a bridle on his handsome head, straightened his ears and forelock, removed his halter, and led him out to water.

Mukhorty got frisky as he picked his way out of the dung-strewn sta-ble and, making play with his hind leg, pretended he was trying to kick Nikita, who was running at a trot beside him to the pump.

"Now then, now then, you rascal!" Nikita called out, knowing full well that Mukhorty had carefully thrown out his hind leg just enough to graze his greasy sheepskin coat, not to strike him—a trick Nikita much appreciated.

After a drink of cold water, the horse sighed, and a light spray of transparent drops fell from his strong wet lips into the trough. Then, standing still as if in thought, he suddenly gave a loud snort.

"You needn't drink more if you've had enough. But don't go asking for any later," said Nikita, quite seriously and fully explaining his con-duct to Mukhorty. He ran back to the shed, pulling the playful young horse along by the reins, though Mukhorty wanted to gambol all around the yard.

There was no one else in the yard except a stranger, the cook's hus-band, who had come for the holiday.

"Go and ask which sleigh is to be harnessed—the wide one or the small one—there's a good fellow!"

The cook's husband went into the house, which stood on an iron foundation and was iron-roofed, and soon returned, saying that the small one was to be harnessed. By that time, Nikita had put the collar and brass-studded bellyband on Mukhorty and, carrying a light, painted shaft-bow in one hand, was leading the horse with the other man up to two sleighs that stood in the shed.

"All right, let it be the little one!" he said, backing the intelligent horse into the shafts. Mukhorty kept pretending to bite him the whole time. With the help of the cook's husband, he proceeded to harness the horse. When everything was nearly ready and only the reins had to be adjusted, Nikita sent the other man to the shed for some straw and to the barn for a drugget rug.

"There, that's all right! Now, now, don't bristle!" said Nikita as he took hold of the freshly threshed oat straw brought by the cook's husband and pressed it down into the sleigh. "And now let's spread the sackcloth like this, and the drugget over it. There, that will make for comfortable sitting," he went on, suiting the action to his words and tucking the drugget all around over the straw to form a seat.

"Thank you, dear man. Things always go quicker with two working at it!" he added. Nikita gathered up the leather reins, which were fastened together by a brass ring, and took the driver's seat. He started the impatient horse over the frozen manure that lay in the yard and headed toward the gate.

"Uncle Nikita! I say, Uncle, Uncle!" a high-pitched voice shouted, and a seven-year-old boy in a black sheepskin coat, new white felt boots, and a warm cap ran hurriedly out of the house and into the yard. "Take me with you!" he cried, fastening his coat as he ran.

"All right, come along, darling!" Nikita said. He stopped the sleigh, picked up the master's pale, thin little son, who was radiant with joy, and drove out onto the road.

It was past two o'clock and the day was windy, dull, and frosty—below twenty degrees Fahrenheit. Half the sky was hidden by a lowering dark cloud. It was quiet in the yard, but in the street you could feel the wind more keenly. The snow swept down from a neighboring shed and whirled about in the corner near the bathhouse.

Nikita had just driven out of the yard and was steering the horse toward the house when Vasily Andreevich emerged from the front porch with a cigarette in his mouth and a cloth-covered sheepskin coat tightly cinched low around his waist. He stepped onto the hard-trodden snow, which squeaked under the leather soles of his felt boots, and stood. He drew a final puff of his cigarette, cast it down, and stepped on it. He let the smoke escape through his mustache and, looking askance at the approaching horse, tucked in his sheepskin collar on both sides of his ruddy face (which was clean-shaven except for the mustache) to prevent his breath from moistening the collar.

"See now! The young scamp is there already!" he exclaimed when he saw his little son in the sleigh. Vasily Andreevich was feeling the vodka he had drunk with his visitors, and so he was even more pleased than usual with everything that was his and all that he did. The sight of his son, whom he always thought of as his heir, now gave him great satisfaction. He looked at him, screwing up his eyes and showing his long teeth.

His wife—pregnant, thin and pale, with her head and shoulders wrapped in a shawl so that none of her face could be seen except her eyes—stood behind him in the vestibule to see him off.

"Now really, you ought to take Nikita with you," she said timidly, stepping out from the doorway.

Vasily Andreevich did not answer. Her words evidently annoyed him and he frowned angrily and spat.

"You have money on you," she continued in the same plaintive voice. "What if the weather gets worse! Do take him, for goodness sake!"

"Why? Don't I know the way well enough? Do I really need to take along a guide?" exclaimed Vasily Andreevich, uttering every word very distinctly and compressing his lips unnaturally, as he tended to do when talking to buyers and sellers.

"Really, you ought to take him. I beg you in God's name!" his wife repeated, wrapping her shawl more closely around her head.

"There, she sticks to it like a leech! Where am I to take him?"

"I'm all ready to go with you, Vasily Andreevich," said Nikita cheerfully. "But they'll have to feed the horses while I'm away," he added, turning to his master's wife.

"I'll look after them, Nikita dear. I'll tell Simon," replied the mistress.

"Well, Vasily Andreevich, shall I come with you?" said Nikita, awaiting a decision.

"It seems I must humor my old lady. But if you're coming you'd better put on a warmer cloak," said Vasily Andreevich, smiling again as he winked at Nikita, whose short sheepskin coat was torn under the arms and at the back, greasy and out of shape, frayed to a fringe around the skirt, and had endured many things in its lifetime.

"Hey, dear man, come and hold the horse!" shouted Nikita to the cook's husband, who was still in the yard.

"No, I'll do it myself, I'll do it myself!" shrieked the little boy, pulling his hands, red with cold, out of his pockets and seizing the cold leather reins.

"Only don't be too long dressing yourself up. Look alive!" shouted Vasily Andreevich, grinning at Nikita.

"Just a moment, Father, Vasily Andreevich!" replied Nikita, and he ran quickly, in his felt boots with their soles patched with felt, scurrying pigeon-toed across the yard and into the workmen's hut.

"Arinushka! Get my coat down from the stove. I'm going with the master," he said as he ran into the hut and took his girdle down from the nail on which it hung.

The workmen's cook, who had had a nap after dinner and was now getting the samovar ready for her husband, turned cheerfully to Nikita and, roused by his haste, moved as quickly as he did. She pulled his miserable worn-out cloth coat down from the stove where it was drying and hurriedly shook it out and smoothed it down.

"There now, you'll have a chance of a holiday with your good man," said Nikita, who, out of kindhearted politeness, always said something to anyone he was alone with.

Then, drawing his worn narrow girdle around him, he drew in his breath, pulling in his lean stomach still more, and girdled himself as tightly as he could over his sheepskin.

"There now," he said, now addressing not the cook but the girdle, and he tucked the ends in at the waist, "now you won't come undone!" And working his shoulders up and down to free his arms, he put the coat over his sheepskin, arched his back more strongly to ease his arms, poked himself under the armpits, and took down his leather-covered mittens from the shelf. "Now we're all right!"

"You ought to wrap your feet up, Nikita. Your boots are very bad."

Nikita stopped as if he had suddenly realized this.

"Yes, I ought to. But they'll do like this. It isn't far!" And he ran out to the yard.

"Won't you be cold, Nikita?" said the mistress as he came up to the sleigh.

"Cold? No, I'm quite warm," answered Nikita as he pushed some straw up to the front of the sleigh to cover his feet. He stowed the whip, which the good horse would not need, on the floor of the sleigh.

Vasily Andreevich, who was wearing two fur-lined coats, one over the other, was already in the sleigh, his broad back filling nearly its whole rounded width. He took the reins and immediately urged the horse on. Nikita jumped in just as the sleigh started and got seated in front on the left side, with one leg hanging over the edge.

2

The good stallion pulled the sleigh along at a brisk pace over the smooth-frozen road through the village. The runners squeaked slightly as they went.

"Look at him hanging on there! Hand me the whip, Nikita!" shouted Vasily Andreevich, evidently enjoying the sight of his "heir," who was hanging on to the back of the sleigh, standing on the runners. "I'll give it you! Be off to mamma, you dog!"

The boy jumped down. The horse quickened his pace and, suddenly changing gait, broke into a fast trot.

The Crosses, the village where Vasily Andreevich lived, consisted of six houses. As soon as they passed the blacksmith's hut, the last in the village, they realized that the wind was much stronger than they had thought. The road was hardly visible under the snow. The tracks left by the sleigh-runners were immediately covered in snow and the road was only distinguishable by its being higher than the rest of the ground. There was a swirl of snow over the fields, and the line where sky and earth met couldn't be seen. The Telyatin forest, usually clearly visible, now loomed up only occasionally and dimly through the driving snowy dust. The wind came from the left, insistently blowing the mane on Mukhorty's sleek neck to one side and carrying even his fluffy tail, which was tied in a simple knot. Nikita's wide coat-collar was pressed close to his cheek and nose as he sat on the windy side.

"This road doesn't give him a chance—it's too snowy," said Vasily Andreevich, who prided himself on his good horse. "I once drove to Pashutino with him in half an hour."

"What?" asked Nikita, who couldn't hear, owing to his raised collar.

"I said I once went to Pashutino in half an hour," shouted Vasily Andreevich.

"It goes without saying that he's a good horse," replied Nikita.

They were silent for a while. But Vasily Andreevich felt like chatting.

"Well, did you tell your wife not to give the cooper any vodka?" he began in the same loud tone, convinced that Nikita must feel flattered to be talking with so clever and important a person as himself. He was so pleased with his joke that it did not enter his head that the remark might be unpleasant to Nikita.

The wind once again prevented Nikita from hearing his master's words.

Vasily Andreevich repeated the joke about the cooper in his loud, clear voice.

"That's their business, Vasily Andreevich. I don't pry into their affairs. As long as she doesn't mistreat our boy, God be with them."

"Indeed," said Vasily Andreevich. "So, will you be buying a horse in spring?" he went on, changing the subject.

"Yes, I can't avoid it," answered Nikita, turning down his collar and leaning back toward his master.

The conversation was growing more interesting and he didn't want to miss a word.

"The lad's growing up. He must begin to plough for himself, but so far we've always had to hire someone," he said.

"Well, why not have the lean-rumped one? I won't charge you much for it," shouted Vasily Andreevich, feeling animated, and consequently starting on his favorite occupation—that of horse-dealing—which absorbed all his mental powers.

"Or maybe you could lend me fifteen rubles and I'll buy one at the horse market," said Nikita, who knew that the horse Vasily Andreevich wanted to sell him would be dear at seven rubles, but that if he took it from him it would be charged at twenty-five, and then he would be unable to draw any wages for half a year.

"It's a good horse. I think of your interest as of my own—according to conscience. Brekhunov isn't a man to wrong anyone. Let the loss be mine. I'm not like others. Honestly," he shouted, using the voice with which he hypnotized his customers and dealers, "it's a real good horse!"

"Quite so!" said Nikita with a sigh, convinced there was nothing more to listen to. He again released his collar, which immediately covered his ear and face.

They drove on in silence for about half an hour. The wind blew sharply onto Nikita's side and arm where his sheepskin was torn.

He huddled up and breathed into his collar, which covered his mouth, and was not wholly cold.

"What do you think—shall we go through Karamyshevo or by the straight road?" asked Vasily Andreevich.

The road through Karamyshevo was better-traveled and was well marked with a double row of high stakes. The straight road was shorter but little used and had no stakes, or only poor ones covered with snow.

Nikita thought a while.

"Though Karamyshevo is longer, it's better going," he said.

"But by the straight road, when once we get through the hollow by the forest, it's good going—sheltered," said Vasily Andreevich, who wanted to take the shortest route.

"Just as you please," said Nikita and again let go of his collar.

Vasily Andreevich did as he had said, and after about a third of a mile they came to a tall oak stake that had a few dry leaves still dangling on it, and there he turned left.

They turned directly into the wind, and snow was beginning to fall. Vasily Andreevich, who was driving, puffed up his cheeks and blew the breath out through his mustache. Nikita dozed.

So they went on in silence for about ten minutes. Suddenly Vasily Andreevich spoke.

"Eh, what?" asked Nikita, opening his eyes.

Vasily Andreevich didn't answer, but bent over, looking behind them and then ahead of the horse. The sweat had curled Mukhorty's coat between his legs and on his neck. He had slowed to a walk.

"What is it?" Nikita asked again.

"What is it? What is it?" Vasily Andreevich mimicked him angrily. "There are no stakes to be seen! We must have gone off the road!"

"Well, pull up then and I'll look for it," said Nikita. He jumped down lightly from the sleigh and, taking the whip from under the straw, went off to the left from his own side of the sleigh.

The snow wasn't deep that year, so that it was possible to walk anywhere, but still in places it was knee-deep and it got into Nikita's boots.

He went about testing the ground with his feet and the whip, but he couldn't find the road anywhere.

"Well, how is it?" asked Vasily Andreevich when Nikita came back to the sleigh.

"There's no road on this side. I'll have to go to the other side and try there," said Nikita.

"There's something over there in front. Go and have a look."

Nikita went to what had appeared dark, but found that it was earth that the wind had blown from the bare fields of winter oats and had strewn over the snow, discoloring it. Having searched to the right also, he returned to the sleigh, brushed the snow from his coat, shook it out of his boots, and seated himself once more.

"We must go to the right," he said decidedly. "The wind was blowing on our left before, but now it's straight in my face. Drive to the right," he repeated with decision.

Vasily Andreevich took his advice and turned to the right, but there was still no road. They went on in that direction for some time. The wind was as fierce as ever and it was snowing lightly.

"It seems, Vasily Andreevich, that we have gone quite astray," Nikita suddenly remarked, as if it were a pleasant thing. "What is that?" he added, pointing to some potato vines that showed up from under the snow.

Vasily Andreevich halted the perspiring horse, whose broad flanks were heaving.

"What is it?"

"Why, we're on the Zakharov lands. See where we've got to!"

"Nonsense!" retorted Vasily Andreevich.

"It's not nonsense, Vasily Andreevich. It's the truth," replied Nikita.

"You can feel that the sleigh is going over a potato field, and there are the heaps of vines that have been carted here. It's the Zakharov factory land."

"Dear me, how we've gone astray!" said Vasily Andreevich. "What do we do now?"

"We must go straight on, that's all. We'll come out somewhere—if not at Zakharova, then at the proprietor's farm," said Nikita.

Vasily Andreevich agreed, and drove on as Nikita suggested. So they went on for a considerable while. At times they went onto bare fields and the sleigh-runners rattled over frozen lumps of earth. Sometimes they got onto a winter-rye field or a fallow field, on which they could see stalks of wormwood and straws sticking up through the snow and swaying in the wind; sometimes they went onto deep and even white snow, above which nothing was to be seen.

The snow was falling from above and sometimes rose up from below. The horse was evidently exhausted; his hair was all curled up from sweat and was covered with hoarfrost, and he went at a walk. Suddenly he stumbled and sat down in a ditch or watercourse. Vasily Andreevich wanted to stop, but Nikita cried to him:

"Why stop? We've got in and must get out. Hey, my pet! Hey, darling! Giddyap, old fellow!" he shouted in a cheerful tone to the horse, who kept jumping out of the sleigh and himself getting stuck in the ditch.

The horse gave a start and quickly climbed out onto the frozen bank. It was evidently a ditch that had been dug there.

"Where are we now?" asked Vasily Andreevich.

"We'll soon find out!" Nikita replied. "Go on, we'll get somewhere."

"Why, this must be the Goryachkin forest!" said Vasily Andreevich, pointing to something dark that appeared amid the snow in front of them.

"We'll see what forest it is when we get there," said Nikita.

He saw that near the black thing they had noticed, some dry, oblong willow leaves were fluttering, and so he knew it was not a forest but a settlement, but he didn't wish to say so. And in fact they had not gone twenty-five yards beyond the ditch before something in front of them, evidently trees, showed up black, and they heard a new and melancholy sound. Nikita had guessed right: it was not a wood but a row of tall willows with a few leaves still fluttering on them here and there. They had evidently been planted along the ditch around a threshing floor.

Coming up to the willows, which moaned sadly in the wind, the horse suddenly planted his forelegs above the height of the sleigh and drew up his hind legs, pulling the sleigh onto higher ground, and turned to the left, no longer sinking up to his knees in snow. They were back on a road.

"Well, here we are, but heaven only knows where!" said Nikita.

The horse kept going straight along the road, through the drifted snow, and before they had gone another hundred yards the straight line of the dark wattle wall of a barn showed up black before them, its roof heavily covered with snow, which poured down from it. Past the barn, the road turned into the wind and they drove into a snowdrift. Ahead of them was a lane with houses on either side; evidently the snow had been blown across the road, and they had to drive through the drift. And so in fact it was. Having driven through the snow, they came out into a street. At the last house of the village, some frozen clothes were hanging on a line—shirts, one red and one white, trousers, leg bands, a petticoat—and were fluttering wildly in the wind. The white shirt in particular struggled desperately, waving its sleeves about.

"There now, either a lazy woman or a dead one has not taken her clothes down before the holiday," remarked Nikita, looking at the fluttering shirts.

3

On the edge of town the wind still raged and the road was thickly covered with snow, but in the center of the village it was calm, warm, and cheerful. At one house a dog was barking; at another a woman covered her head with her coat and came from somewhere and ran into a hut, stopping at the threshold to have a look at the passing sleigh. In the middle of the village, girls could be heard singing.

Here in the village there seemed to be less wind and snow, and the frost was less keen.

"Why, this is Grishkino," said Vasily Andreevich.

"So it is," responded Nikita.

It really was Grishkino, which meant that they had gone too far to the left and had traveled some six miles, not quite in the direction they aimed at, but in the general direction of their destination, for all that.

From Grishkino to Goryachkin was about four more miles.

In the middle of the village they almost ran over a tall man walking down the middle of the street.

"Who are you?" shouted the man, stopping the horse. He recognized

Vasily Andreevich and immediately took hold of the shaft, went along it hand over hand until he reached the sleigh, and placed himself in the driver's seat.

He was Isay, a peasant of Vasily Andreevich's acquaintance, and well known as the principal horse thief in the district.

"Ah, Vasily Andreevich! Where are you off to?" said Isay, enveloping Nikita in the odor of the vodka he had drunk.

"We were going to Goryachkin."

"And look where you've got to! You should have gone through Molchanovka."

"Should have, but didn't manage it," said Vasily Andreevich, holding in the horse.

"That's a good horse," said Isay, glancing shrewdly at Mukhorty. With a practiced hand he tightened the knot high in the horse's bushy tail.

"Are you going to stay the night?"

"No, my friend. I must be getting on."

"Your business must be pressing. And who is this? Ah, Nikita Stepanych!"

"Who else?" replied Nikita. "But I say, good friend, how are we to avoid going astray again?"

"Where can you go astray here? Turn back and go straight down the street, and when you come out keep straight on. Don't bear left. You'll come out onto the high road, and then turn right."

"And where do we turn off the high road? As in summer, or the winter route?" asked Nikita.

"The winter route. As soon as you turn off you'll see some bushes, and opposite them there's a roadmark—a large oak, with branches—and that's the way."

Vasily Andreevich turned the horse around and headed out of the village.

"Why not stay the night?" Isay shouted after them.

But Vasily Andreevich didn't answer and started the horse. Four miles of good road, two of which lay through the forest, seemed easy to manage, especially since the wind was apparently quieter and the snow had stopped.

Having driven along the trodden village street, darkened here and there by fresh manure, past the yard where the clothes were hung out and where the white shirt had broken loose and was now attached only by one frozen sleeve, they again came within range of the weird moan of the willows, and again emerged onto the open fields. The storm, far from ceasing, seemed to have grown even stronger. The road was completely covered with snowdrifts, and only the stakes showed that they had not lost their way. But the stakes ahead of them were not easy to see, with the wind blowing in their faces.

Vasily Andreevich squinted his eyes, lowered his head, and looked out for the roadmarks, but trusted mainly to the horse's sagacity, letting it lead the way. And the horse really didn't lose the road but followed its windings, turning now to the right and now to the left and sensing the road under his feet, so that, even as the snow fell thicker and the wind stiffened, they still managed to see roadmarks, now to the left and now to the right of them.

So they traveled on for about ten minutes, when suddenly, through the slanting screen of wind-driven snow, something black appeared, moving in front of the horse.

It was another sleigh with fellow-travelers. Mukhorty overtook them and struck his hoofs against the back of the sleigh in front of them.

"Pass on . . . Hey there, get in front!" cried voices from the sleigh.

Vasily Andreevich swerved aside and passed the other sleigh.

In it sat three men and a woman, evidently visitors returning from a feast. One peasant was whacking the snow-covered rump of their little horse with a long switch, and the other two were sitting in front, waving their arms and shouting something. The woman, completely wrapped up and covered with snow, sat drowsing and bumping at the back.

"Who are you?" shouted Vasily Andreevich.

"From A-a-a . . ." was all that could be heard.

"I say, where are you from?"

"From A-a-a-a!" one of the peasants shouted with all his might, but it was impossible to make out who they were.

"Get along! Keep up!" shouted another, relentlessly beating his horse with the switch.

"So you're coming from a feast, it seems?"

"Go on, go on! Faster, Simon! Get in front! Faster!"

The wings of the sleighs bumped against one another and almost got jammed but managed to separate, and the peasants' sleigh fell behind.

Their shaggy, big-bellied horse was all covered with snow and was breathing heavily under the low shaft-bow. Evidently using the last of its strength, it vainly endeavored to escape from the switch, hobbling on its short legs through the deep snow, which it threw up under itself.

With the nether lip of its young-looking muzzle drawn up like that of a fish, its nostrils distended, and its ears pressed back in fear, the horse kept up for a few seconds near Nikita's shoulder and then fell behind.

"Just see what liquor does!" said Nikita. "They've tired that little horse to death. What pagans!"

For a few minutes they heard the panting of the tired little horse and the drunken shouting of the peasants. Then the panting and the shouts died away, and around them nothing could be heard but the whistling of the wind in their ears and, now and then, the squeak of their sleigh-runners over a windswept part of the road.

This encounter cheered and enlivened Vasily Andreevich, and he drove on more boldly, without examining the roadmarks, urging on the horse and trusting in him.

Nikita had nothing to do, and as usual in such circumstances he nodded off, making up for much sleepless time. Suddenly the horse stopped and Nikita nearly fell forward onto his nose.

"You know, we're off the track again!" said Vasily Andreevich.

"How's that?"

"Why, there are no roadmarks to be seen. We must have gone off the road again."

"Well, if we've lost the road, we must find it," said Nikita curtly. He got out and, stepping lightly on his pigeon-toed feet, went poking around in the snow.

He walked about for a long time, disappearing and reappearing, and finally he came back.

"There is no road here. Maybe it's farther on," he said, getting into the sleigh.

It was already growing dark. The snowstorm had not worsened but had not subsided either.

"If we could only hear those peasants!" said Vasily Andreevich.

"Well, they haven't caught up to us. We must have gone far astray. Or maybe they have lost their way, too."

"Where should we go then?" asked Vasily Andreevich.

"Why, we must let the horse take its own way," said Nikita. "He will take us right. Let me have the reins."

Vasily Andreevich gave him the reins, the more willingly because his hands were beginning to feel frozen in his thick gloves.

Nikita took the reins, but only held them, trying not to shake them and rejoicing at his favorite's sagacity. And indeed the clever horse, turning first one ear and then the other, now to one side, now to the other, began to wheel around.

"The only thing he can't do is talk," Nikita kept saying. "See what he's doing! Go on, go on! You know best. That's it, that's it!"

The wind was blowing from behind now and felt warmer.

"Yes, he's clever," Nikita continued, admiring the horse. "A Kirgiz horse is strong but stupid. But this one—just see what he's doing with his ears! He doesn't need any telegraph. He can pick up a scent a mile off."

Before another half hour had passed, they saw something dark ahead of them—a wood or a village—and stakes again appeared on the right. They had evidently come out onto the road.

"Why, that's Grishkino again!" Nikita exclaimed.

And indeed, there on their left was that same barn with the snow flying from it, and farther on the same line with the frozen laundry, shirts and trousers, still fluttering desperately in the wind.

Again they drove into the street and again it grew quiet, warm, and cheerful, and again they saw the manure-strewn street and heard voices and songs and the barking of a dog. It was already so dark that there were lights in some of the windows.

Halfway through the village, Vasily Andreevich turned the horse toward a large double-fronted brick house and stopped at the porch.

Nikita went to the lighted, snow-covered window, through which passed a light that made the flying snowflakes glitter, and he knocked at it with his whip.

"Who's there?" a voice replied to his knock.

"From Kresty, the Brekhunovs, dear fellow," answered Nikita. "Please come out for just a minute."

Someone moved from the window, and a minute or two later there was the sound of the passageway door as it came unstuck, then the latch of the outer door clicked and a tall white-bearded peasant, with a sheepskin coat thrown over his white holiday shirt, pushed his way out, holding the door firmly against the wind. Behind him was a lad in a red shirt and high leather boots.

"Is that you, Andreevich?" asked the old man.

"Yes, my friend, we've gone astray," said Vasily Andreevich. "We were trying to get to Goryachkin but found ourselves here. We went a second time but lost our way again."

"Just see how you've gone astray!" said the old man. "Petroushka, go and open the gate!" he added, turning to the lad in the red shirt.

"All right," said the lad in a cheerful voice, and he ran back into the passageway.

"But we're not staying the night," said Vasily Andreevich.

"Where will you go in the night? You'd better stay!"

"I'd be glad to, but I must go on. It's business, and it can't be helped."

"Well, warm yourself at least. The samovar is just ready."

"Warm myself? Yes, I'll do that," said Vasily Andreevich. "It won't get any darker. The moon will rise and it will be lighter. Let's go in and warm ourselves, Nikita."

"Well, why not? Let us warm ourselves," replied Nikita, who was stiff with cold and anxious to warm his frozen limbs.

Vasily Andreevich went indoors with the old man, and Nikita drove through the gate opened for him by Petroushka, who guided him as he backed the horse under the penthouse. The ground was covered with manure, and the tall bow over the horse's head caught against the beam. The hens and the rooster had already settled to roost there, and clucked peevishly, clinging to the beam with their claws. The disturbed sheep shied away and rushed aside, trampling the frozen manure under their hooves. The dog yelped desperately with fright and anger and then burst out barking like a puppy at the stranger.

Nikita talked to them all, excusing himself to the fowls and assuring them that he wouldn't disturb them again. He rebuked the sheep for being frightened without knowing why, and kept soothing the dog, while he tied up the horse.

"Now that will be all right," he said, knocking the snow off his clothes. "Just hear how he barks!" He turned to the dog and said, "Be quiet, stupid! Be quiet. You're troubling yourself over nothing. We're not thieves, we're friends."

"And these are, it's said, the three domestic counselors," remarked the lad, and with his strong arms he pushed under the pent-roof the sleigh that had remained outside.

"Why counselors?" asked Nikita.

"That's what is printed in Paulson. A thief creeps to a house—the dog barks, that means 'Be on your guard!' The rooster crows, that means, 'Get up!' The cat licks herself—that means, 'A welcome guest is coming. Get ready to receive him!'" said the lad with a smile.

Petroushka could read and write and knew Paulson's primer, his only book, almost by heart, and he was fond of quoting sayings he thought suited the occasion, especially when he had had something to drink, as today.

"That's so," said Nikita.

"You must be chilled through and through," said Petroushka.

"Yes, I am rather," said Nikita, and they went across the yard and through the passageway into the house.

4

The household to which Vasily Andreevich had come was one of the richest in the village. The family had five allotments, not including the other land they rented. They had six horses, three cows, two calves, and some twenty sheep. There were twenty-two members belonging to the homestead: four married sons, six grandchildren (one of whom, Petroushka, was married), two great-grandchildren, three orphans, and four daughters-in-law with babies in tow. It was one of the few homesteads that remained undivided, but even here the dull work of internal disintegration which would inevitably lead to separation had already begun, starting as usual among the women. Two sons were living in Moscow as water-carriers, and one was in the army. At home now were the old man and his wife; their second son, who managed the homestead; the eldest, who had come from Moscow for the holiday, and all the women and children. Besides these members of the family, there was a visitor, a neighbor who was godfather to one of the children.

Over the table in the room hung a shaded lamp that brightly lit up the tea things, a bottle of vodka, and some refreshments, while also illuminating the brick walls, which in the far corner were hung with icons surrounded on both sides by pictures. At the head of the table sat Vasily Andreevich in a black sheepskin coat, sucking his frozen mustache and observing the room and the people around him with his prominent hawklike eyes. With him sat the old, bald, white-bearded master of the house in a white homespun shirt, and next to him the son home from Moscow for the holiday—a man with a sturdy back and powerful shoulders, and clad in a thin print shirt—and the second son, also broad-shouldered, who acted as head of the house, and then a lean red-haired peasant, the neighbor.

Having had a drink of vodka and something to eat, they were about to take tea; the samovar standing on the floor beside the brick oven was already humming. The children could be seen in the top bunks and on the top of the oven. A woman sat on a lower bunk with a cradle beside her. The old housewife, her entire face covered with wrinkles—even her lips—was waiting on Vasily Andreevich.

Nikita entered the house as she was offering her guest a small tumbler of thick glass which she had just filled with vodka.

"Don't refuse, Vasily Andreevich, you mustn't! Wish us a merry feast. Drink it, dear!" she said.

The sight and smell of vodka, especially now, when he was chilled through and tired out, much disturbed Nikita's mind. He frowned, and after shaking the snow off his cap and coat, stopped in front of the icons as if not seeing anyone, crossed himself three times, and bowed to the icons. Then he turned to the old master of the house and bowed, first to him, then to all those at table, then to the women who stood by the oven, and muttered: "A merry holiday!" He took off his outer things without looking at the table.

"Why, you're all covered with hoarfrost, old fellow!" said the eldest brother, looking at Nikita's snow-covered face, eyes, and beard.

Nikita took off his coat, shook it once more, then hung it up beside the oven and came up to the table. He too was offered vodka. He went through a moment of painful hesitation and nearly took up the glass and emptied the clear fragrant liquid down his throat, but he glanced at Vasily Andreevich, remembered his oath (and the boots that he had sold for drink), recalled the cooper, remembered his son for whom he had promised to buy a horse by spring, sighed, and declined it.

"I don't drink, thank you kindly," he said, frowning, and sat down on a bench near the second window.

"How's that?" asked the eldest brother.

"I just don't drink," replied Nikita without lifting his eyes but looking down at his scanty beard and mustache and picking the icicles out of them.

"It's not good for him," said Vasily Andreevich, munching a cracknel biscuit after emptying his glass.

"Well, then, have some tea," said the kindly old hostess. "You must be chilled to the bone, good soul. Why are you women dawdling so with the samovar?"

"It's ready," said one of the young women, and after flicking her apron at the top of the samovar, which was now boiling over, she carried it with effort to the table, raised it, and set it down with a thud.

Meanwhile Vasily Andreevich was telling how he had lost his way, how they had come back twice to this same village, and how they had gone astray and had met some drunken peasants. Their hosts were surprised, explained where and why they had missed their turn, told them who the tipsy people they had met were, and told them how they ought to go.

"A little child could find the way to Molchanovka from here. All you have to do is take the right turn from the high road. There's a bush you can see just there. But you didn't even get that far!" said the neighbor.

"You'd better stay the night. The women will make up beds for you," said the old woman persuasively.

"You could go on in the morning and it would be pleasanter," said the old man, seconding what his wife had said.

"I can't, my friend. Business!" said Vasily Andreevich. "Lose an hour and you can't catch it up in a year," he added, remembering the grove and the dealers who might snatch that deal from him. "We shall get there, shan't we?" he said, turning to Nikita.

Nikita didn't answer for some time, apparently still intent on thawing out his beard and mustache.

"If only we don't get lost again," he replied gloomily. He was gloomy because he passionately longed for some vodka, and the only thing that could assuage that longing was tea, and he had not yet been offered any.

"But we have only to reach the turn and then we shan't go wrong. The road will lead through the forest the whole way," said Vasily Andreevich.

"It's just as you wish, Vasily Andreevich. If we're to go, let's go," said Nikita, taking the glass of tea he was offered.

"We'll drink our tea and be off."

Nikita said nothing but only shook his head and carefully poured some tea into his saucer. He warmed his hands over the steam. His fingers were always swollen with hard work. Then he bit off a tiny bite of sugar, bowed to his hosts, said, "Your health!" and drew in the steaming liquid.

"If somebody would see us as far as the turning," said Vasily Andreevich.

"Well, we can do that," said the eldest son. "Petroushka will harness the horse and go that far with you."

"Well, then, put in the horse, lad, and I shall be thankful to you for it."

"Oh, what for, dear man?" said the kindly old woman. "We are heartily glad to do it."

"Petroushka, go and put in the mare," said the eldest brother.

"All right," replied Petroushka with a smile. He promptly snatched his cap down from a nail and ran off to harness the horse.

While the horse was being harnessed the talk returned to the point at which it had stopped when Vasily Andreevich drove up to the window. The old man had been complaining to his neighbor, the village elder, about his third son, who had not sent him anything for the holiday though he had sent a French shawl to his wife.

"The young people are getting out of hand," said the old man.

"And how they do!" said the neighbor. "There's no managing them! They know too much. There's Demochkin now, who broke his father's arm. It's all from being too clever, it seems."

Nikita listened, watched their faces, and evidently would have liked to share in the conversation, but he was too busy drinking his tea and only nodded his head approvingly. He emptied one tumbler after another and grew warmer and warmer and more and more comfortable. The talk continued on the same subject for a long time—the harmfulness of a household dividing up—and it was clearly not an abstract discussion but concerned the question of a separation in that house: a separation demanded by the second son, who sat there morosely silent.

It was evidently a sore subject and it absorbed them all, but out of propriety they did not discuss their private affairs before strangers.

At last, however, the old man could not restrain himself, and with tears in his eyes declared that he would not consent to a breakup of the family during his lifetime, that his house was prospering, thank God, but that if they separated they would all have to go begging.

"Just like the Matveevs," said the neighbor. "They used to have a proper house, but now they've split up and none of them has anything."

"And that is what you want to happen to us," said the old man, turning to his son.

The son made no reply and there was an awkward pause. The silence was broken by Petroushka, who, having harnessed the horse, had returned to the hut a few minutes before this and had been listening all the time with a smile.

"There's a fable about that in Paulson," he said. "A father gave his sons a broom to break. At first they could not break it, but when they took it twig by twig they broke it easily. And it's the same here." He gave a broad smile. "I'm ready!" he added.

"If you're ready, let's go," said Vasily Andreevich. "And as to separating, don't you allow it, Grandfather. You got everything together and you're the master. Go to the justice of the peace. He'll say how things should be done."

"He carries on so, carries on so," the old man continued in a whining tone. "There's no doing anything with him. It's as if the devil possessed him."

Nikita had meanwhile finished his fifth tumbler of tea and laid it on its side instead of turning it upside down, hoping to be offered a sixth glass. But there was no more water in the samovar, so the hostess did not fill it up for him. Besides, Vasily Andreevich was putting his things on, so there was nothing for it but for Nikita to get up too, put back into the sugarbowl the lump of sugar he had nibbled all around, wipe his perspiring face with the skirt of his sheepskin, and put on his overcoat.

Having put it on, he sighed deeply, thanked his hosts, said goodbye, and went out of the warm bright room into the cold dark passageway, through which the wind was howling and where snow was blowing through the cracks of the shaking door, and from there into the yard.

Petroushka stood in his sheepskin in the middle of the yard by his horse, repeating some lines from Paulson's primer. He said with a smile:

> Storms with mist the sky conceal,
> Snowy circles wheeling wild.
> Now like savage beast 'twill howl,
> And now 'tis wailing like a child.

Nikita nodded approvingly as he gathered the reins.

The old man, seeing Vasily Andreevich off, brought a lantern into the passageway to light the way, but it blew out at once. And even in the yard it was evident that the snowstorm had become more violent.

"Well, this is some weather!" thought Vasily Andreevich. "Perhaps we may not get there after all. But there is nothing to be done. Business! Besides, we've got ready, our host's horse has been harnessed, and we'll get there with God's help!"

Their aged host also thought they shouldn't go, but he had already tried to persuade them to stay and had not been listened to.

"It's no use asking them again," he thought. "Maybe age has made me timid. They'll get there all right, and at least we shall get to bed in good time and without any fuss."

Petroushka paid no heed to danger. He knew the road and the whole district so well, and the lines about "snowy circles wheeling wild" described what was happening outside so aptly, that he felt downright cheerful.

Nikita didn't wish to go at all, but he had been accustomed to not having his own way, and to serving others, for so long that there was no one to hinder the departing travelers.

5

Vasily Andreevich went over to his sleigh, found it with difficulty in the darkness, climbed in, and took the reins.

"Go on in front!" he cried.

Petroushka kneeled in his low sleigh and started his horse. Mukhorty, who had been neighing for some time, now caught the scent of a mare ahead of him and started after her, and they drove out into the street. They drove again through the outskirts of the village, along the same road; past the yard where the frozen linen had hung (which, however, was no longer to be seen); past the same barn, which was now snowed up almost to the roof, and from which the snow was still endlessly pouring; past the same dismally moaning, whistling, and swaying willows, and again entered into the sea of blustering snow raging from above and below. The wind was so strong that when it blew from the side and the travelers steered against it, it tilted the sleighs and turned the horses to one side.

Petroushka drove his good mare in front at a brisk trot and kept shouting lustily. Mukhorty pressed after her.

After traveling so for about ten minutes, Petroushka turned around and shouted something. Neither Vasily Andreevich nor Nikita could hear anything over of the wind, but they guessed that they had arrived at the turning. In fact, Petroushka had turned right, and now the wind that had blown from the side blew straight in their faces, and through the snow they saw something dark on their right. It was the bush at the turn.

"Well now, God speed you!"

"Thank you, Petroushka!"

"Storms with mist the sky conceal!" shouted Petroushka as he disappeared.

"There's a poet for you!" muttered Vasily Andreevich, pulling at the reins.

"Yes, a fine lad—a true peasant," said Nikita.

They drove on.

Nikita wrapped his coat closely about him and pressed his head down so close to his shoulders that his short beard covered his throat. He sat silently, trying not to lose the warmth he had obtained while drinking tea in the house. Before him he saw the straight lines of the shafts, which constantly deceived him into thinking they were on a well-traveled road, and the horse's swaying hind quarters with his knotted tail blown to one side, and, farther ahead, the high shaft-bow and the swaying head and neck of the horse with its waving mane. Now and then he caught sight of a signpost, so that he knew they were still on a road and that there was nothing for him to be concerned about.

Vasily Andreevich drove on, leaving it to the horse to keep to the road. But Mukhorty, though he had had a breathing-space in the village, ran reluctantly, and seemed now and then to get off the road, so that Vasily Andreevich had to repeatedly correct him.

"Here's a stake to the right, and another, and here's a third," Vasily Andreevich counted, "and here in front is the forest," he thought as he looked at something dark in front of him. But what had seemed to him a forest was only a bush. They passed the bush and drove on for another hundred yards but there was no fourth signpost, nor any forest.

"We should reach the forest soon," thought Vasily Andreevich. Animated by the vodka and the tea, he did not stop but shook the reins, and the good obedient horse responded, now ambling, now slowly trotting in the direction in which he was sent, though he knew he wasn't heading the right way. Ten minutes went by, but still no forest.

"There now, we must be lost again," said Vasily Andreevich, pulling up.

Nikita silently got out of the sleigh and, holding his coat, which the wind now wrapped closely about him and now almost tore off, started to feel about in the snow, going first to one side and then the other.

Three or four times he was completely out of sight. At last he returned and took the reins from Vasily Andreevich's hand.

"We must go to the right," he said sternly and peremptorily as he turned the horse.

"Well, if it's to the right, go to the right," said Vasily Andreevich, yielding up the reins to Nikita and thrusting his freezing hands into his sleeves.

Nikita did not reply.

"Now then, my friend, stir yourself!" he shouted to the horse, but in spite of the shake of the reins Mukhorty moved only at a walk. The snow in places was up to his knees, and the sleigh moved in fits and starts behind him.

Nikita took the whip that hung over the front of the sleigh and struck Mukhorty once. The good horse, unaccustomed to the whip, sprang forward and moved at a trot, but immediately fell back into an amble and then to a walk.

So they went on for five minutes. It was dark and the snow whirled from above and rose from below, so that sometimes the shaft-bow could not be seen. At times the sleigh seemed to stand still and the field to run backwards. Suddenly the horse stopped abruptly, evidently aware of something close in front of him. Nikita again threw down the reins, sprang lightly out, and ventured ahead to see what had brought Mukhorty to a standstill. Hardly had he made a step in front of the horse before he slipped and went rolling down an incline.

"Whoa, whoa, whoa!" he said to himself as he fell. He tried to stop his fall but could not, and only stopped when his feet plunged into a thick layer of snow that had drifted to the bottom of the hollow.

The fringe of a snowdrift that hung on the edge of the hollow was disturbed by Nikita's fall and came showering down on him and got inside his collar.

"What a thing to do!" said Nikita reproachfully, addressing the drift and the hollow. He shook the snow from under his collar.

"Nikita! Hey, Nikita!" shouted Vasily Andreevich from above.

But Nikita did not reply. He was too busy shaking out the snow and searching for the whip he had dropped when rolling down the incline. He found the whip and tried to climb straight up the bank where he had rolled down, but it was impossible—he kept rolling down again—so he had to go along at the foot of the hollow to find a way up. About twenty feet farther on he managed with difficulty to crawl up the incline on all fours, then he followed the edge of the hollow back to the place where the horse should have been. He couldn't see either the horse or the sleigh, but as he walked against the wind he heard Vasily Andreevich's shouts, and Mukhorty's neighing, calling him.

"I'm coming! I'm coming! What are you cackling for?" he muttered.

Only when he had come right up to the sleigh could he make out the horse, and Vasily Andreevich standing beside it and looking gigantic.

"Where the devil did you vanish to? We must go back, if only to Grishkino," he reproached Nikita.

"I'd be glad to get back, Vasily Andreevich, but which way do we go? There is such a ravine here that if we once get in it we won't get out again. I got stuck so fast there myself that I could hardly get out."

"What shall we do, then? We can't stay here! We must go somewhere!" said Vasily Andreevich.

Nikita said nothing. He sat down in the sleigh with his back to the wind, took off his boots, shook out the snow that had got into them, and, using some straw from the bottom of the sleigh, carefully plugged a hole in his left boot.

Vasily Andreevich remained silent, as though now leaving everything to Nikita. Nikita put his boots on again and drew his feet into the sleigh. He put on his mittens, took up the reins, and directed the horse along the side of the ravine. But they hadn't gone a hundred yards before the horse again stopped short. The ravine was in front of him again.

Nikita again climbed out and again trudged about in the snow. He did this for a considerable time and at last appeared from the opposite side to that from which he had started.

"Vasily Andreevich, are you alive?" he called out.

"Here!" replied Vasily Andreevich. "Well, what now?"

"I can't make anything out. It's too dark. There's nothing but ravines. We must drive against the wind again."

They set off once more. Again Nikita went stumbling through the snow, again he fell in, again he climbed out and trudged about, and at last, quite out of breath, he sat down beside the sleigh.

"Well, how now?" asked Vasily Andreevich.

"Why, I'm quite worn out and the horse won't go."

"Then what's to be done?"

"Why, wait a minute."

Nikita went away again but soon returned.

"Follow me!" he said, going in front of the horse.

Vasily Andreevich no longer gave orders but implicitly did what Nikita told him.

"Here, follow me!" Nikita shouted. Stepping quickly to the right and seizing the reins, he led Mukhorty down toward a snowdrift.

At first the horse held back, then he jerked forward, hoping to leap the drift, but he lacked the strength and sank in up to his collar.

"Get out!" Nikita called to Vasily Andreevich, who was still sitting in the sleigh. Nikita took hold of one shaft and moved the sleigh closer to the horse. "It's hard, brother!" he said to Mukhorty, "but it can't be helped. Make an effort! Now, now, just a little!" he shouted.

The horse gave a tug, then another, but failed to clear himself and settled down again as if considering something.

"Now, brother, this won't do!" Nikita admonished him. "Now once more!"

Again Nikita tugged at the shaft on his side, and Vasily Andreevich did the same on the other side.

Mukhorty lifted his head and gave a sudden jerk.

"That's it! That's it!" cried Nikita. "Don't be afraid—you won't sink!"

One plunge, another, and a third, and at last Mukhorty was out of the snowdrift. He stood still, breathing heavily and shaking the snow off himself. Nikita wanted to lead him farther, but Vasily Andreevich, in his two fur coats, was so out of breath that he couldn't walk any farther and dropped into the sleigh.

"Let me catch my breath!" he said, unfastening the kerchief with which he had tied the collar of his fur coat at the village.

"It's all right here. You lie there," said Nikita. "I'll lead him along." And with Vasily Andreevich in the sleigh, he led the horse by the bridle about ten paces down and then up a slight rise, and stopped.

The place where Nikita stopped was not completely in the hollow, where the snow sweeping down from the hillocks might have buried them altogether, but still it was partly sheltered from the wind by the side of the ravine. There were moments when the wind seemed to let up a little, but not for long, and, as if to make up for the respite, the storm swept down with tenfold vigor and tore and swirled all the more fiercely. One such gust struck them at the very moment when Vasily Andreevich, having recovered his breath, got out of the sleigh and went up to Nikita to consult him as to what they should do. They both bent down involuntarily and waited until the violence of the squall passed. Mukhorty likewise laid back his ears and shook his head discontentedly. As soon as the violence of the blast abated a little, Nikita took off his mittens, stuck them into his belt, breathed onto his hands, and undid the straps of the shaft-bow.

"What's that you're doing there?" asked Vasily Andreevich.

"Unharnessing. What else is there to do? I have no strength left," said Nikita as though excusing himself.

"Can't we drive somewhere?"

"No, we can't. We'd just kill the horse. Why, the poor beast is not himself now," said Nikita, pointing to the horse, which was standing submissively, waiting for what might come, with his steep wet sides heaving heavily. "We'll have to stay here for the night," he said, as if preparing to spend the night at an inn. He proceeded to unfasten the collar-straps. The buckles came undone.

"But won't we freeze?" remarked Vasily Andreevich.

"Well, if we do we can't help it," said Nikita.

6

Although Vasily Andreevich felt quite warm in his two fur coats, especially after struggling in the snowdrift, a cold shiver ran down his back on realizing that he really did have to spend the night where they were. To calm himself he sat down in the sleigh and got out his cigarettes and matches.

Nikita meanwhile unharnessed Mukhorty. He unstrapped the belly-band and the backband, took off the reins, loosened the collar-strap, and removed the shaft-bow, talking to him all the time to encourage him.

"Now come out! Come out!" he said, leading him clear of the shafts. "Now we'll tie you up here and I'll put down some straw and take off your bridle. When you've had a bite you'll feel more cheerful."

But Mukhorty was restless and evidently not comforted by Nikita's remarks. He shifted from foot to foot and pressed close against the sleigh, turning his back to the wind and rubbing his head on Nikita's sleeve. Then, as if not to pain Nikita by refusing his offer of the straw he put before him, he hurriedly snatched a wisp from the sleigh, but immediately decided that now was no time to think of straw and threw it down, and the wind instantly scattered it, carried it away, and covered it with snow.

"Now we'll set up a signal," said Nikita. He turned the front of the sleigh into the wind and tied the shafts together with a strap and set them up on end in front of the sleigh. "There now, when the snow covers us up, good folk will see the shafts and dig us out," he said, slapping his mittens together and putting them on. "That's what the old folks taught us!"

Vasily Andreevich meanwhile unfastened his coat and, holding its skirts up for shelter, struck one sulfur match after another on the steel box. But his hands trembled, and one match after another either failed to kindle or was blown out by the wind just as he was lifting it to the cigarette. At last a match did ignite, and its flame briefly illuminated the fur of his coat, his hand with the gold ring on the bent forefinger, and the snow-sprinkled oat-straw that stuck out from under the drugget. The cigarette lighted, and he eagerly took a whiff or two, inhaled the smoke, and let it out through his mustache. He would have inhaled again but the wind tore off the burning tobacco and whirled it away, as it had done with the straw.

But even these few puffs had cheered him.

"If we must spend the night here, we must!" he said with decision. "Wait a bit, I'll arrange a flag as well," he added, picking up the kerchief he had thrown down in the sleigh after having earlier removed it from around his collar. He took off his gloves, stood up on the front of the sleigh, and, stretching to reach the strap, tied the handkerchief to it with a tight knot.

The kerchief immediately began to flutter wildly, now clinging around the shaft, now suddenly streaming out, stretching and flapping.

"Just see what a fine flag!" said Vasily Andreevich, admiring his handiwork and letting himself down into the sleigh. "We would be warmer together, but there's not enough room for two," he added.

"I'll find a place," said Nikita. "But first I must cover up the horse— he sweated so, poor thing. Let go!" he added, drawing the drugget from under Vasily Andreevich.

He got the drugget, folded it in two, and, after taking off the breechband and pad, covered Mukhorty with it.

"Anyhow it will be warmer, silly!" he said, putting the breechband and the pad back on the horse, over the drugget. Then, having finished that business, he returned to the sleigh and said to Vasily Andreevich: "You won't need the sackcloth, will you? And let me have some straw."

And having taken these things from under Vasily Andreevich, Nikita went behind the sleigh, dug out a hole for himself in the snow, put some straw into it, wrapped his coat well around himself, and covered himself with the sackcloth. He pulled his cap well down, seated himself on the straw he had spread out, and leaned against the wooden back of the sleigh to shelter himself from the wind and snow.

Vasily Andreevich shook his head disapprovingly at what Nikita was doing, as in general he disapproved of the peasant's stupidity and lack of education, and he began to settle himself down for the night.

He smoothed the remaining straw over the bottom of the sleigh, putting more of it under his side. Then he thrust his hands into his sleeves and settled down, sheltering his head in the corner of the sleigh from the wind in front.

He did not wish to sleep. He lay and thought. He mulled over the one thing that constituted the sole aim, meaning, pleasure, and pride of his life: how much money he had made and might still make, how much other people he knew had made and possessed, and how those others had made it and were making it, and how he, like them, might still make much more. The purchase of the Goryachkin grove was a matter of immense importance to him. On that one deal he hoped to make perhaps ten thousand rubles. He mentally reckoned the value of the timber he had inspected in autumn, and the five acres on which he had counted all the trees.

"The oaks will go for sleigh-runners. The undergrowth will take care of itself, and there'll still be some thirty *sazheens* of firewood left on each *desyatin*," he said to himself. "That means there will be at least two hundred and twenty-five rubles' worth left on each *desyatin*. Fifty-six *desyatins* means fifty-six hundreds, plus fifty-six hundreds, and fifty-six tens, and another fifty-six tens, and then fifty-six five . . ." He figured it would all come out to more than twelve thousand rubles, but couldn't add it all up exactly without an abacus. "But I won't offer ten thousand anyhow. I'll offer about eight thousand, with a deduction on account of the glades. I'll grease the surveyor's palm—give him a hundred rubles, or a hundred and fifty, and he'll reckon that there are some five *desyatins* of glade to be deducted. And he'll let it go for eight thousand. Three thousand in cash down. That'll move him, no worries!" he thought, and he pressed his pocketbook with his forearm.

"God only knows how we missed that turn. The forest ought to be there, and a watchman's hut, and dogs barking. But the damned things don't bark when they're wanted." He turned his collar down from his ear and listened, but as before only the whistling of the wind could be heard, the flapping and fluttering of the kerchief tied to the shafts, and the pelting of the snow against the woodwork of the sleigh. He covered up his ear again.

"If I had known, I would have stayed the night. Well, no matter, we'll get there tomorrow. It's only one day lost. And the others won't travel in such weather." Then he remembered that on the ninth he had to receive payment from the butcher for his oxen. "He meant to come himself, but he won't find me, and my wife won't know how to receive the money. She doesn't know the right way of doing things," he thought, recalling how at their party the day before she had not known how to treat the police officer who was their guest. "Of course she's only a woman! Where could she have seen anything? In my father's time what was our house like? Just a rich peasant's house: just an oat mill and an inn—that was the whole property. But what have I done in these fifteen years? A shop, two taverns, a flour mill, a granary, two farms leased out, and a house with an iron-roofed barn," he thought proudly. "Not as it was in Father's time! Who is talked of in the whole district now? Brekhunov! And why? Because I stick to business. I take trouble, not like others who lie in bed or waste their time on foolishness while I'm burning the midnight oil. Blizzard or no blizzard, I start out. So business gets done. They think making money is a joke. No, take pains and rack your brains! You get overtaken out of doors at night, like this, or stay awake night after night until the thoughts swirling in your head make the pillow turn," he meditated with pride. "They think people succeed through luck. After all, the Mironovs are now millionaires. And why? Take pains and God gives. If only He grants me health!"

The thought that he might himself be a millionaire like Mironov, who began with nothing, so excited Vasily Andreevich that he felt a need to talk to somebody. But there was no one to talk to. . . . If only he had made it to Goryachkin he would have talked to the landlord and shown him a thing or two.

"Just see how it blows! It will snow us in so deep that we won't be able to get out in the morning!" he thought, listening to a gust of wind that blew against the front of the sleigh, bending it and lashing the snow against it. He sat up and looked around. All he could see through the swirling darkness was Mukhorty's dark head, his back covered by the fluttering drugget, and his thick knotted tail; while all around, in front and behind, was the same fluctuating whity darkness, sometimes seeming to lighten up a little and sometimes growing denser still.

"A pity I listened to Nikita," he thought. "We ought to have driven on. We would have come out somewhere, if only back at Grishkino and stayed the night at Taras's. As it is we must sit here all night. But what was I thinking about? Oh yes, that God gives to those who take trouble, but not to loafers, lie-abeds, or fools. I must have a smoke!"

He sat down again, got out his cigarette case, and stretched out flat on his stomach, screening the matches with the skirt of his coat.

But the wind found its way in and snuffed out match after match. At last he got one to burn and lit a cigarette. He was very glad that he had managed to do what he wanted, and though the wind smoked more of the cigarette than he did, he still got two or three puffs and felt more cheerful. He again leaned back, wrapped himself up, started reflecting and remembering, and then, suddenly and quite unexpectedly, nodded off.

Suddenly something seemed to give him a push and he awoke. Whether it was Mukhorty pulling some straw out from under him, or something within him startling him, in any event it woke him, and his heart was beating faster and faster until the sleigh seemed to tremble under him. He opened his eyes. Everything around him was just as before. "It looks lighter," he thought. "I expect it won't be long before dawn." But he at once remembered that it was lighter because the moon had risen. He sat up and looked at the horse. Mukhorty was still standing with his back to the wind, shivering all over. One side of the drugget, which was completely covered with snow, had been blown back, the breechband had slipped down, and Mukhorty's snow-covered head with its waving forelock and mane was now more visible. Vasily

Andreevich leaned over the back of the sleigh and looked down at Nikita, who was sitting in the same position in which he had settled himself. The sackcloth with which he was covered, and his legs, were thickly covered with snow.

"If only that peasant doesn't freeze to death! His clothes are so wretched. I may be held responsible for him. What shiftless people they are—such a want of education," thought Vasily Andreevich, and he felt like taking the drugget off the horse and putting it over Nikita, but it would be very cold getting out and moving about and, moreover, the horse might freeze to death. "Why did I bring him with me? It was all her stupidity!" he thought, recalling his unloved wife. He rolled over into his old place at the front of the sleigh. "My uncle once spent a whole night like this," he reflected, "and was all right." But another case came at once to his mind. "But when they dug Sebastian out he was dead—stiff like a frozen carcass. If only I had stayed the night in Grishkino, none of this would have happened!"

He wrapped his coat carefully around himself so that none of the warmth of the fur should be wasted but would instead warm him all over, neck, knees, and feet. He shut his eyes and tried to sleep again. But try as he might, he did not get drowsy; on the contrary, he was wide awake and animated. Again he began counting his gains and the debts owed to him; again he bragged to himself, feeling pleased with himself and his position; but all this was continually disturbed by a stealthily approaching fear and the unpleasant regret over not staying in Grishkino.

"How different it would be to be lying warm on a bench!"

He turned over several times looking for a more comfortable position more sheltered from the wind. He wrapped up his legs tighter, shut his eyes, and lay still. But either his legs in their strong felt boots began to ache from being bent in one position, or the wind blew in somewhere; and, after lying still for a short time, he again began to recall the disturbing fact that he might now have been lying quietly in the warm hut at Grishkino. He sat up again, turned around, muffled himself up, and then settled down once more.

At one point he thought he heard a distant cockcrow. Feeling glad, he turned down the collar of his coat and listened with strained attention; but in spite of all his efforts, nothing could be heard but the wind whistling between the shafts, the flapping of the kerchief, and the snow pelting against the frame of the sleigh.

Nikita sat just as he had done all along, not moving and not even answering Vasily Andreevich, who had addressed him a couple of times.

"He doesn't care a bit—he's probably asleep!" thought Vasily Andreevich with vexation, looking behind the sleigh at Nikita, who was covered with a thick layer of snow.

Vasily Andreevich got up and lay down again some twenty times. It seemed to him that the night would never end. "It must be getting near morning," he thought, getting up and looking around. "Let's have a look at my watch. It will be cold to unbutton, but if I only know that it's getting near morning I shall at any rate feel more cheerful. We could begin harnessing."

In the depth of his heart, Vasily Andreevich knew that it could not yet be near morning, but he was growing more and more afraid and wished both to find out and yet to deceive himself. He carefully undid the fastening of his sheepskin, pushed in his hand, and felt about for a long time before he got to his waistcoat. With great difficulty he managed to draw out his silver watch, with its enameled flower design. He tried to make out the time. He couldn't see a thing without a light. Again he went down on his knees and elbows, as he had done when he lighted a cigarette, got out his matches, and proceeded to strike one. This time he went to work more carefully, and feeling with his fingers for a match with the largest head and the greatest amount of phosphorus, lit it on the first try. He brought the face of the watch under the light and could hardly believe his eyes: it was only ten minutes past midnight! Almost the whole night was still before him.

"Oh, how long the night is!" he thought, feeling a cold shudder run down his back. He fastened his fur coats again and wrapped himself up, and he snuggled into a corner of the sleigh, intending to wait patiently. Suddenly, above the monotonous roar of the wind, he clearly distinguished another new and living sound. It steadily strengthened, and, after becoming quite distinct, diminished just as gradually. Beyond all doubt it was a wolf, and he was so near that the movement of his jaws as he modulated his howl was carried downwind. Vasily Andreevich turned back the collar of his coat and listened attentively. Mukhorty too strained to listen, cocking his ears, and when the wolf had ceased its howling he shifted from foot to foot and gave a premonitory snort. After this, Vasily Andreevich couldn't fall asleep again or even calm himself. The more he tried to think of his accounts, his business, his reputation, his worth and his wealth, the more and more was he mastered by fear; and his thoughts were dominated by regrets over not staying overnight at Grishkino.

"The devil take the forest! Things were all right without it, thank God. Ah, if we had only put up for the night!" he said to himself. "They say it's drunkards that freeze," he thought, "and I have had some drink." He noticed that he was beginning to shiver, without knowing whether it was from cold or fear. He tried to wrap himself up and lie down as before but could no longer do so. He couldn't stay in one position. He wanted to get up and do something to master the gathering fear that was rising in him and against which he felt powerless. Again he got out his cigarettes and matches, but only three matches were left and they were bad ones. The phosphorus rubbed off all three of them without lighting.

"The devil take you! Damned thing! Curse you!" he muttered, not knowing whom or what he was cursing, and he flung away the crushed cigarette. He was about to throw away the matchbox too, but checked the movement of his hand and put the box in his pocket instead. He was seized with such unrest that he could no longer remain in one spot. He climbed out of the sleigh and stood with his back to the wind. He shifted his belt again, fastening it lower down in the waist and tightening it.

"What's the use of lying and waiting for death? Better mount the horse and get away!" The thought suddenly occurred to him. "The horse will move when he has someone on his back. As for him," he thought of Nikita, "it's all the same to him whether he lives or dies. What is his life worth? He won't grudge his life, but I have something to live for, thank God."

He untied the horse, threw the reins over his neck, and tried to mount, but his coats and boots were so heavy that he failed. Then he clambered up onto the sleigh and tried to mount from there, but the sleigh tilted under his weight and he failed again. At last he drew Mukhorty nearer to the sleigh, cautiously balanced on one side of it, and managed to pull himself on his stomach across the horse's back. After lying like that for a while he shifted forward once and again, threw a leg over, and finally seated himself, supporting his feet on the loose breechband. The shaking of the sleigh awoke Nikita. He got up, and it seemed to Vasily Andreevich that he said something.

"Listen to such fools as you! Am I to die like this for nothing?" exclaimed Vasily Andreevich. And tucking the loose skirts of his fur coat in under his knees, he turned the horse and rode away from the sleigh in the direction in which he thought the forest and the forester's hut must be.

7

From the time he had covered himself with the sackcloth and seated himself behind the sleigh, Nikita had not stirred. Like all those who live in touch with nature and have known want, he was patient and could wait for hours, even days, without growing restless or irritable. He heard his master call him, but did not answer because he did not want to move or talk. Though he still felt some warmth from the tea he had drunk and from his energetic struggle when clambering about in the snowdrift, he knew that this warmth would not last long and that he had no strength left to warm himself again by moving about, for he felt as tired as a horse when it stops and refuses to go further in spite of the whip, and its master sees that it must be fed before it can work again. The foot in the boot with a hole in it had already grown numb, and he could no longer feel his big toe. Besides that, his whole body began to feel colder and colder.

The thought that he might, and very probably would, die that night occurred to him, but did not seem particularly unpleasant or dreadful.

It did not seem particularly unpleasant, because his whole life had been not a continual holiday, but on the contrary an unceasing round of toil of which he was beginning to feel weary. And it did not seem particularly dreadful, because besides the masters he had served here, like Vasily Andreevich, he always felt dependent on the Chief Master, who had sent him into this life, and he knew that when dying he would still be in that Master's power and would not be ill-used by Him.

"It seems a pity to give up what one is used to and accustomed to. But there's nothing to be done, I shall get used to the new things."

"Sins?" he thought, and remembered his drunkenness, the money that had gone on drink, how he had offended his wife, his cursing, his neglect of church and of the fasts, and all the things the priest blamed him for at confession. "Of course they are sins. But then, did I take them on of myself? That's evidently how God made me. Well, and the sins? Where am I to escape to?"

So at first he thought of what might happen to him that night, and then did not return to such thoughts but gave himself up to whatever recollections came into his head on their own. Now he thought of Martha's arrival, of the drunkenness among the workers and his own renunciation of drink, then of their present journey and of Taras's house and the talk about the breaking up of the family, then of his own lad, and of Mukhorty, now sheltered under the drugget, and then of his master, who made the sleigh creak as he tossed about in it. "I expect you're sorry yourself that you started out, dear man," he thought. "It would seem hard to leave a life such as his! It's not like the likes of us."

Then all these recollections began to grow confused and got mixed in his head, and he fell asleep.

But when Vasily Andreevich, getting on the horse, jerked the sleigh, against the back of which Nikita was leaning against, and it shifted away and hit him in the back with one of its runners, he awoke and had to change his position whether he liked it or not. He straightened his legs with difficulty and shook the snow off them and got up, and an agonizing cold immediately penetrated his whole body. On making out what was happening, he called to Vasily Andreevich to leave him the drugget, which the horse no longer needed, so that he might wrap himself in it.

But Vasily Andreevich didn't stop, but disappeared amid the powdery snow.

Left alone, Nikita considered for a moment what he should do. He felt that he hadn't the strength to go off in search of a house. It was no longer possible to sit down in his old place—it was by now all filled with snow. He felt he couldn't get any warmer in the sleigh either, for there was nothing to cover himself with, and his coat and sheepskin no longer warmed him at all. He felt as cold as though he had nothing on but a shirt. He became frightened. "Lord, heavenly Father!" he muttered and was comforted by the consciousness that he was not alone but that there was One who heard him and would not abandon him. He gave a deep sigh and, keeping the sackcloth over his head, he got inside the sleigh and lay down in the place where his master had been.

But he couldn't get warm in the sleigh either. At first he shivered all over, then the shivering ceased and little by little he began to lose consciousness. He did not know whether he was dying or falling asleep, but felt equally prepared for the one as for the other.

8

Meanwhile Vasily Andreevich, with his feet and the ends of the reins, urged the horse on in the direction in which for some reason he expected the forest and forester's hut to be. The snow covered his eyes and the wind seemed intent on stopping him, but he leaned forward and, constantly lapping his coat over and pushing it between himself and the cold harness pad, which prevented him from sitting properly, he kept urging the horse on. Mukhorty ambled on obediently though with difficulty, in the direction in which he was driven.

Vasily Andreevich rode for about five minutes straight ahead, as far as he could tell, seeing nothing but the horse's head and the white waste, and hearing only the whistle of the wind about the horse's ears and his coat collar.

Suddenly a dark patch showed up in front of him. His heart beat with joy and he rode toward the object, already seeing, in his mind's eye, the walls of village houses. But the dark patch wasn't stationary, it kept moving; and it was no village but some tall stalks of wormwood that were sticking up through the snow on the boundary between two fields and were desperately tossing about under the pressure of the wind, which beat them all to one side and whistled through them. The sight of that wormwood tormented by the pitiless wind made Vasily Andreevich shudder, he knew not why, and he hurriedly urged the horse on, unaware that when he rode up to the wormwood he had quite changed his direction and was now heading the opposite way, though still imagining that he was riding toward where the hut should be. But the horse kept angling to the right, and Vasily Andreevich kept guiding it to the left.

Again something dark appeared in front of him. Again he rejoiced, convinced that now it was certainly a village. But once more it was the same boundary line overgrown with wormwood, once more the same wormwood desperately tossed by the wind and carrying unreasoning terror to his heart. Not only was it the same wormwood, but beside it was a horse's track partly snowed over. Vasily Andreevich stopped, stooped down, and looked carefully. The track was only partially covered with snow, and could be none but his own horse's hoofprints. He had evidently gone around in a small circle. "I shall perish like that!" he thought. Trying not to give way to his terror, he kept urging the horse on, peering into the snowy darkness, in which he saw only flitting and fitful points of light. Once he thought he heard the barking of dogs or the howling of wolves, but the sounds were so faint and indistinct that he didn't know whether he heard them or merely imagined them, and he stopped and listened intently.

Suddenly some terrible, deafening cry resounded near his ears, and everything shivered and shook under him. He seized Mukhorty's neck, but that too was shaking all over and the terrible cry grew even more frightful. For several seconds Vasily Andreevich was unable to collect himself or understand what was happening. It was only that Mukhorty, whether to encourage himself or to call for help, had neighed loudly and resonantly. "Ugh, you wretch! How you frightened me, damn you!" thought Vasily Andreevich. But even when he understood the cause of his terror he couldn't shake it off.

"I must calm myself and think things over," he said to himself, but yet he couldn't stop, and he continued to urge the horse on, not noticing that he was now going with the wind instead of against it. His body, especially between his legs where it touched the pad of the harness and wasn't covered by his overcoats, was getting painfully cold, especially when the horse walked slowly. His legs and arms trembled and his breathing came fast. He saw himself perishing amid this dreadful snowy waste and could see no means of escape.

Suddenly the horse under him tumbled into something and, sinking into a snowdrift, plunged and fell on his side. Vasily Andreevich jumped off, and in so doing dragged to one side the breechband on which his foot was resting, and twisted around the pad, which he held on to as he dismounted. As soon as he had jumped off, the horse struggled to his feet, plunged forward, gave one leap and then another, neighed again, and, dragging the drugget and the breechband behind him, disappeared, leaving Vasily Andreevich alone on the snowdrift.

The latter pressed on after the horse, but the snow was so deep and his coats were so heavy that, sinking above his knees at each step, he stopped breathless after taking not more than twenty steps. "The grove, the oxen, the leasehold, the shop, the tavern, the house with the iron-roofed barn, and my heir," thought he. "How can I leave all that? What does this mean? It cannot be!" These thoughts flashed through his mind. Then he thought of the wormwood tossed by the wind, which he had twice ridden past, and he was seized with such terror that he did not believe in the reality of what was happening to him. "Can this be a dream?" he thought, and tried to wake up but could not. It was real snow that lashed his face and covered him and chilled his right hand, which had lost its glove, and this was a real desert in which he was now left alone like that wormwood, awaiting an inevitable, speedy, and meaningless death.

"Queen of Heaven! Holy Father Nicholas, teacher of temperance!" he thought, recalling the service of the day before and the holy icon with its black face and gilt frame, and the tapers which he sold to be set before that icon and which were almost immediately brought back to him scarcely burnt at all, and which he put away in the storage chest. He prayed to that same Nicholas the Wonder-Worker to save him, promising him a thanksgiving service and some candles. But he clearly and indubitably realized that the icon, its frame, the candles, the priest, and the thanksgiving service, though very important and necessary in church, could do nothing for him here, and that there was and could be no connection between those candles and services and his present disastrous plight. "I must not despair," he thought. "I must follow the horse's tracks before they're snowed under. He'll lead me out, or I may even catch him. Only I must not hurry, or I shall get stuck fast and be more lost than ever."

But in spite of his resolution to go quietly, he rushed forward and even ran, continually falling, getting up, and falling again. The horse's tracks were already hardly visible in places where the snow wasn't deep. "I'm lost!" thought Vasily Andreevich. "I shall lose the tracks and not catch the horse." But at that moment he saw something black. It was Mukhorty, and not only Mukhorty but the sleigh with the shafts and the kerchief. Mukhorty, with the sackcloth and the breechband twisted around to one side, was standing not in his former place but nearer to the shafts, shaking his head, which the reins he was stepping on drew downward. It turned out that Vasily Andreevich had sunk in the same ravine Nikita had previously fallen into, and that Mukhorty had been bringing him back to the sleigh and he had got off his back no more than fifty paces from where the sleigh was.

9

Having stumbled back to the sleigh, Vasily Andreevich caught hold of it and for a long time stood motionless, trying to calm himself and catch his breath. Nikita was not in his former place, but something, already covered with snow, was lying in the sleigh and Vasily Andreevich concluded that this was Nikita. His terror had now quite left him, and if he felt any fear it was lest the dreadful terror should return that he had experienced when on the horse and especially when he was left alone in the snowdrift. He had to avoid that terror at any cost, and he must do something to keep it away—occupy himself with something. The first thing he did was turn his back against the wind and open his fur coat. Then, as soon as he recovered his breath a little, he shook the snow out of his boots and out of his left glove (the right glove was hopelessly lost and by this time probably lying somewhere under a foot of snow); then, as was his custom when going out of his shop to buy grain from the peasants, he pulled his girdle low down and tightened it and prepared for action. The first thing that occurred to him was to free Mukhorty's leg from the rein. He did that and tethered him to the iron clamp at the front of the sleigh where he had been before; as he was going around the horse's hind quarters to put the breechband and pad straight and cover him with the cloth, he noticed something moving in the sleigh and Nikita's head rose up from under a layer of snow. Nikita, who was half frozen, rose with great difficulty and sat up, moving his hand before his nose in a strange manner just as if he were driving away flies. He waved his hand and said something, and seemed to Vasily Andreevich to be calling him. Vasily Andreevich left the sackcloth unadjusted and went up to the sleigh.

"What is it?" he asked. "What are you saying?"

"I'm dy . . . ing, that's what," said Nikita brokenly and with difficulty. "Give what is owing to me to my lad, or to my wife, no matter."

"Why, are you really frozen?" asked Vasily Andreevich.

"I feel it's my death. Forgive me, for Christ's sake . . ." said Nikita in a tearful voice, continuing to wave his hand before his face as if driving away flies.

Vasily Andreevich stood silent and motionless for half a minute. Then suddenly, with the same resoluteness with which he used to shake hands when making a good purchase, he took a step back, rolled up his sleeves, and began raking the snow off Nikita and out of the sleigh. Having done this he hurriedly undid his girdle, opened out his fur coat, and, having pushed Nikita down, lay down on top of him, covering him not only with his fur coat but with the whole of his body, which glowed with warmth. He pushed the skirts of his coat between Nikita and the sides of the sleigh and held down the hem of the coat with his knees. Vasily Andreevich lay like that, face down, with his head pressed against the front of the sleigh. Here he no longer heard the horse's movements or the whistling of the wind, but only Nikita's breathing. For a long time Nikita lay motionless, then he sighed deeply and moved.

"There, and you say you're dying! Lie still and get warm, that's our way . . ." began Vasily Andreevich.

But to his great surprise he could say no more, for tears came to his eyes and his lower jaw began to quiver rapidly. He stopped speaking and only gulped down the risings in his throat. "Seems I was badly frightened and have gone quite weak," he thought. But this weakness was not only unpleasant, but gave him a peculiar joy such as he had never felt before.

"That's our way!" he said to himself, experiencing a strange and solemn tenderness. He lay like that for a long time, wiping his eyes on the fur of his coat. The wind kept turning up the right skirt of his coat, and each time he would respond by tucking it back under his knee.

But he longed so passionately to tell somebody of his joyful condition that he said: "Nikita!"

"It's comfortable, warm!" came a voice from beneath.

"There, you see, my friend, I was going to perish. And you would have been frozen, and I should have . . ."

But again his jaws began to quiver and his eyes brimmed with tears, and he could say no more.

"Well, never mind," he thought. "I know about myself what I know."

He remained silent and lay like that for a long time.

Nikita kept him warm from below and his fur coats from above. Only his hands, with which he kept the skirts of his coat down around Nikita's sides, and his legs, which the wind kept uncovering, began to freeze, especially his right hand, which had no glove. But he did not think of his legs or his hands but only of how to warm the peasant who was lying under him. He looked out several times at Mukhorty and could see that his back was uncovered and the drugget and breechband were lying on the snow, and that he ought to get up and cover him, but he couldn't bring himself to leave Nikita and disturb for even a moment the joyous condition he was in. He no longer felt any kind of terror.

"No fear, we shan't lose him this time!" he said to himself, referring to his getting the peasant warm with the same boastfulness with which he spoke of his buying and selling.

Vasily Andreevich lay in that way for one hour, another, and a third, but he was unconscious of the passage of time. At first, impressions of the snowstorm, the sleigh-shafts, and the horse with the shaft-bow shaking before his eyes, kept passing through his mind; then he remembered Nikita lying under him; then recollections of the festival, his wife, the police officer, and the box of candles began to mingle with these; then again Nikita, this time lying under that box; then the peasants, customers, and traders, and the white walls of his house, with its iron roof, with Nikita lying underneath, presented themselves to his imagination. Afterward all these impressions blended into one nothingness. As the colors of the rainbow unite into one white light, so all these different impressions mingled into one, and he fell asleep.

For a long time he slept without dreaming, but just before dawn the visions recommenced. It seemed to him that he was standing by the box of candles and that Tikhon's wife was asking for a five-kopek taper for the Church festival. He wished to take one out and give it to her, but his hands would not move, being held tight in his pockets. He wanted to walk around the box but his feet would not move and his new clean galoshes had grown to the stone floor, and he could neither lift them nor get his feet out of the galoshes. Then the box of tapers was no longer a box but a bed, and suddenly Vasily Andreevich saw himself lying in his bed at home. He was lying in his bed and couldn't get up. Yet it was necessary for him to get up because Ivan Matveich, the police officer, would soon call for him and he had to go with him—either to bargain for the forest or to put Mukhorty's breechband straight.

He asked his wife: "Nikolaevna, hasn't he come yet?" "No, he hasn't," she replied. He heard someone drive up to the front steps. "It must be him." "No, he's gone past." "Nikolaevna! I say, Nikolaevna, isn't he here yet?" "No." He was still lying on his bed and couldn't get up, but was always waiting. And this waiting was uncanny and yet joyful. Then suddenly his joy was completed. He whom he was expecting came; not Ivan Matveich the police officer, but someone else—yet it was he whom he had been waiting for. He came and called him; and it was he who had called him and told him to lie down on Nikita. And Vasily Andreevich was glad that that one had come for him.

"I'm coming!" he cried joyfully, and that cry awoke him, but woke him up not at all the same person he had been when he fell asleep. He tried to get up but could not, tried to move his arm and could not, tried to move his leg and also could not, tried to turn his head and could not. He was surprised but not at all disturbed by this. He understood that this was death, and he wasn't at all disturbed by that, either.

He remembered that Nikita was lying under him and that he had got warm and was alive, and it seemed to him that he was Nikita and Nikita was he and that his life was not in himself but in Nikita. He strained his ears and heard Nikita breathing and even snoring slightly. "Nikita is alive, so I too am alive!" he said to himself triumphantly.

And he remembered his money, his shop, his house, the buying and selling, and Mironov's millions, and it was hard for him to understand why that man, called Vasily Brekhunov, had troubled himself with all those things with which he had been troubled.

"Well, it was because he didn't know what the real thing was," he thought, concerning that Vasily Brekhunov. "He didn't know, but now I know and know for sure. Now I know!" And again he heard the voice of the one who had called him before. "I'm coming! Coming!" he responded gladly, and his whole being was filled with joyful emotion. He felt free, and as if nothing could hold him back any longer.

After that, Vasily Andreevich neither saw, heard, nor felt anything more in this world.

All around the snow still eddied. The same whirlwinds of snow circled about, covering the dead Vasily Andreevich's fur coat, the shivering Mukhorty, the sleigh, now scarcely visible, and Nikita lying at the bottom of it, kept warm beneath his dead master.

10

Nikita awoke before daybreak. He was aroused by the cold that had begun to creep down his back. He had dreamed that he was coming from the mill with a load of his master's flour and when crossing the stream had missed the bridge and let the cart get stuck. And he saw that he had crawled under the cart and was trying to lift it by arching his back.

But, strange to say, the cart did not move; it stuck to his back and he could neither lift it nor get out from under it. It was crushing the whole of his loins. And how cold it felt! Evidently he must crawl out.

"Stop that!" he exclaimed to whoever was pressing the cart down on him.

"Take out the sacks!" But the cart pressed down colder and colder, and then he heard a strange knocking, awoke completely, and remembered everything. The cold cart was his dead and frozen master lying upon him. And the knock was produced by Mukhorty, who had struck the sleigh twice with his hoof.

"Andreevich! Hey, Andreevich!" Nikita called cautiously, beginning to realize the truth, and straightening his back. But Vasily Andreevich did not answer and his stomach and legs were stiff and cold and heavy like iron weights.

"He must have died! May the Kingdom of Heaven be his!" thought Nikita.

He turned his head, dug through the snow about him, and opened his eyes. It was daylight; the wind was whistling as before between the shafts, and the snow was falling in the same way, except that it was no longer driving against the frame of the sleigh but silently covered both sleigh and horse deeper and deeper, and neither the horse's movements nor his breathing could any longer be heard.

"He must have frozen too," thought Nikita of Mukhorty, and indeed those hoof knocks against the sleigh, which had awakened Nikita, were the last efforts the already numbed Mukhorty had made to keep on his feet before dying.

"O Lord God, it seems Thou art calling me too!" said Nikita. "Thy Holy Will be done. But it's uncanny. . . . Still, a man can't die twice and must die once. If only it would come soon!"

And he again drew in his head, closed his eyes, and became unconscious, fully convinced that now he was certainly and finally dying.

It wasn't until noon that day that peasants dug Vasily Andreevich and Nikita out of the snow with their shovels, not more than seventy yards from the road and less than half a mile from the village.

The snow had hidden the sleigh, but the shafts and the kerchief tied to them were still visible. Mukhorty, buried up to his belly in snow, with the breechband and drugget hanging down, stood all white, his dead head pressed against his frozen throat: icicles hung from his nostrils, his eyes were covered with hoarfrost as though filled with tears, and he had grown so thin in that one night that he was nothing but skin and bones.

Vasily Andreevich was stiff as a frozen carcass, and when they rolled him off Nikita his legs remained apart and his arms stretched out as they had been. His bulging hawk eyes were frozen, and his open mouth was full of snow under his clipped mustache. But Nikita, though chilled through, was still alive. When he had been brought to, he felt sure that he was already dead and that what was taking place with him was no longer happening in this world but in the next. When he heard the peasants shouting as they dug him out and rolled the frozen body of Vasily Andreevich off of him, he was at first surprised that in the other world peasants should be shouting in the same old way and had the same kind of body, and then when he realized that he was still in this world he was sorry rather than glad, especially when he found that the toes on both his feet were frozen.

Nikita lay in the hospital for two months. They cut off three of his toes, but the others recovered so that he was still able to work and went on living for another twenty years, first as a farm laborer, then in his old age as a watchman. He died at home as he had wished, just this past year, under the icons with a lighted taper in his hands. Before he died, he asked his wife's forgiveness and forgave her for the cooper. He also took leave of his son and grandchildren, and died sincerely glad that he was relieving his son and daughter-in-law of the burden of having to feed him, and that he was now really passing from this life, of which he was weary, into that other life which every year and every hour grew clearer and more desirable to him. Whether he is better or worse off there where he awoke after his death, whether he was disappointed or found what he expected there, we shall all soon learn.

ACKNOWLEDGMENTS
AND PERMISSIONS

Gathering together this anthology was an act of love, an expression of affection for these writers and the wisdom, insight, creativity, and daring they bring to their work.

We thank, first, our families; then the many friends, colleagues, and teachers, past and present, who have supported us and nudged us along. Among those who have furthered us in our task preparing this book are: Mark Albion, Marek Fuchs, Emily G. Kahn, Sydney Lewis, Toinette Lippe, Daniel Menaker, Alan Rinzler, Robin Rolewicz, Patrick Samway, Michael Shinagel, Isabelle Storey, John Updike, and Amanda Urban.

This would have been a lesser book, and longer in coming, without the determined efforts of Rachel Greenhaus, who accomplished tasks that are too often thankless. We salute the unsung heroes in the permissions offices of publishers and literary agencies who dutifully and graciously replied to our queries, generated the necessary paperwork, and kept things moving until we had what we needed.

At The New Press we have been favored with two particularly talented editors, Diane Wachtell and Priyanka Jacob; we're grateful to them for their early and abiding belief in this project and for their commitment to publishing in the public interest. We extend our thanks to our production editor, Sarah Fan, for her keen eye. And we celebrate The New Press's founding publisher, André Schiffrin, whose editorial acumen and resourceful, humane approach to publishing have kept important books coming for more than half a century.

Grateful acknowledgment is made to the following sources for permission to reprint previously published and unpublished material: